Roman and m

townhouses o

London waterfront

Excavations at Governor's House,

City of London

MoLAS Monograph Series

1 Excavations at the Priory and Hospital of St Mary Spital, London,
Christopher Thomas, Barney Sloane and Christopher Phillpotts
ISBN 1 901992 00 4

2 The National Roman Fabric Reference Collection: a handbook,
Roberta Tomber and John Dore
ISBN 1 901992 01 2

3 The Cross Bones burial ground, Redcross Way, Southwark, London:
archaeological excavations (1991–1998) for the London
Underground Limited Jubilee Line Extension Project,
Megan Brickley and Adrian Miles with Hilary Stainer
ISBN 1 901992 06 3

4 The eastern cemetery of Roman London: excavations 1983–1990,
Bruno Barber and David Bowsher
ISBN 1 901992 09 8

5 The Holocene evolution of the London Thames: archaeological
excavations (1991–1998) for the London Underground Limited,
Jubilee Line Extension Project, Jane Sidell, Keith Wilkinson,
Robert Scaife and Nigel Cameron
ISBN 1 901992 10 1

6 The Limehouse porcelain manufactory: excavations at 108–116
Narrow Street, London, 1990, Kieron Tyler and Roy Stephenson,
with J Victor Owen and Christopher Phillpotts
ISBN 1 901992 16 0

7 Roman defences and medieval industry:
excavations at Baltic House, City of London,
Elizabeth Howe
ISBN 1 901992 17 9

8 London bridge: 2000 years of a river crossing,
Bruce Watson, Trevor Brigham and Tony Dyson
ISBN 1 901992 18 7

9 Roman and medieval townhouses on the London waterfront:
excavations at Governor's House, City of London,
Trevor Brigham with Aidan Woodger
ISBN 1 901992 21 7

Roman and medieval townhouses on the London waterfront

Excavations at Governor's House, City of London

Trevor Brigham with Aidan Woodger

MoLAS Monograph 9

Museum of London Archaeology Service

Published by the Museum of London Archaeology Service

Copyright © Museum of London 2001

A CIP catalogue record for this book is available from the British Library

Production and series design by Tracy Wellman
Typesetting and design by Tracy Wellman, Susan Banks
Reprographics by Andy Chopping
Editing by Monica Kendall
Series editing by Sue Hirst/Susan M Wright

Printed by the Lavenham Press

Front cover: Roman wall in Building 3 cut by later chalk wall associated with
Buildings 14 and 15; the 'Agas' woodcut map (1561–70); stamped leather sandal
Back cover: tiebacks forming the supporting structure for Waterfront 2; enamelled
Roman disc brooch; 12th-century chalk foundation of Building 13

CONTRIBUTORS

Principal authors	Trevor Brigham, Aidan Woodger
Roman pottery	Robin Symonds
Post-Roman pottery	Lyn Blackmore
Building material	Terence Paul Smith
Finds	Angela Wardle
Non-shoe leather	Jackie Keily
Shoe leather	Penny MacConnoran
Roman glass	John Shepherd, Sasha Smith
Prehistoric environment	Jane Sidell
Animal bone	Charlotte Ainsley
Botanical remains	Lisa Gray
Goldworking	Megan Dennis, Malcolm Ward
Dendrochronology	Ian Tyers, Gretel Boswijk
Timber technology	Damian Goodburn
Graphics	Steven Cheshire, Kate Pollard, Sophie Lamb, Susan Banks
Photography	Edwin Baker, Andy Chopping, Maggie Cox, Liv Renolin
Project managers	Dick Malt, Barney Sloane, Gordon Malcolm, Peter Rowsome
Editor	Monica Kendall

CONTENTS

FIGURES

TABLES

SUMMARY

In 1969 Peter Marsden recorded substantial masonry in a watching brief during the construction of Suffolk House, Upper Thames Street, which he interpreted as the remains of a substantial Roman townhouse attached to the 'Governor's Palace' under Cannon Street Station. A proposed redevelopment of the site by Argent Real Estate led to an opportunity for further archaeological investigation of the site, which consisted of an evaluation in 1994–5 and an excavation and watching brief in 1996–7. The new building was renamed Governor's House. The scheduled status of the 'Palace' area meant that preservation was of paramount importance, and the archaeological works were therefore designed as part of a package of mitigation measures to reduce damage to the remaining archaeological resource to a minimum.

Despite the limited scope of the investigations, a hitherto unsuspected prehistoric marsh was recorded. A pair of structures in the south-west constructed from timbers apparently felled in AD 84 were tiebacks for a north–south quay standing to c 2.1m OD. This was probably the east end of a river wharf under Upper Thames Street, which stretched about 120m to the mouth of the Walbrook where the west end had been recorded at Cannon Street Station in 1988. In the eastern part of the site was a post-and-plank revetment constructed between c AD 100–20 and standing to c 1.3m OD, partly built using salvaged building timbers. Further reclamation to the south of Suffolk House probably took place in AD 125–6 when a box-drain was cut across the top of the post-and-plank revetment, extending beyond the limit of excavation. These structures almost certainly predated the major building phases. Later in the 2nd century a system of hollowed quartered oak pipes carried water to the west.

Walls and floors of a number of buildings were recorded on the terraces overlooking the river, including two early structures which predated the townhouse phase. One of these, in the north-east, may have been a goldworker's premises, a second to the west was rebuilt, perhaps to form the north wing of the townhouse. Extra details of the townhouse were added to the 1969 observations, particularly in the area of the west wing where an underfloor heating system was recorded. Part of the drum and capital of a Roman Tuscan order column, first observed in 1994, was recovered in 1996 from a medieval pit overlying the south-east corner of the building. Remains of one or two contemporary buildings to the east of the townhouse were also encountered.

Roman occupation of the site apparently continued at least into the late 4th century when the townhouse was demolished, although the walls survived to a considerable height.

Early 11th-century pitting was succeeded in the late 11th to early 12th centuries by a series of sunken-floored or cellared buildings which were constructed in dark earth deposits laid over the Roman remains. These were succeeded by later medieval chalk walls and foundations along the Laurence Pountney Lane frontage and south of Rectory House; a chalk and gravel foundation on cleft beech piles from the southern part of the site was of a type found from the early 12th century. Along Suffolk Lane, walls of at least two phases of the 14th-century Pountney's Inn, later the Manor of the Rose, were found. A chalk-lined well and cesspit associated with the manor may have been in use until the 17th century.

Three chapters discuss the development of the site from the prehistoric marsh through the long Roman occupation, to the early and later medieval development (chapters 2–4). The stratigraphic evidence is supported by specialist contributions, the results of which are both integrated with the main text and presented more fully in appendices. An attempt is also made to determine whether or not the results of the two phases of the project were successful in answering the research questions which were outlined before each began and were subsequently updated. The success of the mitigation strategy and its ramifications for future management of the archaeological resource are also considered (chapter 5).

ACKNOWLEDGEMENTS

Thanks are due to the client Argent Real Estate for their support throughout the project, the architects Sidell Gibson Partnership, the Consulting Engineers Arup, Resident Engineers Tarmac/Wimpey and the site contractors JNK and Keltbray.

MoLAS staff who worked on the site and whose excellent recording has facilitated the production of this report were: Bruno Barber, Paul Cox, Andy Daykin, Mike Edwards, Richard Heawood, Damian Goodburn, Kieron Heard, Ken Pitt, Nick Sambrook, Richard Turnbull and Bruce Watson, who also co-supervised the first evaluation. Dana Goodburn-Brown and Kirsten Suenson-Taylor advised and carried out conservation work on site, Richenda Goffin recorded the in situ wall plaster in TP14. Patrick Hunter carried out the monolith and bulk sampling of the marsh deposits. Maggie Cox and Edwin Baker provided the photographic coverage.

Alan Gammon, Lee Hunt and Pat Connolly carried out metal detecting on site.

Site visits were made and opinions expressed by Richard Hughes (Arup Consultant Archaeologist), Ellen Barnes (English Heritage Inspector of Ancient Monuments for London) and Kathryn Stubbs (Planning and Archaeology Officer of the Corporation of London). Particular thanks are due to Gill Andrews, the developer's post-excavation consultant, for commenting on this text and suggesting many improvements. Any mistakes and inaccuracies remaining are the authors' responsibility. The summary was translated into French by Dominique de Moulins and into German by Friederike Hammer. The index was compiled by Susanne Atkin.

Megan Dennis and Malcolm Ward would like to thank Jenny Hall from the Museum of London for her help in locating the goldworking debris from earlier excavations and allowing them to examine it and take small samples, and the Archaeological Conservation Laboratory for allowing them to use their equipment and space while taking samples.

1

Introduction

1.1 Circumstances of the excavation

The site

This report describes some of the major findings of archaeological investigations carried out by the Museum of London Archaeology Service (MoLAS) between 1994–7 at Suffolk House (now Governor's House), with the principal address 5 Laurence Pountney Hill and 154–156 Upper Thames Street, City of London (Figs 1, 2; site code: SUF94, TQ 3271 8077). The site occupies a block of land measuring some 60m east–west and 45m north–south, bounded on the west side by Suffolk Lane, the south side by Upper Thames Street, the east side by Laurence Pountney Lane, and the north side by Laurence Pountney Hill. The site is called Suffolk House in this report, except when the new building is referred to in chapter 5.

Until 1995, the site was occupied by a building designed by CLRP Architects and built during 1969–71. This replaced two late 19th-century buildings, Suffolk and Norfolk Houses, which were separated by a narrow street, Ducksfoot Lane. The property consisted of three adjoining blocks with a cruciform plan. The 12-storey central block had a deep basement with a floor level at 3.15m OD. The five-storey east wing had no basement. The west wing was four storeys high, with no basement, but a car park at ground level terraced into the natural ground slope, and entered at street level from Suffolk Lane. The exterior of the building was faced with grey mosaic tiles (Pevsner & Cherry 1973, 299).

The south-east corner of the property was an area of paved garden constructed over the infilled basements of the previous building, with a large free-standing cooling tower for the air-conditioning system connected to the main building by subsurface ducts.

Ove Arup & Partners designed the foundations of Suffolk House. In the east and west wings these mainly consisted of individual 0.60m perimeter piles supporting square columns, with paired or single 0.75m piles internally, topped by concrete pile caps. Cast ground beams linked the perimeter piles which supported the concrete retaining walls, and also served to connect the individual internal pile caps to the outer circuit. The foundations of the basemented central block consisted of a dense grid of closely spaced 0.75m diameter piles beneath massive pile caps, with clusters of two, three and four piles along the four sides of the block. Each of these had a discrete pile cap supporting the cast columns of the facade (information from site engineering drawings and Hughes 1994a, figs 19–23).

During groundworks in 1969 the pile locations and pile cap trenches were cleared of obstructions by grubbing out all existing foundations in the vicinity. While this work was carried out, Peter Marsden, an archaeologist then working for the Guildhall Museum, carried out a watching brief under difficult conditions to record the archaeological deposits which were being revealed and destroyed (Marsden 1975, 54–60). In addition, an area of mosaic pavement and several walls were revealed and destroyed during excavation work for a tower crane base and service conduit beneath the present car park. As well as site notes, features were plotted on a base plan in relation to the new foundations (see Fig 4).

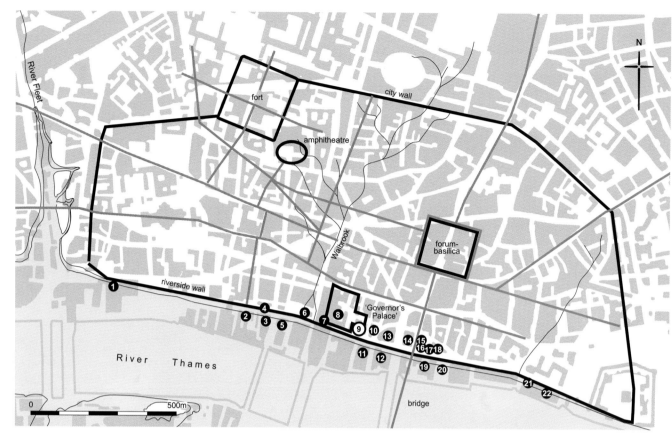

Fig 1 Map of the City of London, showing location of the study area, the principal features of Roman Londinium, and waterfront excavations undertaken by the Museum of London

Key to sites: 1 – Baynard's Castle; 2 – Bull Wharf; 3 – Vintry/Vintner's Place; 4 – Thames Street Tunnel; 5 – Thames Exchange; 6 – Dowgate Hill House; 7 – Cannon Street Station; 8 – Bush Lane; 9 – Suffolk House; 10 – Minster House; 11 – Swan Lane; 12 – Seal House; 13 – Miles Lane; 14 – Regis House; 15 – 37–40 Fish Street Hill; 16 – Pudding Lane; 17 – Peninsular House; 18 – Billingsgate Buildings; 19 – New Fresh Wharf; 20 – Billingsgate Lorry Park; 21 – Old Custom House; 22 – Three Quays House

The Roman 'Governor's Palace' Scheduled Monument

The western and central blocks of Suffolk House lie within the area of the Scheduled Ancient Monument known as the Cannon Street Station Roman Palace (see Fig 2; CoL 1992, 36; Marsden 1975, 62–73). Scheduled Monuments are sites of regional or national archaeological importance. To protect these important archaeological sites from accidental or intentional damage, Scheduled Monument Consent is required from English Heritage before any works are carried out which would have the effect of demolishing, damaging or removing any portion of the monument. To carry out any unauthorised work on a Scheduled Monument is forbidden by the Ancient Monuments and Archaeological Areas Act of 1979 (Spoerry 1993, 3–5).

The main (western) part of the monument under Cannon Street Station consists of a complex sequence of walls, floors and other features recorded from the mid 19th century onwards, which have been interpreted as forming part of an extensive structure. Peter Marsden has suggested that this may have been the palace of the Roman provincial governor, constructed during the Flavian period (AD 69–96), and in use as late as the

3rd century (Marsden 1975). The northern element occupied an upper terrace immediately above Suffolk House, consisting of a collection of walls continuing as far as Cannon Street, but including a massive rectangular hypocausted hall incorporated into a terrace wall along with a semicircular bastion-like feature. This may be considered the original core, as the area to the south remained open marsh and foreshore until the construction of the timber quay also observed at Suffolk House (built AD 84) and its early 2nd-century successors. This reclamation allowed the erection of masonry structures below the upper terrace, which Marsden has interpreted as forming wings around a central 'garden court' with a feature which appeared to have been a large ornamental pool. The general courtyard plan of the complex therefore resembled the main building recorded at Suffolk House, but on a much larger scale. The various wings were modified over time, with the addition of hypocaust systems and a bath suite, before its demolition in the late 3rd or 4th century.

Its interpretation as the 'Governor's Palace' was based on the size, position and quality of the buildings, supported by the presence in pre-'palace' levels of evidence for goldworking, which Marsden argued was under central control. The Suffolk House excavations have produced further evidence for this

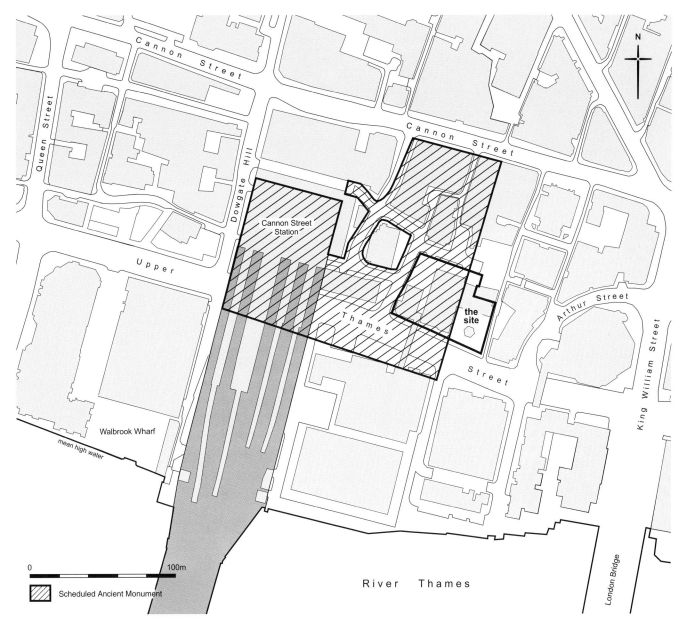

Fig 2 Map showing site location and the boundary of the Cannon Street Station Scheduled Ancient Monument

activity, perhaps associated with one of the buildings on the site.

By inference, the identification of the complex as being the governor's London residence raised the question of the status of the townhouse located at Suffolk House (see 1.2 below). This, it was argued, must have been connected with the 'palace' in some way, perhaps as the domicile of an important provincial official. It was this which influenced its inclusion as part of the Scheduled Monument (Marsden 1975, 54–60).

Some doubt has been cast recently on the original interpretation of the area, partly as a result of further excavations at Cannon Street Station in 1988 (LYD88: *London Archaeol* 6, 1990, 161–2; *Britannia* 22, 1991, 270; Stephenson 1996), but also because of changing views of the way the governorship worked in practice. Although it is not the purpose of this volume to deal with this matter in any great detail, it will be addressed in outline, because the status of the 'palace' site obviously affects the original interpretation of the main Roman building at Suffolk House (see chapter 3).

The archaeological programme

An evaluation supervised by Trevor Brigham and Bruce Watson carried out between 1 November 1994 and 6 January 1995 was followed by an excavation and watching brief conducted between 17 April 1996 and 18 March 1997 under the supervision of Aidan Woodger (see Fig 3).

The evaluation took the form of recording work and limited excavation in nine trial pits (TP1–4, 7–9, 13 and 14; Fig 3) and the monitoring of four geotechnical boreholes. The aim of the evaluation was to confirm the suitability or otherwise of the trial pits as locations for piles. Substantial remains of Roman masonry were found in four trial pits, and medieval walls associated with an important medieval townhouse – Pountney's Inn or the Manor of the Rose – survived along the Suffolk Lane frontage. Small areas of Roman surfaces and pits were removed in two areas but where possible remains were left *in situ*. Conservation work was carried out to protect Roman walls,

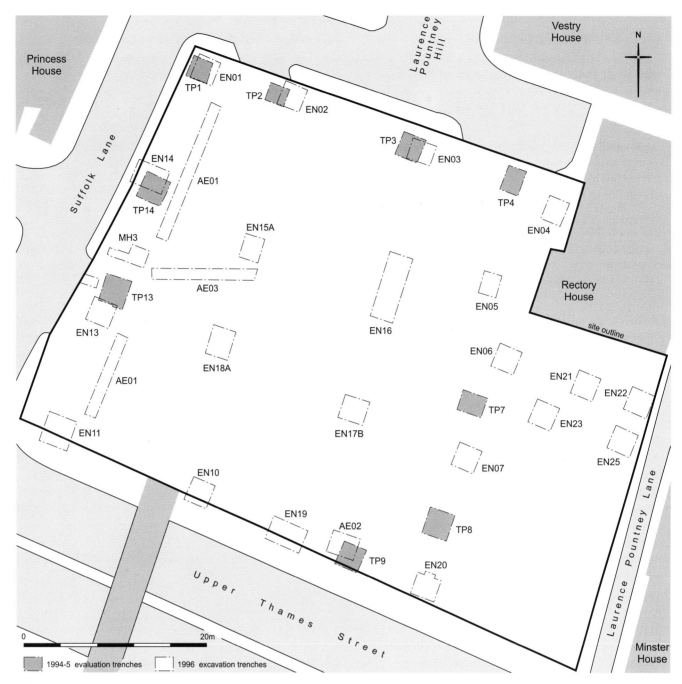

Fig 3 Map showing the 1994–7 areas of investigation

floors and an area of painted wall plaster (Brigham & Watson 1995).

A mitigation strategy was devised by Richard Hughes of Arup (1994a; 1994b) to provide foundations for the new building with the minimum of impact on the archaeological resource. This involved the reuse of the locations of 16 existing piles supporting the 1969 building, the insertion of five piles in areas shown or expected to have little archaeological survival, and four further piles in previously undisturbed areas. In the case of the former, a watching brief was carried out on the enabling and piling works, and where the entirely new areas were to be drilled, four enabling holes (EN4, 5, 11 and 20; see Fig 3) were hand dug by MoLAS from the top of archaeological deposits down to the natural clay, silt, sand or gravel. In addition, a north–south evaluation trench (AEI) was opened to the east of

TP13 and TP14 to investigate the level of survival; a number of features were exposed and recorded, but not excavated.

All of the trial pits and enabling holes were excavated and recorded stratigraphically according to the principles laid down in the Museum of London *Archaeological site manual* (Westman 1994). Because of the depth of the excavations on Upper Thames Street (EN11 and EN20), and because they went into waterlogged deposits, gas detectors were used to ensure adequate air supply in the work area. Water pumps were also required to maintain a workable environment. The holes were shored with interlocking 5.0m long trench sheeting inserted by contractors working for Keltbray, stepping in when they went more than 5.0m below the ground surface. For this reason EN11 and EN20 were broken out over a larger area than necessary for the enabling works in order to allow reasonable working space at depth.

Attempts were made to hand auger below the level of the enabling work ground reduction in the rebored piles. It was difficult, however, to proceed below c 1.0m before hitting tile, stone or other obstructions. Since the upper deposits tended to be 'dark earth', little information other than a minimum depth could be ascertained. The auger did, however, provide useful information in EN11 and EN20 with respect to depths of silts and peats, for which task it was much better suited.

A watching brief was carried out during the reduction of the floor to the formation level of the new slab, which was to be constructed above the level of the 19th-century cellars. Important archaeological deposits and walls were, however, recorded in a section along the Laurence Pountney Lane frontage in the east, and some medieval foundations were recorded at formation level in the eastern annexe. This phase of work was carried out between 16 April and 17 October 1996 (Woodger 1996a; 1996b).

In the following year, the excavation of new drain runs and a sewer connection necessitated further works, including a watching brief during February and March and the excavation of a manhole shaft (MH3) between 10 and 18 March (Woodger 1997).

A Ground Penetrating Radar (GPR) survey was also carried out by MoLAS's Clark Laboratory on 4 October 1996. Two main areas were covered, the area of the east wing of the townhouse and the north-west corner of the site, the southern areas being unsuitable by reason of the waterlogged nature of the deposits. Unfortunately this survey did not provide useful results and is not discussed further (Mackie & McCann 1997).

Although well-stratified sequences of archaeological deposits were investigated, there were severe limitations common to all projects of this nature (see 5.1 for a further discussion of this). The maximum size of the individual areas of investigation was about 3.0m x 3.0m, although most were smaller at between about 1.8–2.5m square. Only about 4% of the area of the site was investigated between 1994 and 1997 and around a third of this was not fully excavated: a number of the evaluation trial pits ceased excavation before reaching Roman levels. The construction of the 1960s' tower removed about a third of the site with minimal recording, including the eastern and southern ranges and the eastern limit of the western range of the townhouse. Furthermore most of the areas where recording took place in 1994–7 were separated laterally by 10m or so of uninvestigated deposits. Although this has led as intended to the preservation of most of the archaeological resource still present, it has severely limited confident interpretation of what is a complex, deeply stratified terraced site; this should be borne in mind when reading the following chapters, and in any future study of the site archive.

Apart from Roman and medieval features along the Suffolk Lane frontage, very few structures can be traced from one area to the next, and as in 1969 very few junctions between walls or the different 'ranges' of the townhouse were observable. Overall interpretation is therefore highly subjective, even though individual sequences may be understandable. The small area of the trenches has resulted in a high proportion of contexts with small to medium finds assemblages, while those trenches which were evaluated but not excavated subsequently, mainly during the 1994 site investigation, have produced no finds to accompany the recorded sequence. A few of the early waterfront dumps provide exceptions to this rule, but even here there are some problems resulting from a conflict with dendrochronological dating, almost certainly as a result of disturbance during reshoring. Clearly, the investigation of a deeply stratified, multi-period site by watching brief or keyhole excavation is highly unsatisfactory in many ways. The problem is further exacerbated on this site since the level of the pre-Roman ground surface varies from −1.0m OD in the south-east to +6.6m OD to the north-west.

Marsden's interpretation of the western part of the site as being occupied by a single structure was bold considering the extent and quality of the evidence, and is potentially open to reinterpretation. The more recent investigation was designed to avoid, as far as possible, the destruction of the Roman remains (and therefore also largely prevented their recording), thus any confirmation or reinterpretation of his work is also highly subjective. In some cases the evidence from the more recent work contradicts the earlier conclusions in its detail. In view of the possibility that a prime site in the Roman city might be under great demand and that buildings could share party walls, it is clear that much more recording work would be necessary to determine how many buildings were really present on the west end of the site over a period of about 350 years. The site under discussion therefore has large areas of 'negative evidence', some of which must ever remain so, but others of which may at some future date become positive.

Despite these reservations and caveats, it has been possible to suggest an overall dated sequence of events with proposed building layouts by combining the results of all the site investigations, answering many of the key research questions posed before work began. These are presented in the relevant chapters dealing with the stratigraphic sequence, and also summarised at the end of the volume, with some suggestions for the direction of future work, should this ever be possible.

1.2 The work of Peter Marsden and earlier observations

Introduction

In 1969 the site was the subject of a watching brief carried out by Peter Marsden for the Guildhall Museum (summarised below). The findings were published under the auspices of the Department of Urban Archaeology of the Museum of London as part of the complex of substantial masonry remains in the area of Cannon Street Station (see Fig 48), which he interpreted as the Roman 'Governor's Palace' (Marsden 1975, 54–60).

Marsden described the findings in blocks of numbered features (Fig 4): the north range (57–64, incorrectly headed

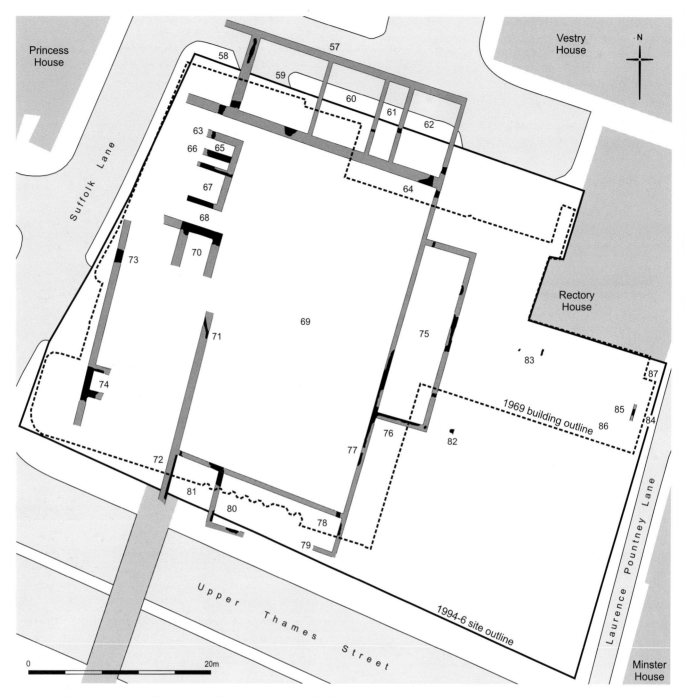

Fig 4 Plan of principal archaeological features recorded during the construction of Suffolk House in 1969 (adapted from Marsden 1975, fig 26)

57–62); the west range (65–74); the south and east ranges (75–81, incorrectly headed 75–82); and isolated features to the east of the proposed main building (82–7). The central part of the proposed townhouse, the site of the main tower in the 1969 development, was removed almost entirely without archaeological recording. This may have greatly influenced its interpretation as a courtyard.

The 1996 watching brief showed that an area of up to about 6.5m around the tower had been removed during the construction of a deep central basement. This would have destroyed about half of the proposed townhouse, leaving only the west wing and a few peripheral elements. Although Marsden accepted that there were few remains in the area, the original reconstruction of the building included a conjectured wall nearly 20m in

length. Not all of Marsden's assumptions have been borne out by the more recent investigations and there are some aspects of the interpretation which are still in need of elucidation.

The 1969 watching brief

The purpose of the 1969 work was to record the archaeological deposits and structures which were revealed and destroyed by the digging of holes to facilitate the grubbing out of existing foundations within the area of new pile positions. 'Unfortunately, no archaeological excavation could be undertaken in the area, and it was not possible to fully watch the clearance of the central part of the site. As a result, the archaeological record is fragmentary, though probably sufficiently complete for an attempted interpretation of the significance of the structures to be made' (Marsden 1975, 54).

The plans and records from the 1969 watching brief are held by the Museum of London Archaeological Archive (GM187). The following summary is taken from Marsden 1975, and contains the original interpretations. An updated synthesis, considering the 1969, 1994 and 1996–7 work, is to be found in chapter 3, with new or extended interpretations as appropriate.

The north range

The north range was thought to have consisted of a line of five rooms (Rooms 58–62). The position of the external (northern) wall of this range was entirely conjectural as it was expected to have been on a very similar alignment to that of the 19th-century walls along the Laurence Pountney Hill frontage. This conjectured northern wall must have been quite substantial as it would also have served as a terrace wall. In Room 58 a white mortar floor was found at c 6.7m OD. In Room 59 there was a buff mortar floor, above which was found a late 3rd-century bronze radiate copy (MoL 92.127/637). The floor was covered 'by a deposit of ash and dark earth ... while above ... was a layer of Roman rubble and mortar fragments, perhaps indicating the destruction of the building' (Marsden 1975, 56). Below the floor in the southern part of the room was a short length of ceramic pipe, interpreted as a drain flowing southwards to remove groundwater coming under the northern wall.

In Room 61 was a buff mortar floor at c 6.7m OD, while in Room 62 was an *opus signinum* floor 0.15m thick at c 6.76m OD, with gravel make-up below. To the south of Room 62 was a yellow mortar floor at 6.3m OD: this was interpreted as part of Room 64 and may have been part of a corridor along the internal side of the northern range. It was considered unlikely to be part of a second set of rooms belonging to the northern range as there was no evidence for any walls further south within this area.

The southern external walls of the north range and the west wall of Room 59 were c 1.0m wide and all constructed of ragstone rubble blocks, bonded by buff mortar, containing some reused brick and fragments of pink mortar. The internal walls were c 0.50m wide with flint and chalk rubble foundations, bonded by brown mortar, with traces of brick string courses above ground level in Room 62. These narrow internal walls were interpreted as secondary additions, suggesting that Rooms 59–62 were originally one large chamber.

The west range

The plan of this range suggested the existence of either several phases of building or several separate but adjoining buildings. Several rooms were identified (Rooms 65–8, 70–4). At the northern end of the range between Room 58 (part of the north range) and Room 65 was a possible corridor or passageway 2.46m wide (Room 63).

The north and south walls of Room 65 at the northern end of the range were constructed of ragstone rubble blocks with

double bonding courses of brick. Within the room was a secondary partition or blocking wall on an east–west alignment (Feature 66), constructed of ragstone rubble blocks and some fragments of Roman brick, bonded by brown mortar.

Later rebuilding during the Roman period largely destroyed Room 67, when the south wall was demolished and it was combined with Room 68 to form one chamber. Natural sand/gravel was located within the room at 4.07m OD, sealed by clayey brickearth, above which was the rubble make-up for a mosaic floor (information from site notes). This 'decorated mosaic pavement' at 4.77m OD was the first floor of the room. Sadly, it 'was in part destroyed by the mechanical excavator without any opportunity having been given to record its design. A narrow zone of the mosaic was measured in the edge of the modern excavation [recorded length 2.1m] to show that originally it had a broad surround of plain red tesserae, while the mosaic border itself was a guilloche pattern ... The tesserae ... were coloured black, red, white and yellow. Fortunately, part of the mosaic remains in situ and could be excavated in future' (Marsden 1975, 57). The following details of the room were obtained from site notes. During the later alterations to Room 67, two layers of *opus signinum* 0.3m and 0.1m thick were laid above the mosaic at up to 5.17m OD. Within the thickness of the lower layer was an east–west drain or flue 2.27m south of the north wall. This was constructed of brick in a clay bed, and was 0.2m wide internally. The north wall survived to 1.45m above this level (7.62m OD), containing at least three double brick bonding courses.

Room 68 was originally a small chamber, but was combined later with Room 67 by demolishing the dividing wall, leaving two underlying rows of foundation piles set 0.45m apart to mark its former position. The south wall of Room 68 was originally 1.7m thick, but was rebuilt subsequently to 0.86m, the site notes suggesting that it survived to 1.06m above the final floor (6.23m OD).

The east wall of Room 70 was 0.91m wide, constructed of ragstone rubble blocks, probably with brick bonding courses at a higher level. The floor of the room was a coarse red tessellated pavement at 4.00m OD.

The plan of the southern portion of the west range was very fragmentary. Three short lengths of wall (Features 71, 73 and the west wall of Room 74) defined the probable east and west limits. Walls 71 and 73 were constructed of ragstone rubble blocks, the eastern wall (Feature 71) was 0.9m wide; to the west was a fragment of pink mortar flooring. The western wall (Feature 73) was 0.6m wide bonded by yellow mortar. It had double string courses of bricks at intervals of about 0.9m. Two yellow mortar floors separated vertically by 1.0m were recorded 1.52m west of Feature 73.

Only one room (74) in the south-west corner of this range was examined. It was 2.0m wide and was interpreted as a probable corridor. Its west and south walls were constructed of ragstone rubble blocks, with double brick courses, bonded by yellow mortar. Within the room was a series of floor surfaces. The earliest floor was a layer of white mortar over 0.46m thick, with bricks set in its top surface. A layer of *opus signinum* at

3.86m OD sealed this. The north wall of Room 74 was built over the *opus signinum* floor, proving that it was a later addition to the building (Marsden 1975, 58).

The east range

This range was thought to have consisted of at least two large rectangular rooms (75–6), although cross-walls may well have existed in the unexamined areas of the site (see Fig 4). Room 75 had a floor of coarse red tesserae set in pink mortar at *c* 4.5m OD. At the northern end of the room was a quarter-round pink mortar moulding at the junction of the wall and floor. Such mouldings are commonly found in plunge baths, where their function was to make a waterproof joint between the wall and floor of the bath. The west wall of Room 76 contained an 'oval opening of a hypocaust flue' (Feature 77), and a second possible flue (Feature 79) was seen at the southern end of this room (Marsden 1975, 58). Later the wall dividing Rooms 75 and 76 was demolished and an *opus signinum* floor laid in the enlarged chamber. As the interior of Room 76 was not examined, the interpretation of these features is uncertain, but it is possible that they represented either a suite of heated rooms or possibly part of a baths complex.

The walls of Rooms 75 and 76 were constructed of ragstone rubble blocks, bonded by yellow mortar with traces of a double course of bricks.

The south range

The plan of this range was very fragmentary, and only two rooms were identified (Rooms 80–1). In Room 80 was a floor of *opus signinum* 0.1m thick, topped by red bricks at *c* 3.35m OD. The foundations of the floor consisted of a layer of buff mortar supported on timber piles. No floors were recorded in Room 81. The walls of both were constructed of ragstone rubble blocks, bonded by yellow or brown mortar, and founded on timber piles. The west wall of Room 81 (Feature 72) was constructed of ragstone blocks bonded by pink mortar; this difference could be explained by the use of pink 'opus signinum-type' waterproof mortar to bond the foundations, as was the case in one of the 1996 trenches (TP14). The use of timber pile foundations here can be explained by the ground conditions: the south range was entirely built on reclaimed land behind the 1st- and 2nd-century waterfronts below the northern fringes of modern Upper Thames Street.

The central area

It is probable that very little archaeological work was undertaken in the area bounded by the four ranges of rooms (Area 69), which was largely destroyed by piling and excavation for massive pile caps. Little could therefore be said about the nature of the archaeology there, with the exception that timber piles were noted across the northern part of the area during groundworks (information from site notes). In the absence of any evidence to the contrary, the area was interpreted as a garden or courtyard.

The area to the east

Very limited archaeological work was undertaken in the eastern area of the site, and the Roman features recorded were of a rather different nature to those in the west.

Three small fragments of Roman brick-built walling bonded by pink mortar were observed (Features 82 and 83). These were thought to represent fragments of other Roman buildings to the east of the main townhouse. Feature 82 was 2.0m east of and parallel to the outer wall of Room 75 in the east wing of the main structure, with 'No floor, just black silt' intervening. This implies the presence of a second building, probably separated from it by a narrow alley. Feature 83 consisted of two fragments of wall core, set 6.25m and 8.0m east of the main building, 10m north of Feature 82.

Along the Laurence Pountney Lane street frontage a sequence of Roman buildings was discovered. The earliest was represented by a dump of burnt daub recorded over an area *c* 6.0m north–south by 2.5m east–west (Features 84, 85, 87). This dump was sealed by a wattle and daub building with *opus signinum* (Feature 84) and white mortar (Feature 86) floors (no level given). This later building also appears to have been destroyed by fire.

These vernacular buildings are almost certainly unconnected with both the main masonry structure and the intervening brick and pink mortar building.

Earlier work

Several earlier observations were made on the site and in the immediate area in the 19th century (*J Brit Archaeol Ass* 1847, 340–1, 345), in 1927 (RCHM 1928, 143) and in 1966 (Guildhall Museum file GM52).

The 19th-century observations

During sewer works in 1846 'were observed some very large Roman walls, built entirely of tiles, 18 inches [0.45m] by 12 [0.3m], and mortar; and some fragments of Samian ware.' In association were coins of mid 1st- and late 3rd-century date. In addition, 'A large space was covered with the coarse pavement made of square red brick tesserae.' Subsequently, walls (one incorporating many fragments of Andernach querns and millstones), tessellated floors and two column bases 15in (0.38m) and 19in (0.48m) in diameter were located. These, however, appear to have been located from St Laurence Church passage northwards towards Cannon Street.

More certainly associated with the site was the important discovery beneath Ducksfoot Lane of 'a large number of Roman flue-tiles, mostly in fragments. These tiles were used to convey heat to those rooms distant from the hypocaust; they were built up in the centre of the wall, as is proved by the mortar, which still adheres to every side.'

The 1927 observations

In 1927 during works to lay electrical cables under the north side of Upper Thames Street (near the middle of the present dual carriageway), two north–south aligned 'composite' baulks of oak sloping southwards were encountered to either side of Suffolk Lane, set 6.1m apart at c 0.5m OD and 1.5m OD. A parallel 0.76m wide wall of flints set in white mortar was recorded 5.5m further east, and a further 5.2m eastwards was a second timber structure of lighter construction than the first. Timbers ran both east–west and north–south. The drum of a 0.61m diameter stone column was also found in the same place.

The 1966 observation

During works on the north side of the site, an east–west medieval foundation of ragstone with a little chalk and flint was discovered to a height of 3.05m. It was not precisely located, but supported the north wall of the 19th-century building which predated Suffolk House, clear evidence of how the medieval structures were constantly reused.

Discussion

The 1969 archaeological work located the fragmentary remains of a large masonry building of Roman date. This was provisionally interpreted by the excavator, Peter Marsden, as a substantial masonry townhouse, possibly connected to the Cannon Street 'palace' complex, since mortar floors were found in the intervening space beneath the present Suffolk Lane. The surviving plan of this structure was fragmentary, but it appears to have consisted of four ranges of rooms grouped around a large rectangular garden or courtyard. It is possible that there was a corridor or colonnaded passage along the internal sides of the four ranges.

It was apparent that the building was of a very high status and some architectural sophistication. For instance, although most rooms had plain mortar floors, some were surfaced with *opus signinum* as either a primary (Rooms 62, 80) or a secondary feature (Rooms 67, 75/76). Room 67 had a decorated mosaic as its original floor, which was subsequently replaced by *opus signinum*. Rooms 75 and 68, by way of contrast, were floored with coarse red tesserae. In the east wing, the presence of one or possibly two flues suggested either the existence of underfloor heating or that the area formed part of a bath suite. This seems to be borne out by the 19th-century observations of flue tiles under the former Ducksfoot Lane.

The building was clearly of several phases of construction as there was evidence of walls being added, or in some cases being demolished (Room 75/76), and of floors being replaced. Unfortunately there was no dating evidence for either the construction or the additions to the building. The discovery of a late 3rd-century coin above the floor of Room 59 in the north range was taken as a possible indicator of the date of its demise, being located in a deposit of ash probably relating to the disuse of the room. It was suggested that the building was constructed during the late 1st or early 2nd century.

The presence of timbers beneath Upper Thames Street in 1927 implies that an early quay was perhaps associated with the townhouse, while the column drum from the same area suggests

that the building may have been colonnaded, at least facing the river. The medieval ragstone wall found in 1966 was almost certainly part of the west wing of the large building complex identified as the Manor of the Rose.

The main components of this earlier work – the Roman and medieval townhouses and the quay – were all present in the 1994–7 investigation, which has enabled them to be more precisely interpreted.

1.3 Organisation of the report

The report attempts to cover as many aspects of the site sequence and areas of specialist interest as possible, although there is an inevitable emphasis on the Roman period, particularly the waterfronts and the townhouse. The prehistoric marsh is also studied in some detail. The analysis of the material collected and recorded was the subject of a series of specialist archive reports (see the bibliography) in accordance with the *Management of archaeological projects* (English Heritage 1991), and these are lodged with the Museum of London, where they may be consulted by prior engagement.

The chronological narrative is broken down into a series of three main chapters, two of which (for the Roman and medieval sequences) are divided into periods, each representing a fundamental change in the nature of the site's development or dating. Within the main periods, the site is presented chronologically within individual land uses (defined as buildings, open areas, waterfronts, roads etc). Dating evidence is both integrated with the text and summarised in specialist discussions. The text is accompanied by period plans and illustrations, which include line drawings and photographs of features and artefacts associated with particular periods or areas of land use. Specialist appendices are also included which contain more detailed back-up data, including tables and catalogues of artefacts and ecofacts. These are cross-referenced to the main text, generally through the use of both subgroup and land-use numbers to enable the reader to access details from several sections.

1.4 Documentary sources

Specialist documentary research for the site was not undertaken, although an outline of the development of the area and its principal buildings has been collated based on initial research carried out at various stages in the project (chapters 3 and 4). This concentrated particularly on the history and layout of the Manor of the Rose and its successors. The main source was a published synthesis (Norman 1901) which was based on deeds, wills, charters, leases, rentals and court rolls relating to the property. The available documentary and cartographic evidence has been used to produce an outline of the development of the western part of the manor, the only part of the property for which substantial remains survived in 1994–7.

1.5 Textual and graphical conventions in this report

This report presents a summary of the archaeological evidence from the site. Where quoted, context numbers are in square brackets [ ], group/subgroup numbers in curved brackets (), finds accession numbers <> and environmental samples {}. The evidence is presented chiefly by major units of land use, Building (B), Open Area (OA), Waterfront (W), or less frequently, Road (R) and Structure (S). In addition, EN = enabling hole; MH = manhole shaft; TP = trial pit. Buildings have usually been identified on the basis of the presence of either an apparently internal surface (for example a brickearth floor), or by the presence of one or more walls (whether of timber or masonry, robbed or present). External surfaces or features (pits, wells, quarries and cesspits) normally define open areas, although in the medieval and post-medieval periods, stone-lined wells and cesspits were often sited within buildings. In cases where there is no structural evidence for buildings,

the available documentary or cartographic evidence has been consulted to determine whether or not they were formerly present.

The synthetic nature of this report has determined that details of horizontal stratigraphy, wall construction, areas of truncation and variations in ground level have not been included on the site plans. Some features described in the text have also been omitted for clarity, particularly where one or more are superimposed. The Research Archive holds the original plans and sections which were used to develop the sequence presented in this volume.

Location map

site outline

Archaeological features

— · — · — · —   **limit of excavation**

wall : found and conjectured

retained wall

surface : found and conjectured

Key to graphical conventions used in this report

2

Natural topography

2.1 Introduction

Evidence for the underlying geology and topography of the site was mainly obtained through a study of borehole data, although some trenches were excavated to the Pleistocene gravel.

London occupies an area close to the centre of a depression in the underlying Cretaceous chalk, the Thames basin. The chalk outcrops around the rim of the basin as the Chilterns and North Downs, the basin itself being infilled by a series of geologically more recent deposits, including the marine sands and clays of the Woolwich and Reading Beds, the Thanet Sands and the London Clay. These were deposited around 55 million years ago in warm marine conditions (Ellison & Zalasiewicz 1996, 92).

Subsequently, around 40 million years ago, a river system occupied the area, and the floodplain consisted of fine sandy deposits, which were mainly eroded later, exposing large areas of the London Clay. Around 2–3 million years ago the Thames followed a course further north, until the Anglian glaciation, which disrupted the area, ultimately leading to the river reaching its present position. Large amounts of sands and gravels were deposited across the eroded surface of the London Clay, and during several phases of downcutting, a series of at least six gravel terraces were formed along the Thames Valley.

The present-day City of London lies on the second 'Taplow' Terrace, which reaches c 10.4m OD, and is capped by the Langley Silts, a fine sandy silt ('brickearth') deposited towards the end of the Devensian, c 17,000 years ago (Gibbard 1994, 94) and reaching c 12.0m OD. These deposits are cut by the rivers Fleet and Walbrook, leaving the brickearth confined to the upper parts of two hills. The site lies at the south-east corner of the eastern hill on the fringe of the brickearth zone. Located very close to the current river is the Shepperton or Floodplain Terrace of a buried channel of the Thames.

2.2 Geology and topography

Open Area 1

London Clay

It is clear from a study of the levels for London Clay (Group 1.1) at Suffolk House that there is a substantial fall in levels from 3.82m OD in the north-west (Borehole 6a) to −5.55m OD in the south (Borehole 8). The contours trend from the north-west towards the south-east for the most part, although there is evidence for a possible valley in the east, leaving the highest surviving area of clay as a plateau extending into the site from the north. This is less visible on a contour survey of the overlying gravel (Fig 5).

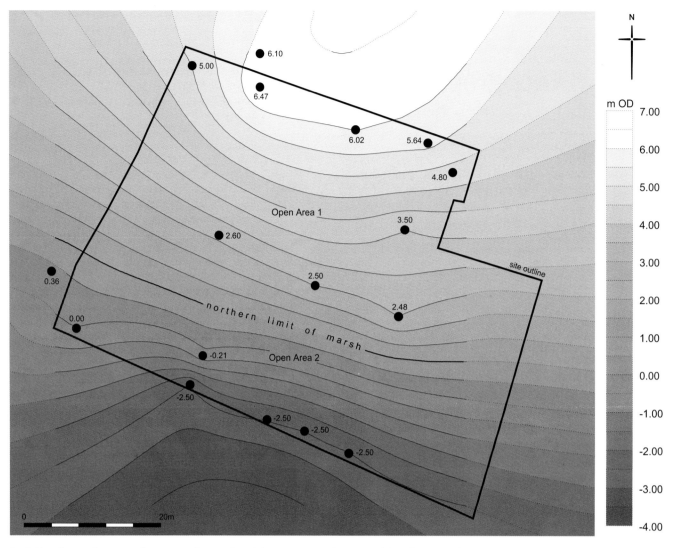

Fig 5 Plan of principal pre-Roman features: natural topography and the approximate northern extent of the prehistoric marsh

Gravels

The terrace gravels (1.2) over most of the area averaged a depth of 2.5m (OA1; see Fig 5). Outside the northern site boundary, Marsden recorded the gravel surface as being at 7.92m OD (Feature 57), but this appears to have fallen away rapidly southwards, probably due in part to later terracing, to above 6.0m OD (TP1–2). Southwards, the gravels continue to slope to a lower terrace. Boreholes 1 and 2 show that this lay at c 2.5–2.6m OD.

Further south, the terrace gravels mingled with finer early foreshore material (1.4), and it seems likely that the two merged in the intertidal zone (between c Ordnance Datum to 1.25m OD) which ran across the central part of the site. A number of observations encountered the top of the foreshore gravel at −2.50m OD to the south of this area (Borehole 8).

Langley Silts

Only one area of possible Langley Silts (natural brickearth) was observed in the north-east at 5.65m OD (1.3). This may, however, represent a small area of redeposited material.

2.3 The prehistoric environment

Introduction

During the excavation of the testpits at Suffolk House, a series of peaty organic sediments (1.5: Open Area 2) were observed underlying the Roman timber quays to some depth (Figs 6, 61; see 6.1 below). These were thought to be an extension of marsh deposits recorded under Cannon Street Station in 1988 (Burch & Hill 1988), which have not yet been examined in detail. The peats survived to c 1.0m OD where they were undisturbed and had not apparently been eroded, allowing the approximate original northern extent to be mapped (see Fig 5). Such deposits are surprisingly rare in the City and therefore the opportunity to collect information on presumably pre-Roman ecology was not one to be missed. Accordingly, two sections were sampled to collect undisturbed blocks of sediment for analysis (these are dealt with more fully in 6.1 below). The specific research questions were to establish details of the natural topography and to construct a more

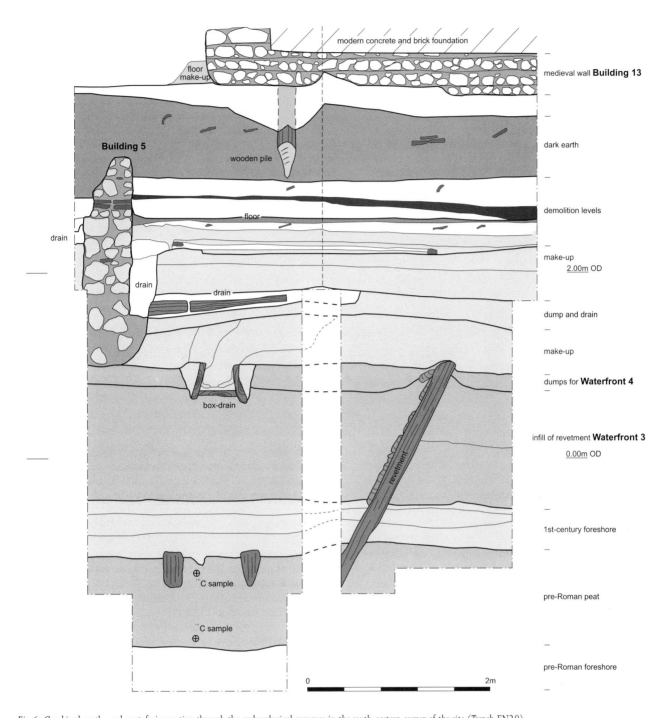

W   E   N   S

modern concrete and brick foundation

floor make-up

medieval wall **Building 13**

Building 5

wooden pile

dark earth

drain

floor

demolition levels

drain

make-up

2.00m OD

drain

drain

dump and drain

make-up

box-drain

dumps for **Waterfront 4**

revetment

infill of revetment **Waterfront 3**

0.00m OD

1st-century foreshore

C sample

pre-Roman peat

C sample

pre-Roman foreshore

0   2m

Fig 6 Combined south- and west-facing section through the archaeological sequence in the south-eastern corner of the site (Trench EN20)

detailed picture of the pre-urban riparian environment (see Woodger 1997). Several ^{14}C samples were submitted for assay to confirm the pre-Roman date, and indeed it was possible to date the onset of peat formation to at least the Neolithic period (see Tables 1, 2). This result proved that the deposits were even rarer in the City than was initially thought. Comparable peats laid down on sites in Southwark, such as at Courage's Brewery directly opposite Suffolk House (Cowan in prep), appear to be of Late Bronze Age or Iron Age date.

Open Area 2

The prehistoric marsh

As might be expected, the prehistoric marsh proved to contain the seeds of damp or wetland-loving species in six out of nine samples (see 6.2 below), including pondweed, celery-leaved crowfoot, gipsy-wort, bur-reed, fine-leaved water dropwort, spike-rush, yellow flag/iris, marshwort and lesser spearwort. These suggest that the water at the confluence of the lower Walbrook and River Thames was clean and normally slow-moving prior to the arrival of the Romans. Seeds of rush and sedge may have come from plants imported for thatching, floor covering or bedding, but these were few in number, and are more likely to have been part of the local flora.

Also present were seeds and catkins of alder, a hazelnut shell and seeds from woodland, scrub or hedgerow habitats. One sample contained remains of wild radish/charlock, found growing in cultivated and rough ground (Stace 1991, 342).

The presence of fig, grape and barley grains suggests contamination from Roman levels.

A complete woodcock skull was recovered, possibly representing local fowling, although as only a single example was found, it is perhaps more likely to have been the result of natural deposition.

Microanalysis of two column samples taken in EN20 indicate that the organic mud formed in situ, a process that ^{14}C samples suggest began in the Late Mesolithic or Early Neolithic period (see Fig 6; Tables 1, 2), c 3900–3350 BC. Pollen from the samples suggest the presence of mixed woodland in the area in the earliest periods, with clearance for more intensive agricultural activities taking place in the Middle Bronze Age (c 1500–1000 BC), represented by a decline in lime.

The formation of the marsh appears to have continued to the pre-Roman Iron Age, c 260–30 BC, although erosion which occurred before the construction of Waterfront 2 in AD 84 suggests that there had been a change from a depositional to an erosional environment. The upper contact horizon was consequently disturbed, and contained an intrusive medieval lead-alloy spangle <168>, as well as a number of Roman artefacts (see Figs 10, 11), including an early to mid 1st-century one-piece 'Nauheim derivative' brooch <141> (<S1>), two iron styli – one <165> (<S17>) of Manning Type 1, the second <174> (<S20>) Type 4 – and a fragment of writing tablet <74>. The marsh also contained a single human bone, the left humerus of an infant probably less than six months, although it is unclear whether this should be viewed as part of the Roman contamination or the pre-Roman marsh itself. Human bones do occur in Roman waterfront deposits, including several examples from Regis House (Conheeney in Brigham & Watson in prep).

2.4 Period discussion

The natural topography of the riverbank is the single most important factor governing the pattern of later development. There is, as yet, no clear evidence for prehistoric exploitation of the shoreline of the City of London in the same way that there is in Southwark. (Several marginal areas which were ploughed in the Bronze Age have been recognised, including sites at Lafone Street, Wolseley Street and Phoenix Wharf. A ring-ditch with cremations dated c 1600 BC – probably the truncated remains of a round barrow – was also excavated on the shoreline at Fennings Wharf. All of these sites are downstream of London Bridge, in areas which were inundated by the rising level of the tidal river in the Iron Age.) The presence of peat deposits in the City may lead to the discovery of such evidence in the future, such as traces of fishing or wildfowling. The single woodcock skull and human infant humerus could represent local occupation, although further examination of larger exposures of peat is required to determine the frequency and distribution of such finds, and whether or not they are intrusive. Organic structures such as fish weirs and traps are often found in such environments, where the conditions for preservation are good. Communities which had access to rivers would certainly have exploited their resources to augment and vary a diet of cereals and animal protein. It may be expected that the position of the marsh at the confluence of the Walbrook and Thames would provide a variety of habitats ranging from fresh to brackish depending on the state of the tide. The evidence, however, seems to point to there being little marine influence during the period of formation, which may well suggest that the tidal head of the river was some distance downstream of the present City.

Despite the limitations of the area investigated, the identification and analysis of the marsh at Suffolk House have therefore proved to be of considerable value in determining the past environment from the Neolithic period to the pre-Roman Iron Age.

3

The Roman period

3.1 Introduction

It has generally been suggested that Roman London was founded on a previously unoccupied site; to be more precise, there were almost certainly Iron Age farmsteads in the area beforehand, successors to later Bronze Age occupation, but the area was largely open ground. What is clear is that early Roman London was the first nucleated settlement in the vicinity of the modern City of London with urban characteristics as defined by past studies (eg Todd 1970; Rodwell & Rowley 1975; Burnham 1987).

It is possible to suggest on the basis of the present evidence that Londinium began as a small planned settlement shortly after the invasion of AD 43, centred around the northern end of the new bridge across the Thames, linking modern Southwark with the City (see Fig 1). Buildings and patterns of landholding with urban, as opposed to rural, characteristics began to develop very quickly, although simple rural buildings would still be apparent, particularly on the fringes. They have, for example, been identified in Neronian or early Flavian levels at Leadenhall Court (LCT84; Milne 1992, 9–12; Milne & Wardle 1993, 30–3). The site of the settlement included creeks on the south bank suitable for offline mooring of smaller vessels, river barges and lighters, while on the north bank, the mouths of the Walbrook, the Fleet and lesser streams would have given additional mooring or beaching facilities. The high ground along the north bank also allowed the creation of artificial terraces suitable for wharves and waterside buildings, and this was quickly exploited. Dendrochronological analysis of a timber revetment at Regis House in 1996 has suggested that work on the waterfront area next to the bridge began at least as early as AD 52, and very probably several years earlier (Brigham & Watson in prep). A small settlement protected from the river by embankments seems to have come into being on the south bank in present-day Southwark at the same time.

There was little evidence for the provision of public facilities in the first decade beyond a localised orthogonal street grid and what appears to have been an open market area below the later forum (Marsden 1987, 70–2).

These features formed the nucleus of a community which was destroyed during the Boudican revolt of AD 60–1, but was subsequently re-established to include the western hill and other marginal areas. There was also a massive investment in the construction of new wharves and waterfront buildings, beginning at Regis House in AD 63–4, but extending both east and west in the following decades.

The later 1st century also saw the construction of the first forum, a timber amphitheatre, and on the waterfront to the west of the site a large public baths complex, all evidence of a flourishing settlement. This work was followed in the early 2nd century by a fort, an enlarged forum and masonry amphitheatre, and in the 3rd century by landward and riverside defensive walls. From the point of view of the site, the most significant addition was the late Flavian complex identified by Peter Marsden as the 'Governor's Palace' (see 1.2 above). Whatever the interpretation, this clearly dominated the area, particularly in the 1st and early 2nd centuries, when it stood largely alone at the mouth of the Walbrook.

A study of the natural topography below Suffolk House and the neighbouring Cannon Street Station clearly shows its restrictive influence on the use made of the area. Immediately downstream of the Walbrook mouth the lower terrace was initially unusable because of the presence of the prehistoric marsh (see 2.3 above), and it was not until reclamation after AD 84 that buildings could extend into this zone from the uppermost terrace. This has ramifications for the development of the 'Governor's Palace' site, where up to 1.0m of marsh deposits were located (Stephenson 1996).

The later history of the town following a second fire in the Hadrianic period is one of change and contraction. The early clay-and-timber strip-buildings which characterised the commercial and residential districts were increasingly replaced by a smaller number of large masonry townhouses set in their own grounds, or at least 'detached', to use the modern term. Many of the larger townhouses were still occupied and even altered or enlarged well into the 4th century. At the same time, public buildings such as the baths and the forum went out of use, the latter being demolished in the later 3rd century, some years after the port facilities had also been largely dismantled. So, although the townhouse recorded at Suffolk House continued in use in the 4th century, as will be demonstrated, the neighbouring 'Governor's Palace' was, significantly, abandoned and levelled. The way government operated in London, whether

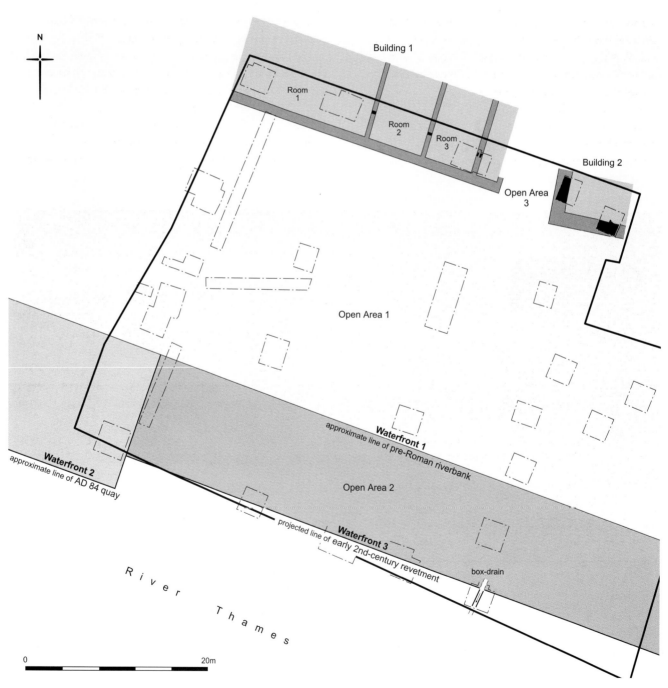

Fig 7 Plan of principal 1st-century archaeological features: Buildings 1–2, Waterfronts 1–3

local or provincial, changed beyond all recognition, at least as far as its outward manifestations such as public works and facilities were concerned. Intervention clearly continued in some form, however, organising, for example, the construction of bastions around the eastern part of the landward defensive wall.

3.2 Waterfront development: *c* AD 50–120

Waterfront 1: *c* AD 50–84

The earliest Roman activity was represented in the south-west (EN11) by a pair of straight-grained oak piles (2.1) driven into the foreshore along the south edge of Open Area 1. While they may have been part of a roughly east–west alignment, the position of these timbers some distance south of where the riverbank is thought to have lain suggests that they were part of an ancillary structure, such as a jetty or mooring installation. No trace was found of the early Roman riverbank itself (Waterfront 1), and the projected line (Fig 7) is based on the evidence of the level the river was expected to reach at high water, which in AD 50 was probably *c* 1.2–1.3m OD. Although the timbers were undated, the structure was superseded by a

quay (Waterfront 2) dated *c* AD 84. Waterfront 1 may have formed one of a series of early revetments dating from shortly after the establishment of the town *c* AD 50. If not, the period of reconstruction and expansion following the Boudican revolt (*c* AD 60–1) is the most likely time at which it was laid out on the basis of evidence from other sites. As such, this evidence adds a small but significant contribution to the study of the early waterfront.

Waterfront 2: timber quay and later reclamation: *c* AD 84–100/120

In the same area, part of a hitherto unknown substantial timber quay (Waterfront 2) is of much greater significance. The quay was represented by two groups of squared east–west land-ties or tiebacks (Figs 8, 9; see also Figs 64, 65) which anchored a north–south return at the eastern end of a riverside wharf, although the frontage did not pass through EN11.

The wharf almost certainly continues as far west as the mouth of the Walbrook stream, where a broadly similar but currently undated structure was recorded at Cannon Street Station (Stephenson 1996, 67; Millett 1990, 165).

The length of the longest tieback timber was about 3.0m, roughly equivalent to those used in the similar 1st-century Pudding Lane II quay (Brigham 1990a, 153, fig 15.3), suggesting

Fig 8 Trench EN11. View of the northern face of the tiebacks forming the supporting structure for Waterfront 2 from the south-east, showing the arrangement of retaining piles and locking bars. The empty dovetail housing for the upper locking bar is clearly visible. The main frontage lies beyond the edge of the trench to the left (0.5m scale)

17

Fig 9 Trench EN11. View of Waterfront 2 under excavation from the south-west, showing the arrangement of the retaining piles and locking bars

that the frontage of the return was not far to the east of the excavation trench. The area beyond, including the main part of the Suffolk House site, presumably took the form of a wide inlet with Waterfront 1 forming the north side, perhaps continuing as far as the Miles Lane site (see Fig 1) where a similar quay had been constructed a few years previously (Miller 1982).

The more substantial southern group comprised a stack of five squared timber baulks (2.3), the lower two of which were inserted into a gravel-filled trench cut into the surface of the prehistoric peat horizon (2.2). Four squared piles at the west end of the horizontal timbers acted to secure them by means of cross-ties or locking bars inserted through dovetail housings cut into the upper face of three of the tiebacks (see Fig 69). These enabled the quay to resist pressure from the weight of its infill, thereby securely anchoring the structure in place on the exposed foreshore.

The second group consisted of a single tieback set 2.0m further north after the partial infilling of the quay with organic rubbish. A roundwood pile was driven into the infill alongside the tieback to retain a locking bar like those in the southern group. The quay survived to about 2.15m OD suggesting that it had not been robbed, although the upper locking bars of both sets of tiebacks had been removed at some time. Other 1st-century structures – such as the Miles Lane and Regis House quays, and the slightly later Pudding Lane/Peninsular House quays – stood to 2.0m OD along the main river frontage, so Waterfront 2 fits into an established pattern. The intention was

clearly to create a level open space or wharf alongside the river, and stretching for some distance inland. This can be demonstrated by the extent of the latest organic infill, which continued some distance north of the main quay (EN13: 2.4). Fragments of oak recovered from the infill may have been the remains of a drain or a baseplate associated with the nearby west wall of Building 3 (see Fig 35).

The structural appearance of the quayfront in the inlet is unknown, and will remain so until future investigations can take place to the east of EN11. Its general nature can, however, be suggested with some confidence from evidence recovered from other sites. Excavations at Pudding Lane, Miles Lane and more recently at Regis House (see Fig 1) have shown that 1st-century waterfront structures without exception used lap joints to attach the tiebacks to the quayfront, which would have consisted of a stack of up to five beams (Milne 1985, 65; Brigham & Watson in prep). The main river frontage of Waterfront 2 must have been very similar structurally, and the fact that no north–south tiebacks were identified in the southern part of EN11 indicates that it passed at least 3.0m to the south of the excavated area. Although its exact line is unclear, the suggested position (see Fig 7) has been determined from the alignment of contemporary quays to the east and west, which generally rested on the contemporary foreshore at Ordnance Datum.

Two north–south squared timber baulks were found in Thames Street in 1927 at the foot of Suffolk Lane as it was before the construction of the present dual carriageway, some distance to the south of the modern frontage (RCHM 1928, 143). The timbers were at approximate levels of 0.5m OD and 2.0m OD, one of the baulks being 660mm x 610mm in section, substantially larger than those seen in 1996. These may have formed part of Waterfront 2, although this cannot be determined until future further investigations take place beneath the street.

The western end of what is presumably the same quay at Cannon Street Station differed in that it apparently had no tiebacks, although it rested on piles driven into the foreshore in the mouth of the Walbrook. This difference in construction may be significant, but until publication of the excavation sequence, a proper understanding of its nature is not possible. The Suffolk House/Cannon Street Station quay formed one of a pair of wharves, each c 120m long, to either side of the Walbrook. The river frontage and west end of the western wharf were recorded in a telecommunications tunnel in Upper Thames Street, where it terminated opposite the tower of St James Garlickhithe (see Fig 1; Flude 1980; Brigham 1990a, 135). There was a similar arrangement to either side of the bridge, with wharves at Miles Lane/Regis House (Brigham & Watson in prep) and Pudding Lane/Peninsular House (Milne 1985). From the early 2nd century, the apparent closure of the inlet at Suffolk House with the construction of Waterfront 3 led to the creation of a single wharf between the bridge and the Walbrook.

Nine tree-ring samples were dated from the tieback structure of Waterfront 2 (see 6.13 below). Six included sapwood, and a seventh [594] had bark edge, giving a combined felling date range of AD 83–105; [594] was felled in AD 84. Since the structure was made from squared baulks of green oak (see Fig 67) and there were no relict joints or other signs of reuse, a construction date of AD 84 seems to be indicated from the timber evidence alone, which does not conflict with the AD 70–160 pottery from the construction trench (2.2). This is considerably earlier than the comparable quay at Pudding Lane, which was probably constructed after c AD 90–5 (Milne 1985, 87).

The pottery assemblage is largely consistent with a date shortly after AD 70, although two sherds of samian ware from Les Martres de Veyre dated AD 100–20, and a sherd of Highgate 'C' dated AD 120–50, were recovered from the surface of the underlying prehistoric peats. The only explanation for their presence is that they had been disturbed from the sides of the trench during the excavation or shoring processes. Four sherds of Highgate 'C' ware with added coarse sand, dated AD 120–40, from the upper levels of the quay (2.3) were probably incorporated when the upper locking bars of the structure were robbed. If so, this would date its disuse to the construction of Waterfront 4, the presumed successor to Waterfront 2, as might be expected. The infill contained few artefacts, although several pieces of leather were found, including a small fragment of a possible stitched garment <328> and a glass beaker fragment <256> (see Fig 13: <G5>).

Foreshore

In the south-east (EN20), foreshore gravel with intermixed rubbish (4.1) was naturally deposited over the eroded pre-Roman peats

in the inlet (OA2) east of the main quay (see Fig 6). The gravel lay between −0.6m and −0.45m OD, just below the contemporary level of the mean low water spring tidal level suggested for the 1st century (Brigham et al 1995, 11). Pottery associated with the deposits was dated to AD 100–20, suggesting that it continued to collect in the early 2nd century. An as of Vespasian of AD 72 was also recovered, together with an earlier issue of Antonia (AD 41–5: <205>). Artefacts (Figs 10, 11) included three mirror fragments <209>–<211> (not illustrated) and two complete iron styli, one <216> (<S19>) of Manning Type 1, the second <137> (<S18>) of Type 2. Those recovered from the surface of the underlying peat (1.5) probably belonged with this group. The few animal bones recovered included a worked cattle tibia which was apparently a waste product of boneworking.

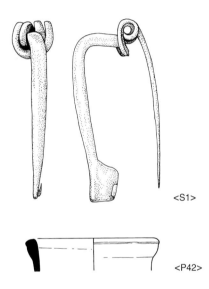

Fig 10 Finds from early foreshore Open Area 2: one-piece brooch <S1> (1:1); 1st-century amphora rim <P42> (1:4)

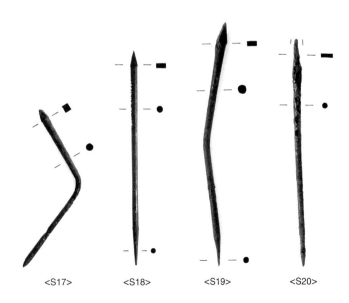

Fig 11 Iron styli <S17>–<S20> from Open Area 2 (1:2)

Waterfront 3: later post-and-plank revetment: *c* AD 100–20

An east–west post-and-plank revetment (Waterfront 3: 4.2) was subsequently constructed across the foreshore (Fig 12 and see Fig 66), blocking the inlet to the east of Waterfront 2 (EN20). The section of revetment recorded consisted of three reused posts with the remains of four levels of planks (see Fig 6). The lower three planks were reused tangentially cleft timbers which had been nailed into place but there was no sign that the upper planking had been similarly fixed; the upper planks were radially cleft, and had not apparently been reused. The base of the structure was at −0.45m OD and the top at about +1.05m OD. It was, however, leaning to the south at an angle of about 25°, apparently as a result of the lack of any form of bracing, and would have stood to at least 1.3m OD (probably nearer *c* 1.5m OD originally, as the tops of the supporting posts were decayed). The new wharf was therefore at least 0.5m below the level of Waterfront 2, apparently a response to a fall in the river level over the intervening period. (The comparable fall in level between the Neronian quay and early 2nd-century revetment at Regis House approaches the same magnitude.)

Five tree-ring samples were dated, three of which included sapwood, and a felling range of AD 90–121 is suggested for one of the planks, putting its original use in the late 1st or early 2nd century. Study of the pattern of the joints and wear on the timber suggests that it had been reused at least once before being incorporated into the revetment, however, and this influences the date of construction, which may be as late as *c* AD 120. The reused piles and lower planking appeared to have been used originally in a timber-framed building of reasonable quality (see 6.4 below; see also Figs 70, 71). The use of such materials and the less substantial nature of Waterfront 3 in comparison with the quay structure suggest a different level of investment and perhaps of function. The substantial quay structure represented by Waterfront 2 was presumably evidence of central planning whereas the flimsier revetment suggests a more local concern, perhaps intended to be of short duration.

Fig 12 *Trench EN20. View of the top of the early 2nd-century Waterfront 3 (centre line of the photograph) from the west, with the timber cradle for a Hadrianic box-drain to the right (0.5m scale)*

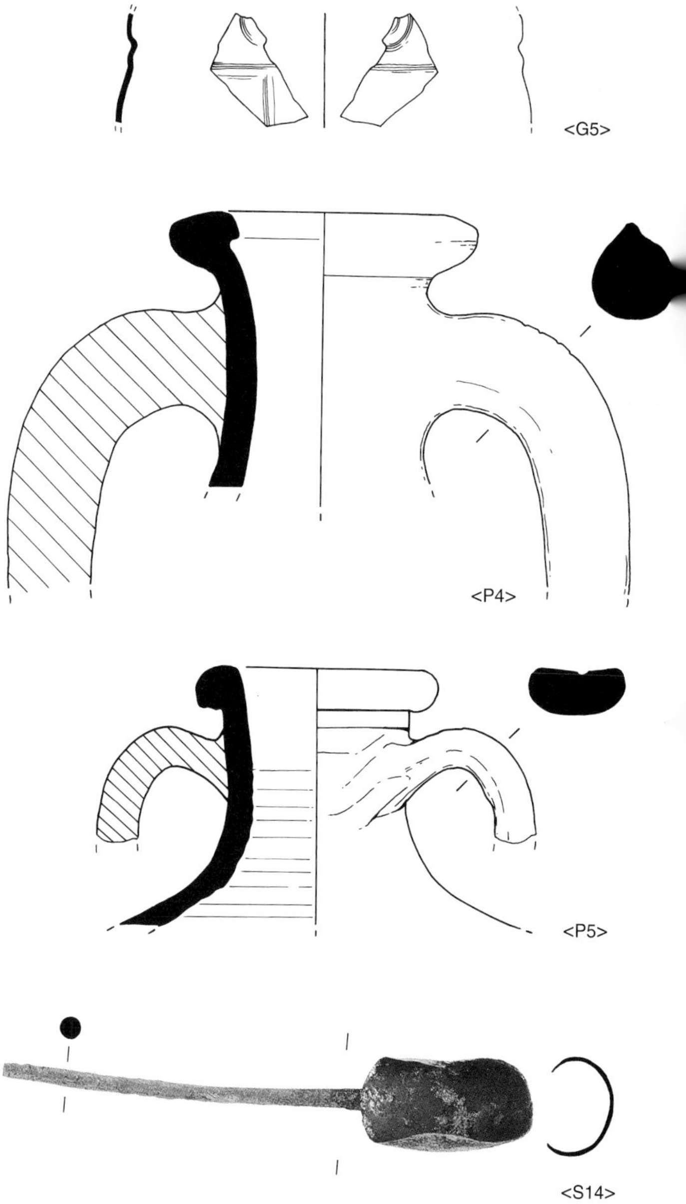

Fig 13 *Finds from Waterfronts 2 and 3: glass beaker fragment <G5> (1:2); early 2nd-century pottery <P4> <P5> (1:4); copper-alloy spoon <S14> (1:1)*

Waterfront 3 was backfilled with organic dumps containing a large assemblage of pottery dated AD 100–20 (Fig 13), which matches the suggested date for the structure itself. An *as* of Titus (AD 79–81: <118>) was also found, together with an almost complete copper-alloy spoon <142> (see Fig 13: <S14>). Bones from the dumps included the remains of cattle, sheep or goat, and chicken. Signs of butchery were present on many of the cattle upper limb bones as well as on a single horse humerus. Peaty gravel (5.7) dumped over the exposed London Clay along the eastern street frontage (EN22) may have been part of the same general layer.

Waterfront 4: a new revetment south of the site boundary: *c* AD 120–40

Dumping behind Waterfront 4

Waterfronts 2 and 3 were replaced subsequently by a new structure constructed beyond the site boundary (Waterfront 4). The nature and position of the waterfront itself can only be surmised (see Fig 35), although baulks aligned north–south and east–west were found to the south of Suffolk House in 1927 under the north side of Thames Street (RCHM 1928, 143). These are thought to have formed part of a quay that was of lighter construction than Waterfront 2, and between 5–10m further south. (A contemporary structure of just this type was

recorded to the south of the early 2nd-century revetment at Regis House in 1931 (Brigham & Watson in prep).)

In the 1996–7 excavation a lower stratum of organic infill deposits dumped over Waterfront 2 in the west (3.2–4; see Fig 61) was followed by the rubble make-up for a compact brickearth wharf surface (EN11: 3.5; BH9: 3.1). The surface must have sloped sharply down from 3.2m OD in this area to the waterfront itself, which was probably c 1.5m OD or a little lower at this period. Two stakes (3.6) may have formed part of a north–south alignment just to the west of the frontage of the redundant Waterfront 2.

Pottery of AD 100–20/40 and AD 90–160 from the dumps and the wharf surface included many discoloured sherds, although it is unclear whether this was a result of the conditions of preservation or burning. Artefacts from the lower dumps (3.3–4; Figs 14–17, 19, 21, 22) included a wooden comb <72> (<S11>), a bone hairpin <182> (<S7>) of Cool Type 6, probably dated AD 50–150, a needle <136> of Type 2, a clasp <181> (<S23>) and a perforated bone counter <233> (<S16>) of Crummy Type 1, with the letters 'A L' visible. Several pieces of stitched leather were found, one of which <410> (<L17>) appears to have been shoemaking waste, others parts of garments, including <412>. The remains of just two nailed shoes were recovered <411> <413>. Two paving bricks, one overfired but complete, may have come from an *opus spicatum* (herringbone-pattern) floor.

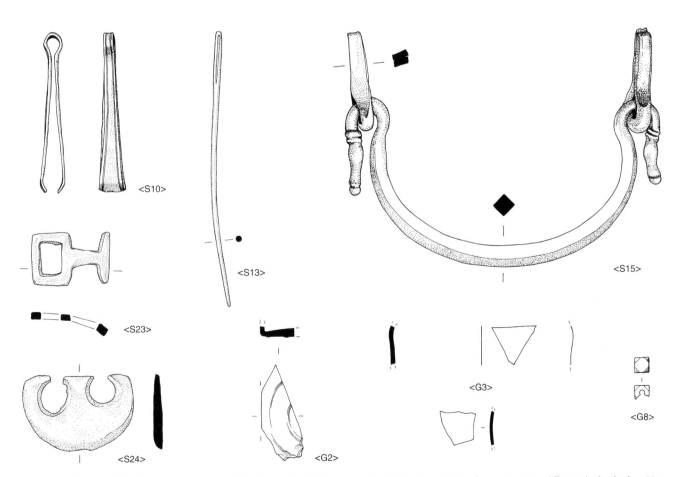

Fig 14 *Finds from lower fills of Waterfront 4: tweezers <S10>; iron needle <S13>; drop handle <S15>; clasp <S23>; pelta mount <S24> (all at 1:1); glass bottle <G2> (1:2); rim-cut beaker <G3> (1:2); glass bead <G8> (1:1)*

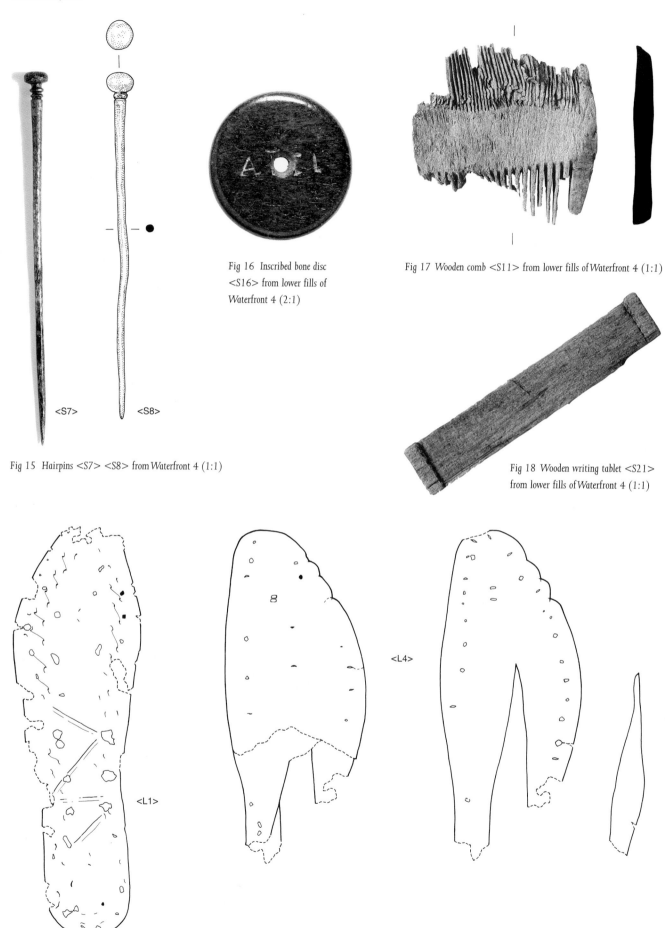

Fig 15 Hairpins <S7> <S8> from Waterfront 4 (1:1)

Fig 16 Inscribed bone disc <S16> from lower fills of Waterfront 4 (2:1)

Fig 17 Wooden comb <S11> from lower fills of Waterfront 4 (1:1)

Fig 18 Wooden writing tablet <S21> from lower fills of Waterfront 4 (1:1)

Fig 19 Leather shoes from lower fills of Waterfront 4: nailed shoe <L1>; sandal <L4>; stitched shoes <L7>–<L9>; one-piece shoes <L10> <L11> (1:2)

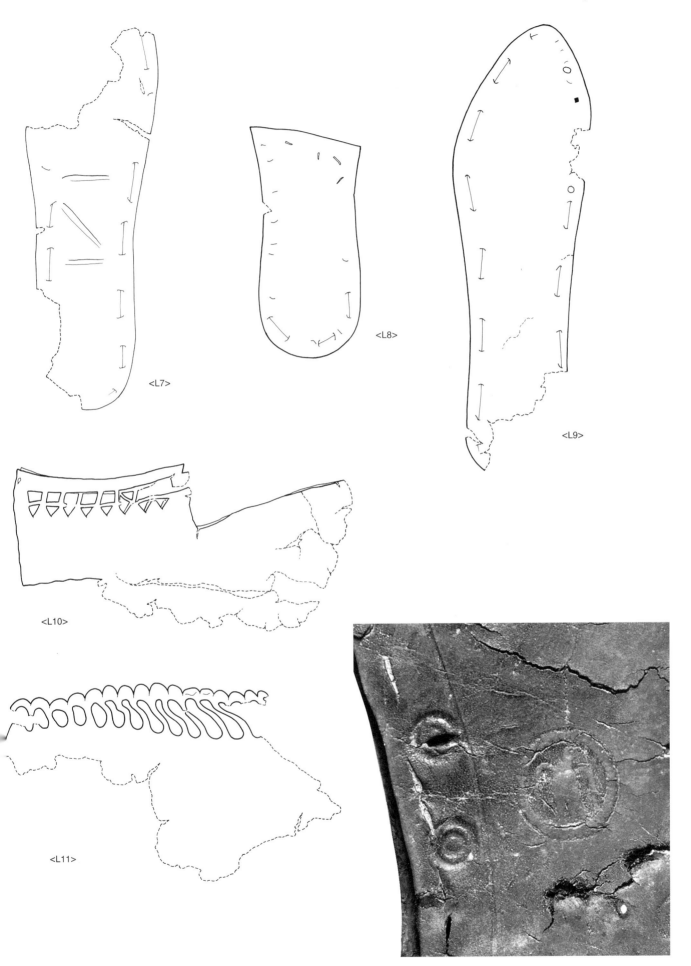

<L7>

<L8>

<L9>

<L10>

<L11>

Fig 20 Stamped sandal <L5> from lower fills of Waterfront 4 (2:1)

23

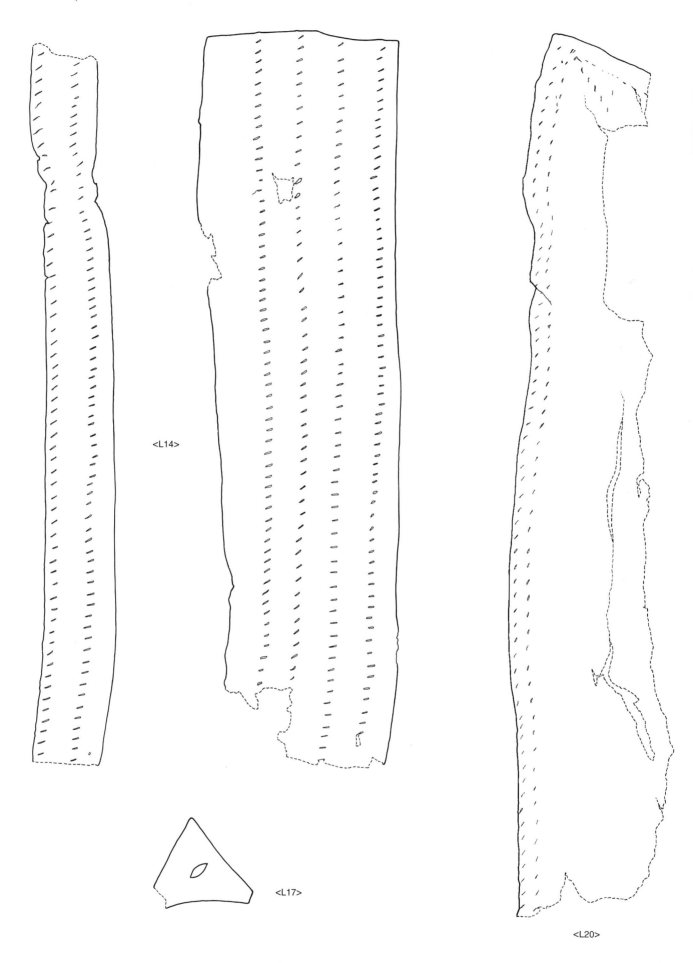

Fig 21 Non-shoe leather from lower fills of Waterfront 4: unidentified <L14>; shoemaking waste <L17>; panel <L20> (1:2)

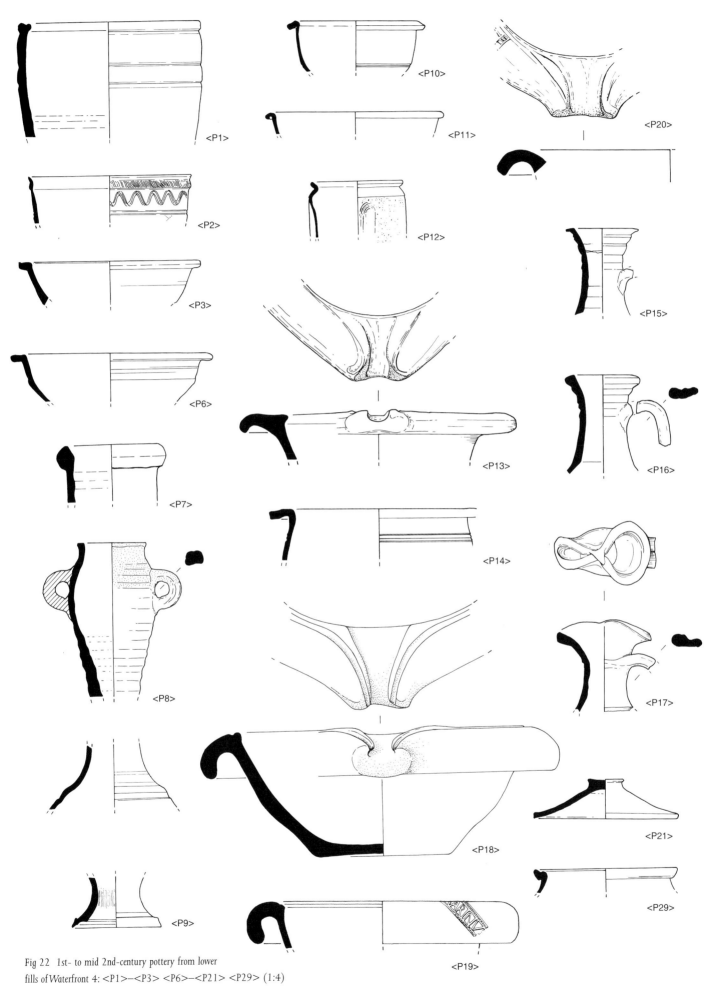

Fig 22 1st- to mid 2nd-century pottery from lower
fills of Waterfront 4: <P1>–<P3> <P6>–<P21> <P29> (1:4)

Environmental sampling indicated that the western infill contained the remains of plants representing a variety of disturbed woodland, scrub or wetland conditions, with evidence of the proximity of grassland and perhaps arable cultivation. Species included wild radish or charlock, corncockle, sorrel and sheep's sorrel, and henbane. There was little evidence for the semi-aquatic or aquatic conditions which might have been expected, perhaps indicating that the deposits were waste collected from a dry-land environment some distance from the waterfront. The presence of a large number of weld or dyer's rocket seeds implies that there may have been a local dyeing industry. Edible plants included coriander, fig, olive, stone pine, walnut and hazelnut, all Roman introductions. A flax seed was also present possibly as a weed rather than representing plants cultivated for linen production. Bones present included the main domesticates and single examples of dog and roe deer. A large number of oyster and winkle shells and a single cuttlefish shell indicated the importance of seafood as part of the diet.

Further east, similar organic waste was dumped in front of and over Waterfront 3 (EN10: 5.12; EN20: 4.4). An east–west fence of four stakes was installed immediately to the south, perhaps to mark the old line of the waterfront. The date of the very large assemblage of pottery recovered from these dumps was AD 100–20, comparable with that from the west. Two coins proved to be residual: an *as* of Domitian (*c* AD 85: <123>), and a very corroded issue of Claudius (AD 45–65: <188>). The deposits also contained a large number of artefacts (see Figs 14, 18–22), including a complete pair of tweezers <124> (<S10>), a rectangular mirror fragment <127>, parts of a bone needle <196> and a pin or needle <203>, three iron needles, one broken <131> (<S13>) <192> <202>, a pelta mount <115> (<S24>), glass fragments including a bottle <236> (<G2>) and a rim-cut beaker <238> (<G3>), and part of a wooden writing tablet <70> (<S21>). A notable find was a fine drop handle with decorated terminals from a box or drawer <138> (<S15>). Part of a hinged strap fitting <128> from *lorica segmentata* armour was also identified. A piece of Carrara marble paving or inlay <274> must have come from a building with some pretensions to grandeur.

Several pieces of leatherwork were recovered (see Figs 19–21): numerous examples of leather footwear and shoe fragments, including parts of 10 nailed shoes such as <419> (<L1>), five sandals including <414> (<L4>), four stitched shoes including <400> (<L7>), <406> (<L8>) and <420> (<L9>), and four

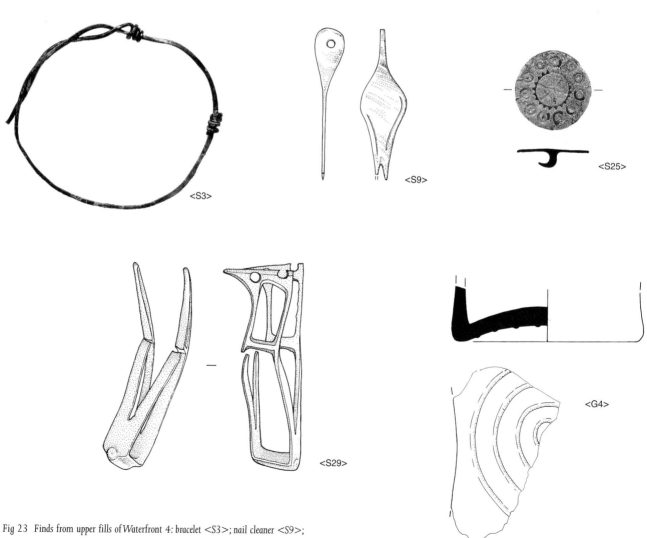

Fig 23 Finds from upper fills of Waterfront 4: bracelet <S3>; nail cleaner <S9>; military stud <S25>; mount/chape <S29> (all 1:1); glass bottle base <G4> (1:2)

one-piece examples such as <391> (<L10>) and <394> (<L11>). Among these were stamped sandals including <418> (<L5>) with both a ring-and-dot motif and a rare eagle in a circle design, and <338> with a series of concentric circles. Parts of possible garments <399> (<L14>), <402> and a panel <397> (<L20>) were also present. A substantial number of animal bones represented the main domesticates as well as a newborn or foetal cattle humerus, which may indicate that animals were kept locally. There was evidence of butchery on the upper limbs of both pig and cattle.

Organic 'peaty' deposits overlying the eastern dumps (5.1) represent a final stage of reclamation, since the pottery (AD 120–30/40) matched the suggested construction date for Waterfront 4. It also produced several coins, among them an *as* of Trajan (AD 96–117: <170>), as well as an earlier issue of Vespasian (AD 72: <106>). An interesting find, presumably kept as a curio or luck-piece, was a quarter *stater* of the Atrebatic

king Eppillus (*c* AD 5–10: <17>). The numerous finds (Figs 23–8) included a typically 2nd-century circular enamelled copper-alloy disc brooch <140> (<S2>), a wire bracelet with an expanding clasp <173> (<S3>), a copper-alloy ring key <108>, a complete nail cleaner <101> (<S9>), two decorated mirror fragments <85> <178>, a ceramic *Firmalampe* <280>, possibly from northern Italy, a trefoil-shaped flagon lid <143>, a possible 1st-century military belt or apron stud <107> (<S25>) and a mount or chape <133> (<S29>), the lower part of a Venus pipeclay figurine <244> (<S26>) and a bone hairpin of Cool Type 6 <104> (<S8>: see Fig 15). A small piece of unalloyed tinfoil sheet with a repoussé decoration <161> is unusual at this early period.

Significantly, two fragments of a Verulamium Region White ware crucible used for cupelling gold were also found <232> (see Fig 73: <S27>). The crucible was one of several from the eastern part of the site.

The range of footwear (see Fig 26) included parts of 13 nailed shoes such as <305> (<L2>), <306> (<L3>), four sandals, one stitched shoe and six one-piece examples, among them <423> (<L12>) and <308> (<L13>), as well as a piece of shoemaking waste. One of the sandals <329> (<L6>) still had the remains of the upper attached, part of a goatskin strap which was probably a repair; it was also stamped with rosettes and reversed 'S' shapes. Several fragments of miscellaneous leather survived (see Fig 27), including an unidentified fragment <337> (<L16>), one with fine stitching <330> (<L15>) which was possibly from a garment, and two pieces of tent panel <317> (<L18>), <326> (<L19>), with a larger fragment <431> (<L21>), which if not a tent panel may have been part of an awning or protective cover. A second piece of Carrara marble <367> was found, also a complete paving brick, which may have come from an *opus spicatum* floor. Animal waste from this deposit included a sawn section of antler and a fragment of sea urchin shell.

The dumping of organic refuse continued for some distance to the north of Waterfront 3 beneath the double basement (EN18: 5.11) as well as further east (TP7: 4.3), where significantly the pottery, dated AD 120–60, was sooted. This may have been burned in the widespread Hadrianic fire which is thought to have occurred in the later 120s (Symonds in prep), and which seems to have affected at least one of the buildings on the eastern part of the site (B4). Non-ferruginous sandstone rubble from these deposits may have been part of a damaged or demolished building, a small fragment of worn sandstone was probably part of a paving slab. The plant remains included evidence for waterlogged conditions, such as sedges and rushes, as well as disturbed or wasteland plants such as elder and nettles. Food waste such as grape pips and hazelnuts were also present. Further north near the south-west corner of Rectory House, a similar deposit was probably part of the same dump sequence, dated AD 50–160 (5.10). Sandy silts (5.6) were deposited further west at the same level (Borehole 8); a complete, although bent, iron razor <5> of Manning knife Type 4 (1st–2nd century) was fortuitously recovered from the borehole.

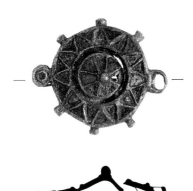

Fig 24 *Enamelled disc brooch <S2> from upper fills of Waterfront 4 (1:1)*

Fig 25 *Ceramic Venus figurine second or waster <S26> from upper fills of Waterfront 4 (1:1)*

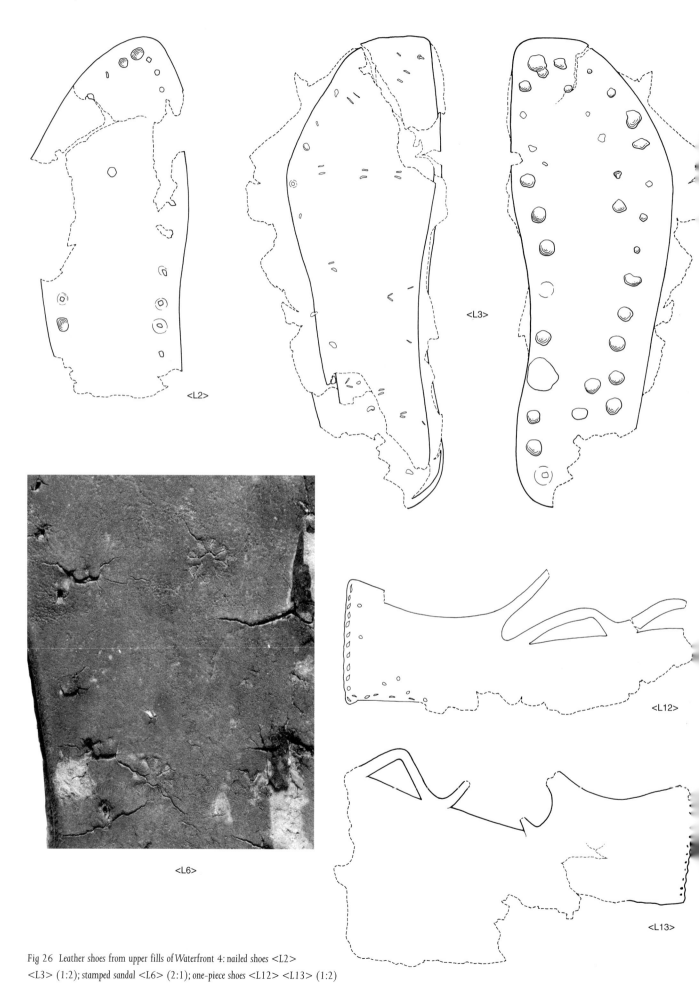

Fig 26 Leather shoes from upper fills of Waterfront 4: nailed shoes <L2>
<L3> (1:2); stamped sandal <L6> (2:1); one-piece shoes <L12> <L13> (1:2)

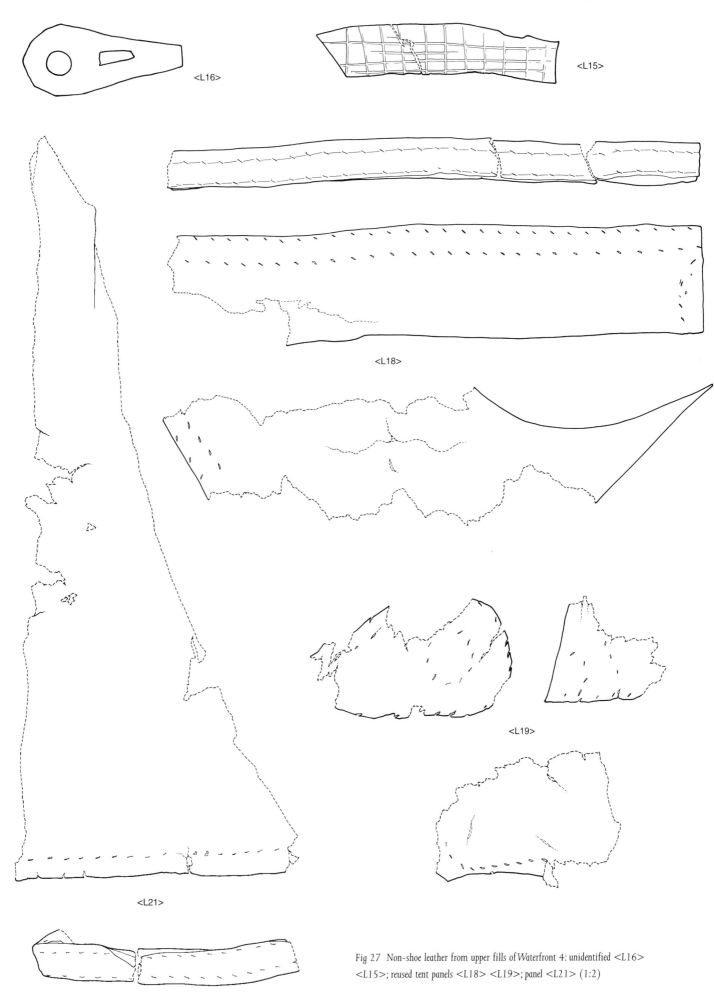

<L16>

<L15>

<L18>

<L19>

<L21>

Fig 27 Non-shoe leather from upper fills of Waterfront 4: unidentified <L16>
<L15>; reused tent panels <L18> <L19>; panel <L21> (1:2)

29

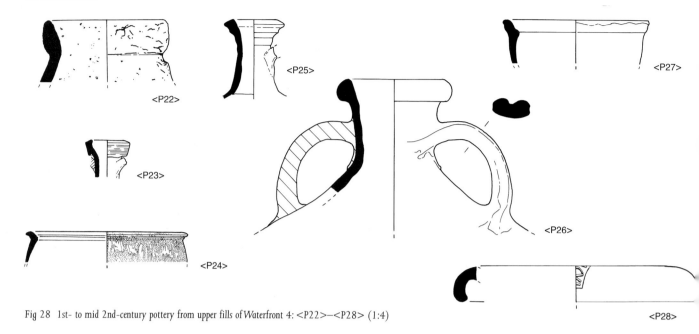

Fig 28 1st- to mid 2nd-century pottery from upper fills of Waterfront 4: <P22>–<P28> (1:4)

Box-drain

In the south-east (EN20) a north–south wooden drain was
inserted into the waterfront dumps (5.2). This consisted of a
simple box structure set on a timber cradle (see Figs 6, 12), and
probably fitted with cross-braces at the top to hold the lid in
place and the sides apart. After its completion, organic dumping
raised the ground surface to 1.55m OD (5.4). The drain silted
up and was eventually blocked (5.3); the fill contained seeds
of disturbed or waste ground, grassland and cultivated land,
including wild fruits (blackberry or raspberry), but more
importantly, charred spelt and chaff. If these represent the
sifting of processed grain, the drain may have been connected
to an area used for the purpose, although it is not possible to
determine whether this was at Suffolk House or further north.
Fragments of planking near Rectory House may have formed
part of a northern continuation of the drain, although this is
uncertain.

The fill of the construction cut contained a little pottery of
AD 120–60, and four timbers were dated, two of which included
some sapwood. One was complete to bark edge and had a
felling date of AD 128, while a second sample came from the
same tree. In view of the absence of evidence for reuse or
seasoning it seems reasonable to take this as the date of
construction. The fact that the box-drain was cut through the
top of Waterfront 3 also provides a *terminus ante quem* for the
demise of the earlier revetment and the construction of
Waterfront 4. These events may only have been a few years
apart, which would suggest a swift southward advance of the
waterfront in the early 2nd century. A similar pace of development
was apparent at Regis House, and the evidence currently
suggests that by AD 140–60 the waterfront had reached the
south side of the present Thames Street dual carriageway. This
shift of c 25–30m over the half-century demonstrates that the
late 1st and early 2nd centuries were a time of the most rapid
expansion elsewhere in the town. The former riverside buildings

on the north side of the modern street, including those at
Suffolk House and the 'palace' site, were therefore left some
distance from the river within the space of a few decades.

There were few finds from the drain apart from a bone
gaming counter <198> of Crummy Type 1 and an iron chisel
<132> (Fig 29: <S22>) recovered from the constructional
backfill. From the overlying make-ups came a piece of Purbeck
marble <636> and fragments of the base and rim of a
Verulamium Region White ware goldworker's crucible <443>;
the latter is significant given the presence of part of a similar
example from the underlying (5.1) dumps.

Fig 29 Iron chisel <S22>
from Waterfront 4 box-drain
(1:2)

Possible drain in the east

On the eastern limit of excavation, some distance behind the
projected line of Waterfront 3 (EN22), fragments of oak planks
and possible posts and beams (5.8) sealed by dark silts (5.9)
were observed, during piling operations, overlying the early

Roman terrace on the eastern streetfront. The timbers may represent a further drain in the area, although it is unclear whether it was contemporary with Waterfront 3 or 4.

Open Area 3

In the earliest period contemporary with Waterfront 1, the northern area remained open (OA3; see Fig 7). In the north-west (TP1) the natural sands and gravels were sealed by gravel make-ups (6.1) cut by quarry pits, followed by the deposition of domestic rubbish, brickearth, mortar, sands and silts (6.2–5) containing pottery of AD 60–120 (6.1) to AD 70–160 (6.4–5). An intrusive coin (<8>) of Valentinian I or Valens (AD 364–78) was probably disturbed from a later pit. Among the few finds was a glass jar fragment <16> (Fig 30: <G1>).

Fig 30 *Glass jar fragment from Open Area 3: <G1> (1:2)*

A little to the east (TP2–3), early quarry pits were backfilled with material containing a high proportion of mortar and painted wall plaster, suggestive of construction or demolition work nearby (6.15, 6.18).

Further east (EN4) the initial gravel make-ups were cut by a single stakehole sealed by a midden, followed by metalled external surfaces (6.26). The deposits in this area were largely dated AD 50–70.

3.3 The buildings: *c* AD 60–400

Building 1

The remains of a building or buildings on the northern terrace were recorded in 1969, and interpreted as the 'northern range' of the townhouse (see Fig 4; Marsden 1975, 54–6). To this can be added further floor and wall fragments observed in 1994 (TP1–3) which help to extend the picture of the structure (see Fig 7). The disparate elements from both investigations are presumed to have formed part of a single building (B1) with a common floor level (*c* 6.7m OD) defined by higher and lower terraces to north and south, and with eastern and western limits which can broadly be determined from other evidence. The 1969 remains were interpreted as consisting of five rooms with three sections of south wall (Feature 64) also acting to support the terrace upon which the building was constructed. The presence of a higher terrace (Feature 57) implied that the north wall of the building lay no further than 5.0m north of the site. While Building 1 may have formed a part of the later main townhouse (B3) as Marsden suggested, the area to the south was not occupied for perhaps around a half-century after occupation

had begun in the north. The 'northern range' has therefore been dealt with separately (see Fig 7).

The western part of Open Area 3 was enclosed and a brickearth hearth up to 1.14m across was constructed, associated with a series of burnt deposits presumably related to its use (6.6–7). These are thought to have constituted the first occupation of Building 1. The date of the hearth's construction and use was the same as that of the underlying area (AD 50–150/60).

A later phase of building was represented by a north–south beam slot terminating in a posthole to the north (6.8), and a contemporary brickearth floor. This was scorched and partially covered by burnt debris, presumably from another hearth (6.9–10). Building material from this area included roof tiles with the flanges removed, perhaps for use as paving, a box-flue tile and several ceramic and stone tesserae, all indicative of higher-quality rooms in the area. Among the few finds was a fragment of a glass cut bowl <17> (Fig 31: <G6>). The area coincides with Marsden's Room 58 (1975, 54) which is said to have had a white mortar floor. The foundation of the east wall, which was not seen in 1994, was of ragstone and mortar with some reused broken bricks and areas of hard pink mortar.

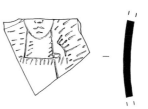

Fig 31 *Glass cut bowl fragment from Building 1: <G6> (1:1)*

The end of the occupation sequence in the room was marked by the excavation of a number of pits, the earliest of which had apparently been backfilled with rubble, including a fragment of white marble inlay and painted wall plaster, suggesting nearby demolition of a high-quality structure (6.11–14). The occurrence of such materials implies that although the room was a low-status area, the nature of some of the building materials found in the area suggests that in its later stages at least, it adjoined a substantial building with underfloor heating and mosaic floors. One possibility is that it formed part of a service wing attached to Building 3, although the difference in floor level of between 2.0–3.0m is too great to be confident of this equation (see Fig 35). If so, intercommunication must have taken place between the ground floor of Building 1 and the first-floor level of the rooms to the south, otherwise by stairs.

The later features seem to represent a resumption of occupation after a long unaccounted period, since they were dated by pottery in the make-up for one of the later floors (6.9) to AD 270–400. A contemporary radiate *antoninianus* (<25>) in the same make-up provides a *terminus post quem* of *c* AD 270–80. Whether this is the result of truncation or a genuine break between the occupation phases is uncertain.

Further east (TP2; Fig 32) was a series of brickearth and mortar surfaces interleaved with bands of occupation silts

Fig 32 Trench TP2. View of the Roman floor sequence in Building 1, from the south-east (0.5m scale)

(6.16). The final floor was sealed by a layer of ash containing what appeared to be metalworking debris; this may have been connected with the reworking of metal fittings prior to demolition, as it was covered by debris (6.17).

This activity coincided with Marsden's Room 59, the eastern foundation of which was built in flint. This material was characteristically used in the Neronian and Flavian periods in London, although Marsden had interpreted it as part of a later phase of modification work to the townhouse (1975, 54–6). Under the mortar floor of the room was a ceramic drainpipe. A late 3rd-century bronze radiate copy (MoL 92.127/637) found on the floor was the only dating evidence from the immediate area, and incidentally the sole piece of dating evidence recovered from the 'townhouse' during 1969 (Marsden 1975, 62).

No floors were seen in Room 60 to the east, which was defined by the wall of Room 59 and a similar flint and chalk foundation for the east wall also recorded in 1969.

East of this in Marsden's Room 62 (Fig 33), the earliest structural activity was represented by the unmortared brickearth and flint foundation (TP3: 6.19) for a superstructure of horizontally laid tegulae (6.20). This may have been aligned at approximately 45° to the general Roman building alignment, and one possibility is that the structure was part of an apsidal wall: it is unlikely to have been a subfloor drain, since a foundation would have been unnecessary. Although undated, the use of roof tile in place of brick, and flint instead of ragstone, places the foundation in the 1st century with the rest of the earliest phase of Building 1. The constructional technique is

Fig 33 Trench TP3. View of two superimposed 2nd-century opus signinum floors of Building 1 from the south, overlying an earlier wall of reused tegulae (right), and an external surface sealing an early quarry cutting natural gravel on the left (0.5m scale)

reminiscent of the small Flavian temple next to the first forum (Marsden 1987, 108–13), where the flanges of the tegulae were turned outwards to mimic brickwork. This particular technique may have been a way of reusing broken or damaged roof tiles which were useless for other practical purposes: while broken bricks could be reused for walling more than once, roof tiles were only of value for their primary purpose while they remained unbroken. A similar use of tegulae was recorded at Regis House, where broken tiles salvaged from the Hadrianic fire levels were employed in post-fire walls and piers (Brigham & Watson in prep).

Whatever the function of the tile structure, it was demolished and sealed by the gravel make-up for an *opus signinum* floor (see Fig 35), separated by a thin band of occupation silts from a second surface, which was inset with small fragments of brick to increase its durability (6.22–3). Marsden also recorded one of these floors.

To the south was an east–west ragstone rubble wall foundation with a triple brick string course forming the base of the superstructure (6.21). Although this had an uncertain relationship with the floor surfaces, it was almost certainly an internal feature within the room, since Marsden noted the south wall of Building 1 further south (Feature 64). It was possibly contemporary with the subdivision of the room by a ragstone foundation (recorded in 1969) to create the narrow Room 61. A further short section of foundation recorded by Marsden would appear to have marked the eastern side of Room 62, and probably of the building itself.

The final floor was sealed by undated deposits of sandy silt, chalk rubble and brickearth reaching 7.51m OD (6.24–5), which may be the remains of demolition debris, although this was possibly of post-Roman date.

In summary, the evidence points to an initial flint-walled phase of perhaps four rooms, which may have been constructed as early as the 60s: the small amount of pottery obtained from the earliest surfaces suggests a date between AD 60–160 for construction and occupation. Later construction work probably removed evidence for the original outer walls of Building 1. It is probable, however, that they were in similar positions to those suggested for the later phase. The positions of the north and south walls were almost certainly governed by the presence of terraces, for example, while the extent of the building in the west may have been determined by an early version of the road which later separated Building 3 and the 'palace' site. The easternmost wall may, however, have been set at an angle of up to 45° to the main alignment, although this is uncertain as it was only seen in section. Whatever the case, the building did not extend across Open Area 3 to join Building 2.

The reconstructed building seems to have had more pretensions. The use of ragstone with brick string courses and the introduction of mortar coloured pink using crushed tile filler indicate a late 1st- or more probably early 2nd-century date. If so, this would place the reconstruction in the same general period as the construction of Building 3. As already suggested, the presence of marble inlay, tesserae and box-flue tile within later dumps in the building also indicates the proximity of high-status structures. The fact that the south wall of Building 1 also acted as the north wall of Building 3 suggests that the latter was a likely source.

Building 1 would appear to have remained in use until the late 3rd or 4th century. Pottery of AD 270–400 and a radiate copy of AD 270–80 from a later floor make-up support this, although as there was little stratigraphic separation between this and the earliest surfaces, some truncation must be postulated.

Building 2: masonry building in the north-east

The south-west corner of Building 2 was recorded to the east of Building 1 (see Fig 7). In TP4 a fragment of north–south mortared chalk foundation (7.7) marked the position of the west wall of the building. This feature cut a deposit of brickearth, which was probably an early pre-construction surface, and perhaps formed the initial floor. It was sealed by demolition debris (burnt brickearth and plaster) cut by a later rubbish pit (7.8–9). In EN4 the floor and a second pit (7.1–2) were cut by a similar foundation for the south wall (7.5). The use of chalk, although unusual, is paralleled for example in the post-Hadrianic fire foundations and superstructure of walls at Regis House (Brigham & Watson in prep). It appears occasionally in 1st-century foundations, often in association with flint, with which it was presumably quarried. The superstructure consisted of a pink-mortared double brick string course just above floor level (5.7m OD), followed by four courses of ragstone and a second double string course. Covering the first surface were occupation dumps containing interleaved charcoal and silt deposits trampled into the earth floors (7.3–4). Part of a shale armlet <75> (Fig 34: <S5>) was recovered from one of these deposits, together with broken combed box-flue tiles, a piece of Purbeck marble <434> and, significantly, a fragment of a Verulamium Region White ware crucible <440> used to melt gold. The presence of the latter may suggest that the charcoal deposits were related to the gold-refining process, particularly as other crucibles were found to the south of the building.

The pottery from the early floor sequence was dated to AD 60/70–100 and a *dupondius* of Vespasian of AD 71 was also recovered. These suggest a later 1st-century construction date for Building 2, although the use of pink mortar in the superstructure could suggest that it had been built early in the 2nd century. Whichever is the case, it is likely that it was at least partly contemporary with the early phases of Building 1, predating the major expansion heralded by Buildings 3–5. Substantial differences in construction suggest that it is unlikely that the buildings on the eastern half of the site formed part of a single complex at any time, in the same way that Buildings 1 and 3 appeared to have become unified (see below).

One of the latest occupation levels contained pottery of AD 350–400, implying a long period of use with final abandonment and demolition taking place in the 4th century, apparently at the same time as the other buildings on the site. The south wall was extensively robbed (7.6) before the earliest recorded medieval activity, possibly after a 'dark earth' type deposit had accumulated or been deposited to the south.

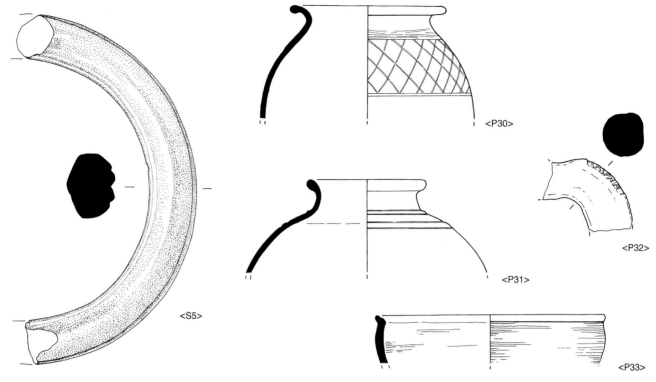

Fig 34 Finds from Building 2: shale armlet <S5> (1:1); 2nd-century pottery <P30>–<P33> (1:4)

Building 3 and Road 1: the townhouse and road to the west

Building 3 is represented by those rooms in Marsden's 'townhouse' which had floors at about the 4.0m OD level, and which occupied the broad central terrace area in the western half of the site. During the recent investigations further evidence for this building was recorded, mainly along the Suffolk Lane and Upper Thames Street frontages in TP9, 13–14, EN10–11, 13–15, 18–19, and MH3 (Figs 35, 36). This is presented below following Marsden's original ordering (see Fig 4), through the western and southern ranges and central courtyard area, and the eastern range. The new evidence adds substantially to the understanding of the history and layout of the western range, although the development of much of the rest of the building remains uncertain.

The west range

The west wall of the building was recorded in several places, the most northerly observation occurring in 1969 (Feature 73). Immediately to the south (MH3; Fig 37) the wall was offset by 0.2m on the eastern side of a brick foundation. Approximately 0.75m thick, the superstructure was of mortared ragstone with double string courses of brick at 0.35m intervals, and with a small internal buttress attached to the east face (8.1). Both faces were limewashed or rendered, but only the eastern side was initially plastered; this was plain, with traces of a red border. The west (external) face was subsequently coated with white

painted plaster (8.5). The wall had been repaired on at least one occasion using broken brick and small fragments of ragstone (8.9).

Further south the wall passed to the west of its expected position, which was instead occupied by a second buttress (TP13: 8.23; see Fig 41). This appeared to continue westwards to join the wall, which may imply that there was a short extension in the area, such as a porch or portico. During piling operations, disturbed masonry – probably from the outer wall – was encountered a little further south between c 3.0–5.7m OD (8.30) with fragments of timber in the underlying deposits which may have been supporting piles or baseplate fragments. Marsden observed the same wall beyond this (Feature 74). Several north–south walls bordering Rooms 65 and 70 which may have formed the east side of the range were recorded in 1969, including Feature 71. None of these were aligned, and it seems that the layout of the wing was complex. This is also reflected in the position of the internal walls of the eastern part of the range.

In the western part of the range, a ragstone wall with brick string courses was revealed standing to 6.92m OD in the southern section of TP14 (8.22; Fig 38). This may have been a later cross-wall similar to others recorded further south, although the eastward continuation recorded in 1969 between Rooms 68 and 70 rested on a much wider foundation, and – if not a rebuild – it was probably a primary feature bonded into the outer wall. The projected line of the outer wall passed the western side of the trench.

Although the superstructure was mainly bonded in pale yellow mortar, the lower brick courses were bonded with pink

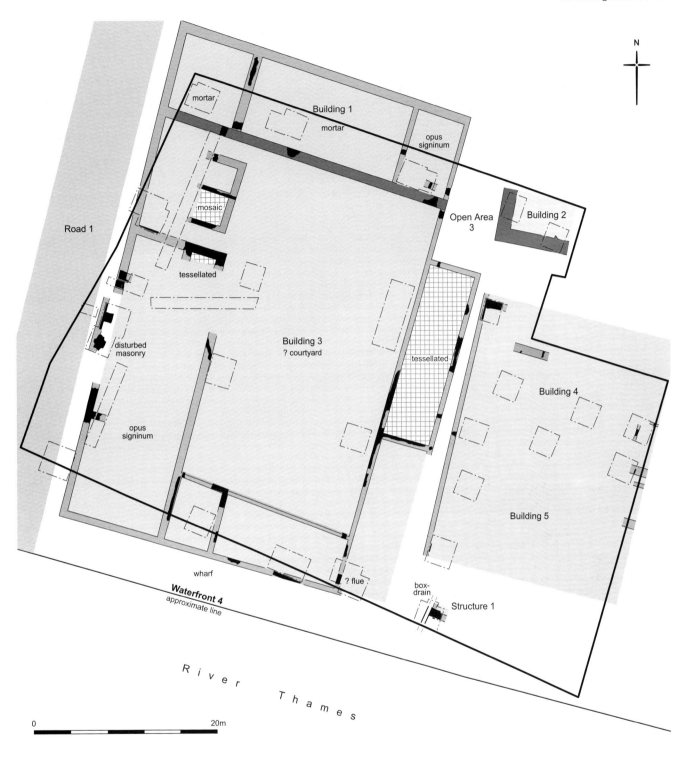

N

Fig 35 Plan of the principal early 2nd-century archaeological features: Buildings 1–5. The plan combines elements of the 1969 investigation with those of 1994–7

mortar, possibly incorporating powdered brick deliberately as a damp-proofing agent, a Romano-British version of pozzolana (in Italy, a hydraulic cement using volcanic dust from Puteoli – modern Pozzuoli – as a setting agent). The lowest part of the visible section consisted of two brick courses, followed by three of ragstone, two of brick and two of ragstone, roughly finished and faced with plaster (Fig 39). Despite being unevenly applied, this showed the remains of painted decoration in the form of alternating vertical panels of red and blue with overpainted

decoration in yellow, Egyptian blue, cinnabar red and green. The green elements took the form of a swag or garland of leaves, with the veins picked out in cream or light yellow. The decoration was badly worn and had been 'pecked' for the application of a later coat; this may still survive at a lower level below undisturbed deposits above the latest Roman floors, which probably lay at c 4.0–4.1m OD.

To the south, the western side of the range appears to have formed a single long room, perhaps extending to a second

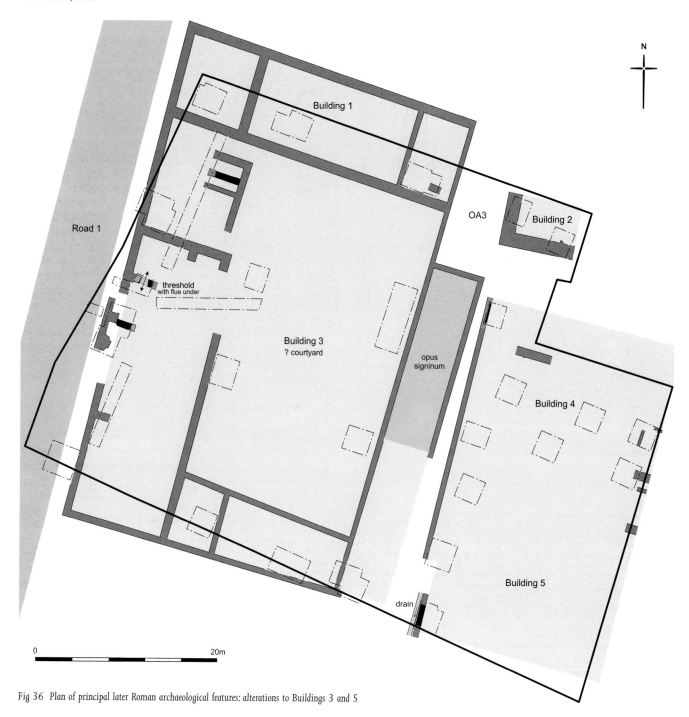

Fig 36 Plan of principal later Roman archaeological features: alterations to Buildings 3 and 5

internal wall (Marsden's Feature 74), but at some time in the lifetime of the building this was subdivided. Two east–west cross-walls were built against the existing buttresses, in MH3 (8.2; Fig 40) and TP13 (3.24; Fig 41), to create three new rooms, and a further wall recorded by Marsden near Feature 74 divided off a smaller area, probably as part of the same process.

The northern cross-wall was cut through later by a doorway and, at a lower level, by a brick flue arch supplying an underground heating system to the south (8.3–4; see Fig 40). Very little of the room to the north was excavated, and the earliest recorded activity seemed to relate to its disuse, represented by dumped soil containing building rubble and a few tesserae (8.16) which may have come from a tessellated floor in Marsden's adjoining Room 70. The area may have

contained a furnace for the heating system with floors consequently at a lower level than elsewhere.

An east–west flue channel to the south of the wall was cheaply constructed of reused mortar and brick fragments and a single brick pila, and had probably been roofed over with further brick. At its western end the flue terminated against a chalk block, although it presumably continued southwards or eastwards. Several mortar and brickearth deposits interleaved with charcoal-rich layers below the level of the top of the flue arch must have been temporary surfaces (8.6–7); the main floor was presumably raised on pilae similar to the example in the flue channel, although none survived. A rectangular cut filled with rubble near the flue may have been associated with modifications to the heating system (8.8).

Fig 37 Trench MH3. View of walls and floors in the western range of Building 3 under excavation, from the east. The wall forming the west side of the range is in the background, the additional east–west cross-wall is in the foreground

Fig 39 Trench TP14. Detail of in situ wall plaster attached to the north face of a Roman east–west cross-wall in Building 3. The plaster has been pecked to key a subsequent coat which has not survived. The area next to the wall was not excavated, and the lower part remains undisturbed (0.2m scale)

Fig 38 Trench TP14. View of Roman east–west cross-wall in Building 3 from the north. The wall has been cut by a later chalk wall associated with Buildings 14 and 15 (1.0m scale)

Fig 40 Trench MH3. View of the additional east–west cross-wall in the western range of Building 3 from the south-west, showing the later threshold (below the 0.2m scale) and the edge of the flue associated with the later heating system cutting the threshold to the east (background)

Fig 41 Trench TP13. View of the internal buttress attached to the west wall of Building 3 (background), with a later abutting east–west cross-wall in the foreground, from the east. The west wall of Building 3 has been robbed to a lower level. Its line passes across the rear wall of the trench behind the buttress. To the right are the arched chalk foundations and a buttress for Buildings 14 and 15 (0.5m scale)

The flue was filled by a soft black sooty deposit, which contained fragments of several broken and burnt Nene Valley Colour-coated ware vessels (Fig 42). The date of these (AD 200–400) implies that the heating system remained in use until at least the 3rd century before the building was finally abandoned. Collapsed wall plaster and rubble, including combed box-flue tiles from the heating system (8.14–15), and fragments of green window glass covered the area. A thick layer of roof tile followed these deposits and further dumps of loose mixed rubble, suggesting that the interior fittings collapsed – or were demolished – first, followed by the roof and finally the masonry shell. The collapse can be dated to AD 300–400 on the basis of pottery recovered from the debris.

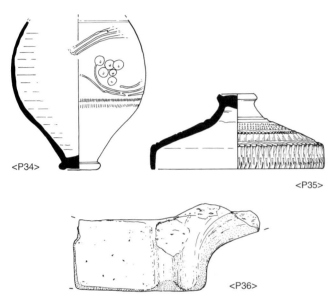

<P34>

<P35>

<P36>

Fig 42 Finds from Building 3: 3rd- to 4th-century pottery <P34>–<P36> (1:4)

The south range

Most of the area of the south wing was completely removed by the construction of the deep central basement and south side of Suffolk House in 1969. Two oak piles (EN10: 8.32) and further timber fragments found a little to the east (EN19: 8.31) may represent the support structures of foundations similar to those recorded by Marsden (1975, 59) in the area of Rooms 80 and 81, but could equally have been related to an earlier waterfront. In the south section of EN19 a 3.2m long stretch of pink-mortared east–west brick wall was observed between about 2.1m and 4.7m OD (8.33), for the most part directly below the modern Thames Street frontage. It was broadly aligned with a fragment recorded by Marsden a little further west (1975, 59), and both may have formed part of the south wall of Room 80, and perhaps also of Building 3 itself.

Significantly, a column drum was found on the north side of Thames Street in 1927 about 10.67m east of Suffolk Lane. The drum was reported to be 0.61m in diameter, and was therefore part of a full-sized column, possibly from a riverside colonnade (RCHM 1928, 143).

The central area

Little further information was recovered concerning the central 'courtyard' area of the building (Marsden's Feature 69). A grey-brown mortar floor was revealed under the modern double basement (EN18: 8.19–21) at about 4.15m OD. This was sealed by a layer that was possibly part of a collapsed roof used as make-up for a later brickearth floor. The location of these deposits immediately to the east of the western range (Feature 71) suggests that the southern part of the 'courtyard' at least was possibly built over. This assertion is supported by the existence of a 'blocked flue' (Feature 77) passing through the west wall of the east range. If there was a courtyard in the area, it was almost certainly considerably smaller than previously represented.

The east range

Although one trench (TP9) was situated in the south end of the east wing, this was not excavated to Roman levels, and no extra information was available to add to the known details of the area. The wing seems to have consisted initially of at least two rooms, later knocked into one (Rooms 75–6), in contrast with the west wing where a larger room was subdivided. A flue in the west wall of Room 76 entered the south wing (Feature 79), demonstrating a relationship between the two areas. During 1996 part of a Tuscan order shelly oolitic limestone dwarf column (Fig 43) was recovered from a medieval pit which overlay the area of the flue (TP9; see Fig 53). The 0.95m fragment consisted of a combined drum and capital, and although not in situ, it would not have been out of place in a building of the status implied by the presence of mosaic and tessellated floors. It may therefore have originated in Building 3 itself, possibly as part of an external portico facing the river.

Fig 43 Detail of Roman stone column capital recovered from an early medieval pit in Trench TP9. Traces of paint or limewash are just visible between the moulded bands on the capital (0.5m scale)

The construction date and development of Building 3

Because Building 3 extended beyond the line of Waterfront 3 it can have been built no earlier than the second quarter of the 2nd century, after Waterfront 4 had reclaimed the area further south. Since it is unlikely that such an expanse of prime riverfront was left vacant for long, a Hadrianic construction date is likely, although the most closely studied of London's masonry townhouses were built in the 3rd century (Perring 1991, 100). If Building 3 followed a courtyard plan, with three or four wings (see below for a discussion of this point), a mid 2nd-century date would place it among the earliest known of this type. Although an example from Blue Boar Lane, Leicester, may predate it, others from Verulamium were only built after a mid 2nd-century Antonine fire (Walthew 1975, 191).

It seems that at least four phases of building can be identified in the west range, which is by far the best-understood part of the structure. These include a primary build incorporating internal buttresses, the insertion of partition walls, the cutting of a doorway through one of the partitions, and the supply of a heating system into the rooms by the insertion of flues. The only major change noted elsewhere was the amalgamation of the rooms in the east wing, which is an apparent reverse of the subdivision of those in the west, perhaps suggesting that the functions of the wings were exchanged.

The difference in floor level between the east and west wings (c 4.1–4.2m OD) and the northern wing or Building 1 (c 6.7m OD) are sufficient to question the interpretation of the remains of the townhouse as a single entity of the courtyard type. Significantly, however, there was an apparent connecting wall between the northern and eastern ranges at the north-east corner of Marsden's Room 64, where the floor level was at about 6.4m OD on the south side of the terrace wall. It is reasonable to assume, as Marsden suggested, that this was repeated in the west. Rooms 63 and 64 would then represent either the ends of a connecting corridor or small rooms, perhaps with stairs, although the ground floor of the northern range may have been designed to communicate with the first floor of the main building. Multi-level buildings of a complex ground plan making the best use of sloping sites were not uncommon in Roman Britain. These include the neighbouring 'Governor's Palace' site and rural structures such as the extensive villa at Great Witcombe, Gloucestershire, where the main house was supported by a massive buttressed retaining wall with wings extending downhill (Clifford 1954).

Certainly Building 1, which appears to have been of fairly low quality prior to the construction of Building 3, was rebuilt at some point, and it has already been suggested that there was sufficient evidence from the latest levels to suggest a relationship with higher-status rooms in the area. The conversion or incorporation of earlier strip-buildings to form more complex townhouses of courtyard or corridor plan was common practice, and may have been adopted as landowners rationalised their properties to match changing trends in the market, or as a result of increased personal wealth (Walthew 1975, 191–2).

If there is uncertainty about its ground plan and structural history, the quality of Building 3 is undoubted, with evidence for heating systems in the east, west and south wings, tessellated pavements and a mosaic floor. The painted plaster examined in TP14 proved to be of a high quality – if unevenly applied – using some expensive imported pigments. The discovery of part of a dwarf column in 1994 and a full-size column drum in the area in 1927 also argues for the presence of colonnades in the south. It is unfortunate that no artefacts were recovered which could be directly associated with the building and its occupants. The existence of such an imposing house at a relatively early period suggests that the residence was both wealthy and influential, since the house occupied a prime site with a large river frontage.

Because excavation halted at Roman levels in the evaluation trenches, for the most part they provided no reliable dating evidence for the development of the building. The presence of burnt Nene Valley Colour-coated ware in one of the flues showed that the heating system was still in use in the 3rd or 4th century. The fact that the walls were left standing and the presence of 4th-century pottery in demolition debris sealing the latest floors may also indicate that the building was still in occupation late in the Roman period. Late Roman occupation of the waterfront area has previously been noted by Morris (1982, 312–13), Milne (1985, 33, 141; 1995, 89) and Perring (1991, 127), and in 1995–6 at Regis House (Brigham & Watson in prep).

Road 1

A 1969 section to the west of Building 3 (Feature 73) included two yellow mortar floors but no metalling, which was thought to infer that the area was internal (Marsden 1975, 58). This led to the conclusion that the townhouse was an integral but distinct part of the main monument to the west (Marsden 1975, 73). The discovery of Road 1 in 1996, however, suggests that the mortar surfaces are more likely to have been earlier external surfaces or repairs.

The earliest deposits recorded in 1996 were an area of redeposited London Clay to the west of MH3, rising against the face of the west wall, possibly to act as waterproofing, and further west an area of black sandy silt (8.10–11) and a rough surface of loose pink mortar. All of these were sealed by silts containing significant quantities of plaster and brick derived either from a destruction phase of Building 3 or from the 'palace' to the west (8.12). Over this was the brickearth base for the metalled surface of the north–south Road 1 which separated Building 3 and the 'palace' site (contra Marsden 1975, 58), and which must have been at least 4.0m in width (8.13). At 5.9m OD this was considerably higher than the floor level of the west wing of the building (c 4.2m OD), although below that of the north wing, Building 1 (6.7m OD). The road was repaired later with a 0.1m layer of white mortar. Combed and roller-stamped box-flue tile fragments were recovered, possibly from the demolition or alteration of Building 3.

To the south, over the hardstanding behind Waterfront 4, a small area of brickearth over gravelly dumps (EN11: 8.34) probably represents the southern continuation of the road make-ups as it sloped down towards the wharf. Further evidence from a borehole immediately adjacent to the west wall of the 'palace' included sandy silt and rubble dumps (Borehole 9: 8.26). If these were make-ups for Road 1 it would increase the potential width of the surface to at least 9.0m.

Pottery from below Road 1 dated to AD 50–160 and an amphora sherd from the resurfacing of AD 50–140 suggest that the road could have been laid out at the same time as Building 3, although this is not conclusive.

Water supply

On Open Area 3 near the south-east corner of the building (EN20), make-up dumps sealing the existing box-drain behind Waterfront 4 raised the ground level by about 0.7m, and a piped water supply was provided (8.17). The recorded remains of the water pipe consisted of two reasonably well-preserved east–west quartered hollowed lengths of oak heartwood with an internal diameter of about 300mm, joined by a tongue and groove and an iron collar or bracket (see Fig 6). The gradient of the pipe suggested that the direction of flow had been westward. It was severed by the foundations of Building 5, by which time other arrangements presumably had been made, but the pipe had in any case already silted up (8.18). Pottery of AD 120–60 was recovered, suggesting that the pipe provided water for Building 3.

Building 4

Building 4, to the east of Building 3, was a masonry-walled structure with floors at about the same level, c 4.0m OD. The structural evidence for the earliest phase of the building was the robber trench for an east–west masonry wall cut through the natural gravel, filled with mixed building rubble and large timber fragments (EN5: 9.1). The feature may represent the original north wall of Building 4, but if so, it must have been separated from Building 2 by a yard or alley. The sole find recovered from the infill was a complete crucible <243> used for melting gold, one of four similar items found on the eastern part of the site (see Fig 73: <S28>). Its location a few metres south of a crucible found in Building 2 implies that one or other of these structures may have been the location of a goldworker's premises. A mortar floor surface to the south of the wall was covered by charcoal which may have been spread from hearths or furnaces used in the goldworking process, although this is speculative (9.2–3). The robber trench contained pottery of AD 50–160, but the earliest occupation deposit was dated AD 120–250, which suggests a construction date no earlier than the AD 120s, and quite possibly nearer the mid 2nd century.

After the robbing had occurred, a new west wall was constructed, presumably to replace a similar precursor, but continuing further north (9.4); it is not clear whether the north wall was also rebuilt nearer to Building 2, or whether the two structures joined and shared a party wall. The new wall was very close to the eastern side of Building 3 recorded in 1969, and seems to have been broadly parallel, presumably separated by a narrow alleyway. The surviving superstructure consisted of a layer of mortared ragstone with a double brick string course

at the same level as the floor, which may have remained in use despite the major alterations. Collapsed masonry in the overlying modern backfill suggests that there was another brick course about 0.6m above the first, and that flint was employed as well as ragstone. Complete new lydion bricks (430mm x 315mm x 35mm) were used which suggests that the reconstruction of the building may have been undertaken for a fairly wealthy individual, since broken bricks were more common, even in public buildings such as the second forum.

An east–west trench cut through the mortar surface contained an oak plank and gravel fill which may have supported a partition south of the original east–west wall, with a contemporary brickearth floor (9.5–6). Alice Holt/Farnham pottery dated the later occupation to the 4th century, supported by residual sherds recovered from the modern deposits in the immediate area. There was no stratigraphic evidence for a hiatus in occupation between the earlier and later phases, indeed the similarity in the levels of the earlier floor with the later brick course suggests continuity of use. An initial construction date in the 2nd century with continued use in the 3rd and 4th centuries, following remodelling, therefore seems reasonable.

The remains of three east–west ragstone walls with brick string coursing were recorded in section on the eastern site boundary, the southernmost of which may mark the limit of Building 4 or a party wall with Building 5 (EN22, EN25: 9.7). The other two walls must therefore have functioned as internal partitions. Further west, Marsden noted two brick wall fragments set in pink mortar (Feature 83), both possibly part of a single east–west feature continuing the alignment of one of the 1996 walls.

The northernmost room was floored with brickearth, sealed by mortar make-ups for a similar surface (9.8–9). Both floors were scorched at some time, although neither event could positively be ascribed to the Hadrianic fire period (c AD 125–30); Marsden recorded four patches of burnt daub, opus signinum and white mortar flooring in the same area (Features 84–7). A pit containing grey silts cut the second brickearth surface (9.10) before dark earth deposits were dumped over the area, suggesting that it was of late Roman date.

There was no sign of an eastern wall, which must have passed somewhere beneath or beyond Laurence Pountney Lane. The floors were not of particularly high quality and there were no other indications that the building was exceptional in any way; a single flue tile or voussoir may have been introduced in imported dump material.

The earliest occasion that the building could have been constructed was after Waterfront 3 had been built at the beginning of the 2nd century and the area reclaimed. The pottery recovered from the earliest occupation levels suggests that this occurred some time after AD 120, which would place it in the period following the construction of Waterfront 4. Like its neighbours, Building 4 seems to have remained in use until the 3rd or 4th century. As already suggested, the presence of scorched floor surfaces and burnt daub could imply that the building was erected just before the Hadrianic fire, which probably occurred c AD 125–30, although other more local fires are equally possible.

Structure 1

Evidence for a further building (B5) was recorded in the south-east (TP8; EN20), but there was some activity in Open Area 3 which constitutes the construction, use and demolition of an earlier structure (Structure 1; see Fig 35). The area overlying an earlier water pipe was sealed by rubbish dumping and levelling for a brickearth surface in preparation for the construction of the structure (10.1). The lower dumps were dated AD 140–250; a single sherd of Portchester D (AD 350–400) was almost certainly intrusive. The brickearth floor contained pottery of AD 180–250, which implies a late 2nd- to mid 3rd-century date for the construction of Structure 1.

Only the south-west corner of the rectangular structure survived, formed by an oak post pad and a linear bed of bricks set in mortar, which also acted as a floor to the east (10.2; see Fig 6). The nature of the evidence suggests that the brick edging and pad supported timber-framed walls, probably with clay or mudbrick infill.

The structure was dismantled and sealed by mixed dumps dated AD 250–400 containing burnt brick and tile which represent its destruction (10.3). The few finds (Fig 44) included two bone hairpins of Crummy Type 3, <199> <231> (<S6>), one of them complete, and an incomplete bone needle <257> (<S12>) of Crummy Type 1.

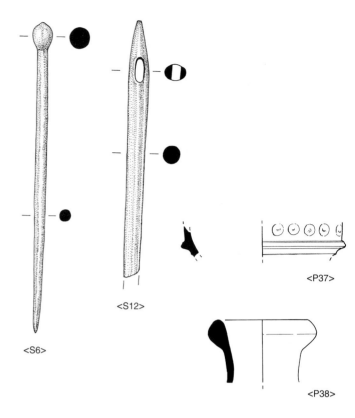

<S12>

<P37>

<S6>

<P38>

Fig 44 Finds from Structure 1: bone hairpin <S6> (1:1); bone needle <S12> (1:1); 2nd- to 4th-century pottery <P37> <P38> (1:4)

Fig 45 Trench EN20. Detail of drain constructed of inverted imbrices with the west wall of Building 5 to the rear, from the east. A section of plaster adhering to the wall has been protected by webbing prior to the wall being removed intact for conservation (0.2m scale)

Tile drain

A tile drain constructed of unused inverted imbrices draining from north to south was built to the west of the demolished Structure 1 (10.4; see Fig 45). After it had silted up, the northern section was apparently robbed as the ground surface to the east was raised to between about 2.4–2.5m OD (10.5).

Building 5

A brickearth and rubble dump containing pottery of AD 120–250 was deposited over the drain area, in order to level the ground surface and act as the construction surface for the west wall of Building 5 (10.6; Figs 45, 46). The mortared flint foundation of the wall supported a superstructure which consisted of a single brick string course, then four layers of flint, probably followed by a second row of bricks. The presence of in situ plaster indicates that the interior lay to the east as expected, whereas the west face – which was offset from the edge of the foundation by about 0.1m – looked out over Open Area 3. Five courses of brick were observed in the southern side of the trench, which probably indicated the proximity of a wall junction or doorway. The depth of the foundation (c 2.0m) suggests that the wall supported a substantial building of more than one storey.

The initial brickearth floor formed a lip against the wall in the manner of a quarter-round moulding at about 2.6m OD (10.7). Adjacent to the west face was a north–south timber dugout drain on horizontal bearers (10.8) which may have been provided to drain rainwater from the roof of the building by means of downpipes, conveying it through an outflow in the contemporary quay.

A second section of wall was found further north (TP8: 10.10). This was built of ragstone, although it too was demolished to about 3.2m OD and must have been part of a different build of the same building. Although the floor level was not reached in this area, given the prevailing slope up to the north and the fact that excavation was halted at about 3.0m OD, it is unlikely to have been significantly different from that in EN20. A third section of wall recorded by Marsden a little to the north (Feature 82) was of brick set in pink mortar. Since the alignment was apparently similar, this was possibly part of the same structure, representing a third type of construction (Marsden 1975, 59). The use of brick suggests an early 2nd-century date for this part of the building, and since brick was often used for quoins, this section may have been close to the north-west corner of the building.

The southern section of foundation contained pottery dated AD 140–200; the superstructure also included a single sherd of AD 120–300. It cannot, however, have been constructed until the demolition of Structure 1, perhaps after AD 250. On balance, it could be suggested that Building 5 was originally confined to the area occupied by the two northern brick and ragstone sections of walling, perhaps being built at the same time as the other buildings in the area. Structure 1 was built either after AD 140 or AD 180, possibly as a separate building, or alternatively as some kind of portico attached to the south-western part of Building 5 in its original form. It was then demolished in the mid 3rd century to allow its extension.

The southern section of wall was deliberately demolished and surrounded by dark earth dumps containing building debris as part of a late terracing operation (EN20: 10.9). Pottery within the dumps was dated AD 250/70–400, which suggests a late 3rd- or 4th-century demolition date for Building 5. Part of a decorated late Roman shale armlet <73> was also recovered (Fig 47: <S4>).

Fig 46 Trench EN20. View of the western flint and tile wall of Building 5 prior to removal, from the east (0.5m scale)

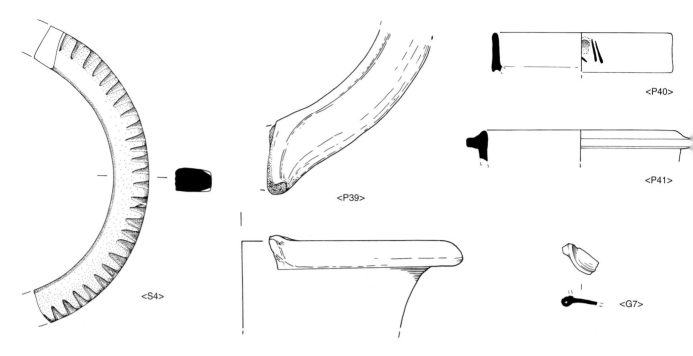

Fig 47 Finds from Building 5: shale armlet <S4> (1:1); 2nd- to 4th-century pottery <P39>–<P41> (1:4); and Open Area 4: glass cut beaker fragment <G7> (1:2)

3.4 The end of the Roman period: c AD 300–400

Open Area 4: 'dark earth'

A thick distinctive layer of dark grey silts was dumped over the remains of the demolished buildings in the eastern area in EN7, EN20 (11.1; see Fig 6) and against the outer wall of Building 2 (EN4: 11.23). Similar deposits were observed across the area during the watching brief (11.17–19, 11.21), where they were cut by at least one pit containing dark earth-like fill near the south wall of Rectory House (11.20). Further north, dark earth was dumped. Environmental samples revealed the presence of plants of waste or disturbed ground and woodland or scrub, including fat hen, elder, campion or catchfly (see 6.10 below). Hemlock and mallow were also recorded, the latter a plant of most dry-land habitats. As well as wild fruits and elder, small amounts of hop, spelt and barley were present, perhaps indicating local cultivation, although possibly at an earlier date. The hops may have intruded from overlying medieval deposits.

Layers of demolition debris and dark earth dumped against and over the west wall of Building 5 also contained seeds representing a disturbed or wasteground habitat, although some charred cereal grains were present (TP8: 11.2). One sample consisted almost entirely of elder seeds in sufficient quantity to indicate an economic use. A crescent-shaped cluster of ragstone blocks and flints, interpreted as the packing for a vertical timber post, may have formed part of a late Roman structure (11.3).

On the western half of the site, dark earth deposits were recorded near the west wall of Building 3 (EN14: 11.16; TP14: 11.24).

On other sites, these 'dark earth' deposits have appeared on analysis to consist of weathered brickearth subsoil and sand, mixed with fine suspended charcoal, which gives the layer its characteristic grey-black colour (Watson 1998a, 101). The 'dark earth' often includes late Roman material, but the bulk of the artefacts recovered are largely of earlier origin which suggests that the dumps incorporate household waste accumulated over a very long period, although the mechanism behind its formation is still not fully understood. Some researchers suggest wholesale dumping, others the biological breakdown and mixing of in situ material including the actual remains of clay-and-timber buildings (see Watson 1998a; Perring 1991, 78–81 for recent discussions). The sand fraction within the matrix is probably derived from brickearth and its by-products, daub and mudbrick, as well as from decayed mortar and plaster.

On balance, the dark earth at Suffolk House was of late 3rd- or 4th-century date, deposited after the demolition of the masonry structures on the site, although clay-and-timber buildings may have been erected.

3.5 Period discussion

The mid 1st century

The waterfront

The construction of the waterfront at Suffolk House (see Fig 7) was a crucial first step towards subsequent developments. As such, it is perhaps the most significant area in which the results of the 1994–7 investigation have added to the understanding of the site. Until the land bounding the river had been protected from the effects of tidal flooding and erosion, there was no prospect of fully utilising the area, whether for building or for the landing of goods. Early revetments were built all along the central part of the north bank, starting at Regis House next to the upstream side of Roman London Bridge (see Fig 1), where a revetment was constructed as early as AD 52 (Brigham & Watson in prep). Downstream of the bridge at Pudding Lane, embankments were probably built around the same time, although the earliest dated structure was a revetment built after AD 59 (Milne 1985, 35); these continued at least as far east as Billingsgate Buildings (Jones & Rhodes 1980).

Waterfront 1 at Suffolk House would have formed part of this pattern, although the only remains were several truncated piles located some distance south of the natural riverbank. There are strong parallels with Regis House where rows of timbers in front of the first waterfront were interpreted as mooring posts and the remains of jetties or landing platforms. There are further examples in the earliest period at Billingsgate Buildings, where lines of piles were positioned on the foreshore c AD 60–70 before the first recognisable revetment was constructed (Jones & Rhodes 1980, 2–5). Such structures would have been necessary to allow vessels to offload, since the depth of water in front of the earliest waterfronts was insufficient for safe handling, and continuous silting would have exacerbated the situation. That large overseas cargo vessels used the river cannot be in doubt, simply because of the high proportion of imported pottery and other goods at sites like Regis House in the first decades. A reference by Tacitus to pre-Boudican Londinium as an important centre for traders and merchandise ('negotiatorum et commeatuum', Annals 14.32) is further evidence, although written retrospectively. At Suffolk House, however, apart from samian, fine wares do not appear in the early years, and it was probably not a significant port site until about the time Waterfront 2 was constructed (see 6.5 below).

The buildings

Despite the construction of waterfronts on a number of sites, there is no structural evidence for a concentration of commercial premises near the river in the first decade of Roman occupation. Regis House is the only waterfront location where buildings of the earliest period have been positively identified. Even on that site with its pre-Boudican waterfront, the buildings appear to have been domestic rather than trade-related. There is no indication that there were any comparable buildings at Suffolk House, which was on the fringes of the original settlement.

The later 1st century

The waterfront

In the immediate post-Boudican period, the bridgehead clearly formed the focus for development of the waterfront. The substantial Neronian quay at Regis House was extended further to Miles Lane within a few years; a block of warehouses and

workshops at Regis House is the earliest known waterfront building in London. In the following decades, the wharf was expanded further along the river frontage in both directions (Brigham 1990, 134–5; Milne 1985, 55–62).

The absence of substantial quays at Suffolk House until the construction of Waterfront 2 suggests that it was not an attractive proposition for landing goods prior to AD 84, although cargoes were undoubtedly routinely handled by lighters, and beaching may have been an option, particularly for flat-bottomed river vessels.

It is probably no coincidence that, following the construction of Waterfront 2, there was an increase in the quantity of imported pottery including fine wares. Samian alone accounted for nearly a quarter of the total (see 6.5 below) and this may be connected to the apparent relationship between the quay and the neighbouring 'palace' site. The new quay and others further upstream of the Walbrook may have made the area as attractive for mercantile activity as sites nearer the bridge, although there was no dedicated riverside storage facility west of Regis House.

Structurally, the quay was virtually identical to that constructed at Pudding Lane, although apparently at least a decade earlier.

The buildings

The development of Suffolk House in the Roman period was clearly driven by the transformation of the waterfront area from sloping irregular marshy ground into a series of level terraces suitable for building.

Buildings 1 and 2 can be placed at the start of the period of expansion. Although the dating evidence is unclear, it is likely that they antedate the construction of Waterfront 2, since there is no need for the quay to have been built to accommodate them. Buildings 3–5 cannot have been constructed until reclamation had taken place in the early 2nd century following the construction of Waterfronts 3–4. An almost identical quay at Pudding Lane, constructed in the 90s, similarly allowed the building of a row of warehouses immediately downstream of the bridge (Milne 1985, 73–5).

Despite problems with the interpretation of the Suffolk House sequence, it does throw some light on the development and status of the neighbouring 'palace' site, which as part of a Scheduled Ancient Monument is unlikely to be available for further work in the foreseeable future. If the substantial quay structure excavated at Cannon Street Station (Stephenson 1996) and Waterfront 2 at Suffolk House were part of the same wharf, as seems likely, this reinforces Marsden's original view that the block of land occupied by the 'palace' was part of a single development. The river frontage of the 'palace' insula coincides exactly with that of this 'palace wharf' (see Fig 48). The Suffolk House quay for the first time provides a terminus post quem of AD 84 for the development of the southern part of the 'palace', which undoubtedly consisted of many phases (Marsden 1975, 62–7). It is significant that Building 3 at Suffolk House lay to the east of the quay, implying that it was part of a separate site developed later. Road 1, which separated Building 3 and the 'palace', was in line with the eastern end of Waterfront 2, and would have been particularly important as a vehicular access route to the river, especially as there seems to have been no such route through the 'palace' itself. Any similar road on the western side of the insula would have had to negotiate the side of the Walbrook Valley, although there is evidence that the northern part of the 'palace' complex continued further west than the end of the wharf in the form of a massive wall and hypocausted room excavated at 3–7 Dowgate Hill (DOW86: *Britannia* 18, 1987, 336). If so, a road here seems unlikely.

The northern block of the 'palace' occupied a continuation of the high terrace immediately north of Building 1, at or above *c* 8.0m OD, which suggests that it could have been contemporary with the earliest buildings at Suffolk House. It lay at a sufficient height above and distance from the river for its development to be independent of events on the waterfront. This northern 'core' consisted of a major terrace wall, with an apparently integral hypocausted hall and apsidal structure, and a complex of walls reaching as far north as Cannon Street. One problem with the suggested 1st-century construction date of this and the wings to the south is the universal use of ragstone and brick in the foundations. Flint was the common foundation material used at this period, for example in Building 1 at Suffolk House, the first forum (Marsden 1987) and the Cheapside baths (Marsden 1976), although the Flavian baths at Huggin Hill made use of ragstone and brick (Rowsome 1999). It has been suggested that the 'palace' and the Huggin Hill baths were both built by the procurator (Selkirk 1988), and it could be postulated that official buildings led the way in the introduction of new techniques and materials. The selection and employment of building materials for different tasks and at different periods is an aspect of Roman London that merits further consideration.

The evidence for goldworking

A feature of the 'palace' site was the presence of gold dust and crucibles related to gold refining in a pre-'palace' phase at Bush Lane House in 1972 (Marsden 1975, 9–13). Marsden suggested that as the mining and refining of precious metals normally came under imperial control, and by inference under that of the emperor's provincial representatives, so an early link between the Cannon Street Station area with the governor's office was seen as a possibility. Whether this was the case or not, further evidence for goldworking was found at Suffolk House during the 1994–7 programme, in the form of one complete crucible and several fragments, all with gold adhering, representing the melting and cupellation processes (see 6.12 below). Notably, these were all found on the eastern part of the site, some distance from the crucibles and gold dust recovered in 1972, and this does suggest working over a larger area than previously envisaged, unless the crucibles had been dispersed. Fragments of two crucibles were found in dumps behind Waterfront 4 in the south-east. A third fragment was obtained from an area of burnt debris identified as hearth rake-out within Building 2, which may have been an actual working area. The single

complete crucible came from the backfill of a robbed wall of the first phase of Building 4 just south of Building 2.

If Building 2 was a late 1st- or early 2nd-century goldworking centre, this would be of considerable interest, since it implies that the construction of the 'palace' may have displaced the pre-Flavian goldworkers in Bush Lane House to a nearby site where refining and working could continue.

The 2nd century

The waterfront

Structurally, Waterfront 3 is typical of the few early 2nd-century waterfronts recorded on other sites. It was far less substantial than the 1st-century quay, and of relatively poor quality in design and in the use of second-hand materials, although timbers observed beneath Thames Street in 1927 imply that the builders of Waterfront 4 returned to the use of squared horizontal beams subsequently (see 1.2 above). Waterfront 4 may have passed as far south as the centre of the modern Thames Street dual carriageway on the basis of observations made near Suffolk Lane in 1927 (RCHM 1928, 143), a considerable distance from its predecessor. One factor which seems to have driven the reclamation process in the 2nd and 3rd centuries was that a progressive fall in river level required the continual extension of the waterfront in an effort to maintain a workable depth of water for shipping (Brigham 1990, 143–9). The Neronian quay at Regis House seems to have set a standard height from foreshore to wharf of 2.0m, which was maintained until the last waterfronts were built nearly 200 years later. The maximum working depth at the normal state of high tide was therefore little more than *c* 1.1–1.3m, which even in optimum conditions was too shallow for fully laden seagoing ships or large rivercraft, suggesting a reliance on the use of lighters. The reduction of the working depth during the lifetime of the quays by falling river levels would have accelerated the cycle of replacement beyond that required on the grounds of decay or structural failure.

There is little evidence for the local environment of the waterfront in the 2nd century. Analysis of the infill of Waterfront 4 suggests that it was collected from drier conditions than those which predominated in the pre-Roman period, but this material could well have originated some distance away. Exotic species within the fill, including fig, olive, stone pine and walnut, were all staple parts of the Roman diet, and typical of such assemblages. The only notable inclusion was the presence of a large number of weld or dyer's rocket seeds. These quite probably came from a dyeing workshop, although again, this may have been some distance from the waterfront. Material from the timber box-drain associated with the same waterfront may be thought more likely to represent local conditions, although the seeds recovered actually suggested that the fill originated in damp meadows or marginal agricultural land, neither of which could be expected on the waterfront at this period. A concentration of charred chaff and cereal grains could, however, have been dumped locally as waste from sieving.

The buildings

One side effect of the continued extension of the waterfront was that buildings which formerly occupied the river frontage faced becoming landlocked. One solution for the owners of such properties was to expand, as was the case with the 'palace', although as the process continued until the 3rd century, this was hardly feasible in the long term.

One of the most significant features of the waterfront in general at this period is the continued lack of dedicated storage space for imported goods. This has already been highlighted in relation to the earliest phase of occupation prior to AD 60–1, but it remained the case during periods for which evidence is available. (Chiefly the 1st–early 2nd centuries and the late 2nd–mid 3rd centuries, since structures of the intervening period lie mainly beneath the modern Thames Street dual carriageway, an area which has rarely been available for detailed examination.) On the north bank, as far as is known, warehouses were confined to two blocks constructed a generation apart at Regis House and Pudding Lane/Peninsular House. Of the other sites examined between the Walbrook stream and Regis House, evidence was recovered for structures of differing levels of complexity, status and size, but all appear to represent domestic buildings. (Apart from Cannon Street Station and Suffolk House these sites include Minster House (Merrifield 1965, gazetteer no. 302, Guildhall Museum file no. GM12) and Miles Lane.) Buildings 3–5 at Suffolk House fit this pattern, as far as can be determined: certainly Building 3 was a high-status residential complex, and there is no evidence that Buildings 4 and 5 were associated with trade either.

It can be assumed from this that the waterfront had two main functions which did not include the provision of large-scale storage. The first of these was to provide a stable, level terrace for building, which is obvious in all cases. The second function, which can only be suggested from the presence of concentrations of imported goods near the waterfront, was to act as an access point for cargoes which were dispersed through the town's street system to storage or retail premises away from the river. These almost certainly included the massive forum complex, private merchants' quarters, shops and public markets or *macella*. With such a pattern of distribution, there was little need for warehousing alongside the wharf itself, with the possible exception of secure or bonded stores for valuable items, or goods awaiting collection for inward and outward conveyance from Londinium. The concentration of sherds of imported pottery at Suffolk House (see 6.5 below) may therefore be a good reflection of items broken in transit or during handling while passing across the quay to a general market, rather than traded specifically on site.

Turning to the 2nd-century development of the 'palace' site (Fig 48), it is significant that the walls to the south of the upper terrace were not bonded into the main terrace wall, indicating, as Marsden suggests, that they were probably later additions. The date of Waterfront 2 gives a *terminus post quem* for this, since it reclaimed a large area of former marsh and foreshore. The whole area occupied by the eastern and southern

wings could therefore have been constructed at the same time, after AD 84. The floor level of the whole area occupied by the 'garden court' and east wing of the 'palace' lay at the same level as the floors of Building 1, *c* 6.4–6.7m OD, although extending much further south. It must therefore be assumed that the east wall of the 'palace' complex supported the terrace, with Road 1 sloping rapidly to connect the higher terraces with the 'palace wharf'. The creation of this terrace, which was at least 30m x 80m in extent, was a major feat of engineering. The massive south wall of the 'garden court' also formed the north side of the south wing, the primary walls of which were integral in some areas. Excavation work in 1988 demonstrated that the south face of the wall was embellished with alternating rectangular and curved niches, unique for London, to which later walls seem to have been attached. The south wing floors were at the same general level as those of the southern part of Building 3, above *c* 3.0m OD, or *c* 3.5m below those of the garden court. A butt joint between the east and south wings shows that they were built separately, although not necessarily a long time apart.

Whether there was a later connection between the two sites depends upon the interpretation of the 'palace'. It has been demonstrated that there was a large degree of planning involved in the 'palace' site, from the construction of the quay to the massive northern terrace wall and tower, and the creation of the 'garden court' and the ranges of rooms to south and east. Something like an official residence or major administrative complex must be envisaged. The presence of a bath suite in the south wing implies a residential function. Recent theories have tended to suggest that the governorship was a peripatetic office, and there need have been no *praetorium* (eg Millett 1998, 9). The procurator was more likely to have been firmly based in Londinium, responsible for much of the town's infrastructure; certainly one of the earliest procurators, Julius Alpinus Classicianus, was buried in London, apparently after playing a leading role in its reconstruction following the Boudican revolt. This degree of control is demonstrated by the number of procuratorial inscriptions and probable brick and tile stamps on the 'palace' site and elsewhere, and conversely by the paucity of inscriptions referring to the governor before the 3rd century. It could be suggested that York, which saw the deaths of two emperors and the creation of a third, was at least as important as London (Selkirk 1988). One possibility, therefore, is that the complex was procuratorial rather than gubernatorial, and that the governor may not have had a large official residence as such, but made use of other facilities when in London, such as the large fort in the north-west corner of the town.

There is nothing to tie Building 3 directly to the 'palace' site; it was, for example, constructed beyond the end of the 'palace wharf' as part of a later infill programme, but it was certainly a substantial townhouse of unusual plan considering its early 2nd-century date. If the building was not actually owned by the imperial estate, something which even further excavation may not elucidate, then it must have been the property of a wealthy merchant or landowner.

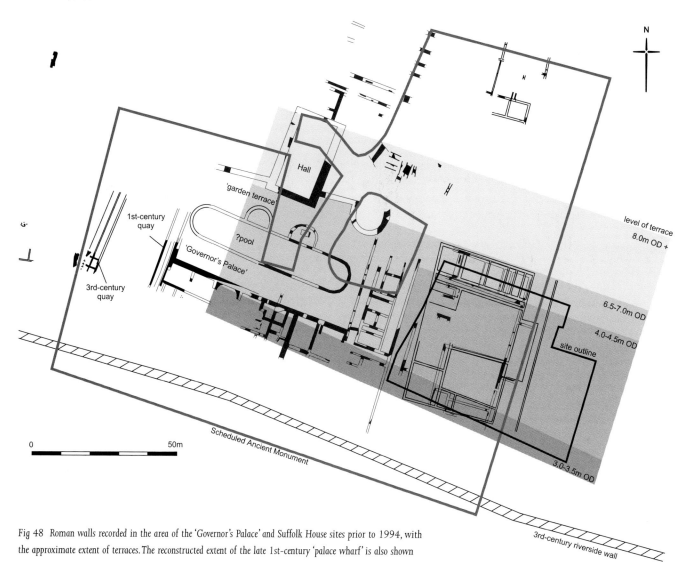

Fig 48 *Roman walls recorded in the area of the 'Governor's Palace' and Suffolk House sites prior to 1994, with the approximate extent of terraces. The reconstructed extent of the late 1st-century 'palace wharf' is also shown*

The 3rd and 4th centuries

The waterfront

The waterfront continued to expand into the second quarter of the 3rd century (Brigham 1990a), reclaiming in excess of 30m in most areas of the central zone. (Broadly the area between modern Queenhithe and Billingsgate.) By this time, Suffolk House and the 'palace' site were situated well back from the river, although the 'palace' insula maintained access through the construction of a new wharf along the Walbrook in the late 2nd or early 3rd century. The decline of the port in the middle of the 3rd century and the construction of a riverside defensive wall within a few years meant in any case that the Thames was no longer as influential in the town's development as it had been. (The inlet at the mouth of the Walbrook was infilled after the wall was built, and the stream canalised.)

The buildings and the dark earth

The evidence for the later periods at Suffolk House consists mainly of alterations to the existing structures. Building 5 (or the southern part of the property at least) was probably the last to be constructed, otherwise there were no major additions to the layout established in the 2nd century. The demolition of all the buildings on the site in the late 3rd or 4th century is part of a pattern which includes the clearance of the 'palace' (Perring 1991, 113), the forum (Brigham 1990b, 77–9) and the amphitheatre (Bateman 1998, 53). (The 'palace' may have been demolished about the same time as the riverside defensive wall was built. Certainly the wharf in the Walbrook mouth which connected the site to the river was dismantled before the Walbrook inlet was infilled as part of the wall-building programme. This can be dated by the presence of hundreds of late 3rd-century radiate copies in the infill of the inlet.) The removal of many large public buildings and the dumping of dark earth on the cleared sites suggest a major change not just in the appearance of the town, but fundamentally in the way that it was governed and the space used by the inhabitants. If the population of Londinium was shrinking, and the remainder increasingly consisted of the landowning classes, Building 3 was just the type of self-contained townhouse which might have been expected to survive until the end of the period, although it is unclear whether it was still occupied in the latter half of the 4th century. Similar structures at Pudding Lane and Billingsgate, for example, may have remained in use until *c* AD 400 (Milne 1985, 33; Merrifield 1983, 247–55). Of the other buildings on the site, less is known, but there is no indication that they approached the quality of Building 3, and there may have been less of a market for such properties in the late period.

Dark earth is not a universal deposit, although it has been recorded on many sites, sealing surfaces from the mid 2nd century onwards. At Suffolk House, it appears to have been deposited at a time when the buildings on site were already in a state of collapse, probably in the late 3rd or 4th century. Whether it represents abandonment or merely a change in usage is still arguable, but a reduction in population is clearly indicated. The botanical remains present suggest that the local habitat was dry, although whether this reflects conditions in the final resting place of the deposit or some other site where the material was collected prior to being transported is unclear, and depends on the extent to which the dark earth formed *in situ*. Like the quay infill, it is perhaps best to see it as an imported deposit, and the artefacts and ecofacts within as intrusive.

4

The medieval and post-medieval periods

4.1 Historical outline

Introduction

Despite some well-documented evidence for early Anglo-Saxon connections with London, most notably the foundation of St Paul's in AD 604, it is now clear that settlement was centred on the Strand area upstream until the very late 9th or early 10th century. At that time, the old walled town was reoccupied as the Alfredian response to repeated Viking attacks (Vince 1990). It has been suggested for some years that two well-documented charters of 889 and 898–9 demonstrate that the harbour area near Queenhithe was probably occupied or developed as part of the early core of a planned settlement (Dyson 1978). Excavations at Bull Wharf in the early 1990s subsequently uncovered waterfront activity of the very late 9th century, beyond the line of the late 3rd-century riverside wall (Ayre & Wroe-Brown in prep).

Documentary research has now established that a series of new streets were laid out (Dyson 1990). Narrow lanes ran north–south to link the waterfront with the centre of the city, including the markets of East and West Cheap (Horsman et al 1988; Vince 1990, 123–9). Suffolk Lane and Laurence Pountney Lane formed part of this new street network: Suffolk Lane overlies the Roman street or alley (R1) between Building 3 and the 'Governor's Palace' site to the west, and the absence of walls may have influenced its position (cf Figs 35, 56). Suffolk Lane had received its present name by 1581. It was previously *Wolsyeslane, Basyngeslane* (1267–8; *Cartulary of St Bartholomew's Hospital,* No. 239) or *Arundelleslane* (1439; *Calendar of Plea and Memoranda Rolls,* 1437–57, 14). A street identifiable as modern Laurence Pountney Lane was first referred to in 1248, and appeared as the 'lane of *St Laurence de Candelwykstrate*' in 1280–1 (Ekwall 1954, 162, 142–3). Ducksfoot Lane, extinguished in 1969, may have been a later addition subdividing the larger block formed by the earlier streets. The presence of late 12th- or early 13th-century structures (Buildings 11 and 13) on its eastern side suggests that it was already in place by that time, perhaps as an alley giving access to the centre of the insula. Its name was possibly a corruption of *Duke's Field Lane,* a reference to the dukes of Suffolk.

Other streets where archaeological work has taken place further east fall into the same pattern, including Fish Street Hill and Botolph Lane (Brigham & Watson in prep; Horsman et al 1988, 112–13) The first elements of the street plan may have predated the construction of the majority of the embankments on the river to the south (Horsman et al 1988), although the late 9th- and 10th-century activity at Queenhithe suggests that the earliest waterfronts were contemporary. The early medieval embankment at Swan Lane, to the south of Suffolk House, was probably of mid 11th-century date, slightly later than the onset of activity at Suffolk House. Other sites, including Vintry and Seal House were all demonstrably a little later.

For details of the late medieval and post-medieval layout, Figs 48–52 should be consulted.

Fig 49 The 'Agas' woodcut map (1561–70)

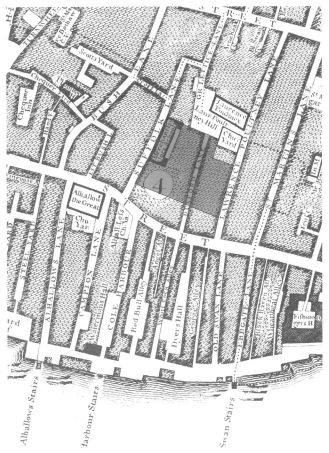

Fig 51 Rocque's survey (1746)

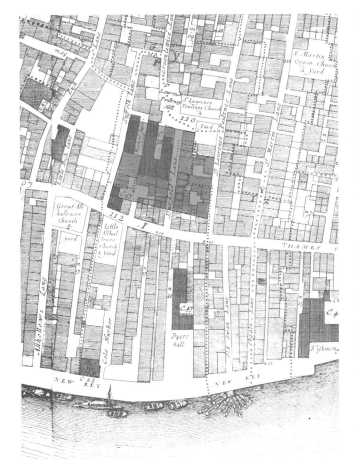

Fig 50 Ogilby and Morgan's survey (1676)

Fig 52 Ordnance Survey (1873)

The church of St Laurence Pountney

Although it was situated to the north of the site, the presence of the church and its graveyard did have an impact on the development of the area, and one of its chief benefactors was also an important figure in the history of Suffolk House. The first reference to the church of St Laurence was in a forged charter purporting to date to 1067 (*Calendar of Charter Rolls*, iv 333), although its actual mid 12th-century origin does at least serve to give a *terminus ante quem* for the establishment of the church and burial ground of St Laurence, Candlewick Street, later Cannon Street (Carlin & Belcher 1989, 88). Repaired *c* 1306, the church was later renamed St Laurence Pountney in posthumous remembrance of Sir John de Pulteney, who founded a chantry chapel in honour of Corpus Christi in 1332, replacing an earlier foundation. The chantry originally had seven chaplains, but was later enlarged as a college for a master, 13 priests and four choristers. It was situated on the north side of the church itself (Norman 1901, 259). The church, which appears as an imposing structure with a steeple on the pre-Great Fire panoramas and maps (eg the 'Agas' map, see Fig 49), was destroyed in the fire of 1666 and never rebuilt (see Fig 50); its site was used as a burial ground until the 1850s, the small parish itself being amalgamated with St Mary Abchurch (see Figs 51, 52).

The burial ground was divided into two by a pathway which still exists: the northern side, including the church site, being the 'church ground'; the southern portion the 'church yard'. Today both the site of the church and the burial ground are public open spaces, maintained by the Corporation of London. There are a number of chest tombs and early monuments remaining, including Henry Strode senior (1683) and his wife Elizabeth (1686), Henry Strode junior (1704) and his sister Sarah Herring (1731) (RCHM 1929, 43–4).

Pountney's Inn or the Manor of the Rose

Sir John de Pulteney (alias Pultney or Pountney), of a Leicestershire family, was a prominent member of the Drapers' Company and Lord Mayor of London in 1331, 1332, 1334 and 1337. His earliest London residence was an imposing 13th-century building on the riverfront at Cold Harbour on the south side of modern Thames Street opposite Suffolk House (Norman 1901, 259). By 1336, however, he had acquired property in the parish of St Laurence, Candlewick Street (Schofield 1995, 193–4), which can be identified in part as Buildings 14–15 (see Figs 50, 56). Sir John either built or, more likely from the archaeological evidence, altered the buildings on the site at this time, as on 6 October 1341 he received a licence to crenellate his London house. This was one of only 11 such licences issued in the period 1305–85 (Schofield 1991, 8–9). The house was subsequently referred to as Pulteney's 'principal messuage' in his will, dated 14 November 1348; both Cold Harbour and the Suffolk Lane properties were, however, referred to at times as Pountney's Inn or Pulteneysin from at least 1365 (Kingsford 1917, 74–8). After his death in 1349 it was occupied as the London house of Edward, the 'Black Prince', although it was

delivered to Sir Nicholas de Loveyne, the new husband of Pulteney's widow, in 1359. After the death without issue of Pulteney's son in 1366, the house passed to the College of St Lawrence Pountney, or Corpus Christi.

In 1385 the College exchanged the house for a property of Richard FitzAlan, earl of Arundel, in Warwickshire. It remained in Arundel hands for a number of years, with an interval between 1397–1406 when it was confiscated following Arundel's execution by Richard II for treason. After being restored to Arundel's son, Thomas, it passed after his death in 1415 through the hands of John Holand, later duke of Exeter, to the de la Pole dukes of Suffolk in 1439. Despite brief reversions to the Crown following the execution of William de la Pole for treason in 1450, and the attainder of his grandson John de la Pole, earl of Lincoln, in 1487, the Suffolks held the house for most of the 15th century until the attainder of another grandson, Edmund, in 1506. This inspired the name of the 19th-century and 1960s' buildings which occupied most of the southern part of the former site of the house, as well as the lane to the west (Suffolke Lane by 1581). John and Edmund were nephews of Edward IV, Yorkist pretenders to the throne and leaders of the White Rose faction. In 1506 the house was granted to Edward Stafford, duke of Buckingham, but after his arrest on a charge of high treason in 1521, it was held by the Crown for four years as a messuage with gardens. In Stafford's time the property was known as the Red Rose, or the Manor of the Rose, showing the Stafford family's switch in allegiance from Richard III to the Lancastrian Henry Tudor. In 1525 it was granted to Henry Courtney, earl of Devon and marquess of Exeter, who in 1530 constructed a gallery with 12 bay windows round the east, north and south sides of the garden and a summerhouse under the south end of the gallery at a cost of £110, exclusive of the cost of materials from an existing gallery (Norman 1901, 268; Kingsford 1917, 76–7). Courtney had little time to enjoy his improvements however: in 1538 he was accused of high treason against Henry VIII and executed the following year, the third owner to have met the same end in less than a century. In 1540 the property was granted to Robert Radcliffe, earl of Sussex and great chamberlain of England, who was related by marriage to the Buckinghams. He predeceased his wife, who continued to occupy the house until her death, whereupon it descended through the male line until 1561, when Thomas Radcliffe sold the property to John Hethe, a cooper.

Several elements of the northern range of Sir John de Pulteney's inn or house have been identified from cartographic evidence (see Fig 56). Firstly, pre-Great Fire depictions – including the 16th- and 17th-century Copperplate and 'Agas' maps (see Fig 49) and panoramas by Braun and Hogenberg and by Hollar – show a tower immediately to the west of St Laurence Pountney church. It appears to have been an imposing crenellated structure several storeys high with paired windows at each level. The southern part of the tower probably encroached on the site in the position later occupied by 4 Laurence Pountney Hill, and an area of modern disturbance at the east end of one testpit (TP2/EN2) may be the robber trench for its west wall.

Secondly, the view by Hollar shows that there was a crenellated east–west range interpreted as the main hall adjoining the northern half of the tower, with five ornate windows in its south wall. The stone-built vaulted undercroft of the range, attributed to the late 13th or early 14th century, was destroyed by redevelopment as recently as 1894 (Norman 1901, 272). This feature was situated immediately to the north of Suffolk House under the southern part of 3 Laurence Pountney Hill, below the present street. The undercroft consisted of a large two-bay space 13.7m x 6.0m reached from the eastern end by a stair, with a cross-passage to the west separating the main area from two smaller rooms on the Suffolk Lane frontage. One of these probably contained a stair giving access to the main hall. The undercroft served as a storage area or workspace below the main hall; the cross-passage perhaps reflected the position of a similar feature on the ground floor, with a kitchen, pantry or buttery at the west end. Norman considered the undercroft to have been late 13th- or early 14th-century work, in which case it belonged to an earlier structure than Pountney's Inn, quite probably identifiable with Building 14.

There are later references from probate sources to a western gatehouse, presumably on the Suffolk Lane frontage immediately south of the hall, at the north end of the streetfront range represented by Buildings 14–15. It is possibly identifiable as a crenellated structure shown on Hollar's panorama close to the likely position of the gate. Behind the streetfront range was a courtyard with a winding stair in the south-east. A garden court probably lay further east. Both the main court and the garden court seem to have been galleried at a later date.

In summary, it appears that Sir John's house consisted of a main western courtyard on Suffolk Lane reached by means of a gatehouse, with ranges of buildings forming a quadrangle (see Fig 56). The northern range contained the hall over an undercroft, with the living quarters perhaps in the tower and eastern range. The south range may have held a chapel with a separate undercroft, the north and west walls of which were recorded in TP13. In the 16th century it is documented that a winding stair from the courtyard gave access to the chapel roof, part of the chapel, and two galleries at the south end, presumably at different levels. The garden court was probably to the east of the main court along Ducksfoot Lane, and was almost certainly surrounded by ancillary buildings such as stores, although in the 16th century it was galleried on the east, north and south sides, with a summerhouse in the south (see above). It may be represented by a yard shown on Ogilby and Morgan's survey of 1676 (see Fig 50) and shown as Laurence Pountney Place on a much later map of the parish, dated 1805 (Norman 1901, pl 33). In the post-Great Fire period the north end was shown giving open access to Laurence Pountney Hill, possibly replacing an earlier entrance. It is likely that most of the foundations of the earlier buildings were reused in the post-Great Fire period, as seems from the 1994–7 investigations to have been the case with the western range. A 19th-century east–west brick wall in TP3 also seems to have coincided with the position of the north wall of the range forming the east side of the garden court.

The Merchant Taylors' School to the present

In 1561 John Hethe divided the property into two units the same year he acquired it, one of which was purchased by William Beswicke, a draper. The other moiety was purchased by Richard Botyl, a merchant tailor, consisting of the west gatehouse, main courtyard, the winding stairs and two galleries at the south end of the yard, and part of the chapel (Kingsford 1917, 77; Norman 1901, 269). Botyl was, however, acting on behalf of the Merchant Taylors' Company, to which he conveyed the property. According to John Stow, Company member Richard Hills contributed £500 towards the purchase of 'the Manor of the Rose', to be used as a grammar school administered by the Merchant Taylors' Company (Kingsford 1971, 113).

The Merchant Taylors' School occupied the existing buildings on this part of the site until the Great Fire of 1666, when the premises were destroyed, together with most of the City. In 1671 the school was rebuilt (Norman 1901, 270), and the work has been attributed to Wren, although no documentary evidence for this has survived (see Figs 51, 52).

The moiety purchased by Beswicke seems to have consisted of four messuages and a garden, and must have included the area of the north range, later 3, 4 and 5 Laurence Pountney Hill, and the garden court, Laurence Pountney Place, with rights to the area beneath the chapel. This part of the moiety passed probably a little before the Great Fire to a Company member, later Master and Lord Mayor, Patience Warde, who rebuilt after the Fire at a cost of nearly £5000, contributing £100 to the reconstruction of the school itself. It remained in the Warde family until in 1859–60 the Merchant Taylors purchased the rest of the original property, possibly to extend the school, although the areas of the former chapel and the north range appear to have remained separate, until in 1875 the buildings were demolished. The school itself was relocated to Charterhouse Square, moving again in 1935 to Sandy Lodge at Northwood in Middlesex. The house containing the crypt, 3 Laurence Pountney Lane, immediately to the north was demolished in 1894.

The area behind the school to the east and west of Ducksfoot Lane was occupied by a number of houses. Several tenements on the eastern side were owned by the Harvey family, which included Dr William Harvey (1578–1657), discoverer of blood circulation. Part of their property at the north-east corner of Ducksfoot Lane was later occupied by Sir Robert Kite, Lord Mayor in 1766–7.

After 1875, two office buildings occupied the site: Suffolk House to the west of Ducksfoot Lane, and Norfolk House to the east. These were damaged during the Second World War, but were repaired subsequently, although office buildings adjoining the south side of Suffolk House were cleared and used as a car park. Finally, in 1969, the existing buildings were cleared in preparation for the construction of a new building, which unified the area by continuing over Ducksfoot Lane. This redevelopment went hand in hand with the widening of Upper Thames Street to form a new dual carriageway.

4.2 Early medieval period:
c AD 1000–1150/1200

Early occupation

The earliest evidence for reoccupation of the site after the long hiatus which followed the Roman withdrawal took the form of a number of pits, which were mainly cut for the disposal of food refuse and cess in the first half of the 11th century (Fig 53). There was no evidence for the construction of buildings in the small areas available for examination, however, until later in the century, although it is unlikely that the local inhabitants would have disposed of their rubbish a very great distance from their houses. It is probable that a pattern of buildings occupying individual burgage plots already existed, which would have

been orientated east–west towards the forerunners of the present-day Suffolk Lane and Laurence Pountney Lane. The largely cellared buildings which were constructed from the 11th century onwards almost certainly removed the slight evidence for the first phase of buildings, which may well have been surface-laid.

The eastern area

In the north-east part of Open Area 4, the latest Roman deposits were cut by a cesspit containing pottery of 1000–1150 (EN4: 12.9). The organic fill included seeds predominantly of woodland, hedgerow or grassland, with some fruits from those areas, such as apple, blackberry/raspberry and elder. This pit also contained a number of human bones, although these were almost certainly slumped from an overlying deposit (27.1) and

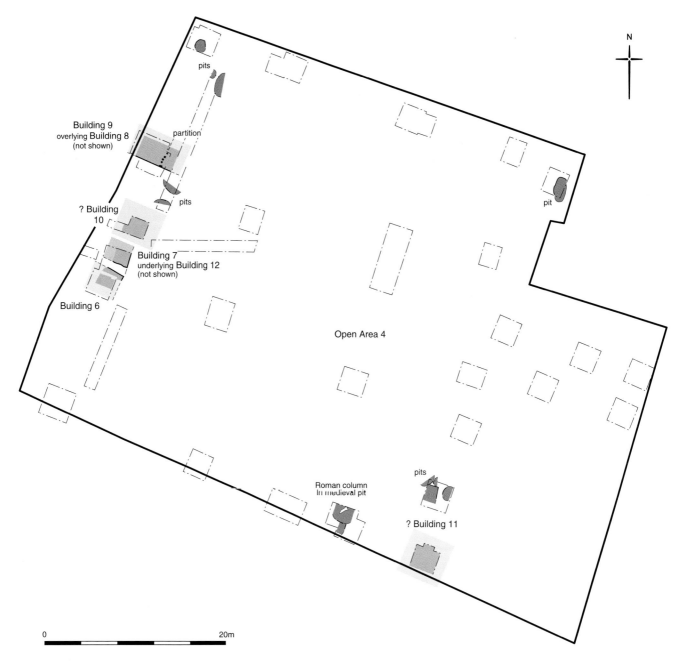

Fig 53 Plan of principal 11th- to 12th-century archaeological features: Buildings 6–12 and areas of pitting

as a result have been assigned to the later medieval period.

Further south, the late Roman dark earth was cut by a series of intercutting pits, the organic fills of which were often well preserved. The lowest recorded fill of the earliest pit located contained weed seeds from both cultivated land and waste ground (TP8: 12.1). The remains of food debris included a number of common wild fruits, as well as cereal bran and grains of bread wheat, spelt and barley, a single grain each of oat and rye, and part of a coriander capsule. The bones of the main domesticates were present, and fish were also represented. A single frog or toad long bone may have been food waste, but is just as likely to represent the wet local environmental conditions that seem to have prevailed. Finds included fragments of two wooden bowls <63> <64> and numerous short lengths of roundwood, with pottery of 970–1050, progressing to later material of up to 1120–50 in the upper fills. The pottery included 12 sherds of an unusual coarse flint-tempered ware (EMFL COAR), probably all from the same mid 11th-century spouted pitcher. Two sherds from a possible Early Medieval Sandy ware (EMS) lamp were also found. Residual Roman material from the disturbed dark earth was well represented, including two coins, one of Constantius II (AD 355–65: <35>), the second a slightly earlier irregular issue (AD 347–50: <34>), and a late Roman blue glass hairpin <371> and glass cut beaker fragment <372> (see Fig 47: <G7>).

A shallow cut intruding into the upper fills was probably a post pit dated 1050–1150, packed with brick, ragstone rubble and flint cobbles; the post had been extracted, and there were no further signs of related structural activity (12.5).

There were three further pits in the vicinity (12.2–4), one with the base cut by a small stakehole, possibly for an upright supporting a lining (12.2). The fills of another were sealed by a thin layer of brickearth containing pottery of 1050–80, which may have been the floor of a building (12.4), possibly associated with the nearby post pit, although the evidence was not conclusive.

Further south were deposits interpreted as belonging to a period of domestic rubbish dumping in an external area, probably with some trees or bushes present (EN20: 12.10). The material was apparently derived from hearths and organic refuse, and contained everyday domestic rubbish such as broken pottery and food waste; the pottery was datable to 1080–1150, and included an unusual spout from an Early Medieval Flinty ware (EMFL) pitcher.

To the west were three pits, again mainly filled with organic refuse (TP9: 12.11–13). The largest contained a stake that may have supported an internal wattle lining, and was datable to 900–1050 (12.13). Above the stake, the fills contained Roman rubble including fragments of oolitic limestone and sandstone, and most notably the 0.91m fragment of Tuscan column capital with an attached broken shaft already mentioned.

The western area

In the north-west corner of the site (TP1) two rubbish pits contained pottery of 1050–1150 (22.1–2; see Fig 58). Further

south, dark earth-like material (12.6) occupied the unexcavated area to either side of the Roman wall in TP13, although this probably consisted of the fills of intercutting pits representing an early stage of reoccupation before the Roman wall and buttress were robbed c 1050–1100 (12.7). Two large stakeholes cutting the robber trench backfill (12.8) may have formed part of an early building, although no other signs of structural activity were observed. In the northern part of AE1 immediately south-east of TP1 was a brickearth surface sealed by dumps consisting largely of Roman brick, which were cut by three pits containing dark earth-type material (11.4–8). Further south near TP14 the dark earth dumps were cut by two pits sealed by the make-up for two successive burnt and trampled brickearth surfaces, cut by a third pit (11.9–14). A brickearth surface to the south of AE1 was sealed by dark earth (EN18: 11.15). The brickearth spreads may have been the floors of an early phase of buildings, although there was no further supporting evidence for this, and they are perhaps more likely to have been thin external spreads, perhaps of hearth material or daub. It is, of course, possible that the features in AE1 were all late Roman, since there is no independent dating evidence available.

Building 6

The post-Roman deposits in TP13 were disturbed by the shallow cut for a sunken-floored building (B6: 13.1; see Fig 53) with layers of sand and crushed chalk forming the first floors. A brickearth hearth dated 1000–1150 was found, with nearby spreads of burnt debris and raked-off ash. The ash was cut by two rubbish pits (13.2) presumably after the building was no longer in use, since the fill of one pit could be dated to a slightly later period (1080–1150). The pottery from the pit contained an Early Medieval Grog-tempered ware (EMGR) spouted pitcher of a form previously unrecorded in the City as well as an imported amphora from Badorf. The area of the building was subsequently covered by an extensive mixed dump of ashy silt, dated 1050–1150 (13.3). No roof tile was found, and the building was probably thatched or shingled.

Building 7

The shallow cellar of a second sunken-floored building (B7: 14.1; see Fig 53) was constructed immediately to the north of Building 6. Not long after its completion, the compaction or settlement of earlier pit fills led to the subsidence of the floor, which was levelled up to allow the laying of a thin brickearth surface dated 1080–1100 (14.2). This was heavily scorched, and this taken together with the presence of burnt plank fragments around the south edge of the cellar cut, suggest that the building burned down. The slab was cut after the fire by two possible post- or stakeholes and two rubbish pits, the latest of which had been lined with brickearth and contained pottery contemporary with the floor (14.3–5).

The building was reconstructed at a higher level and the cellar cut extended westwards (14.6). Continued subsidence into the underlying rubbish pits required the deposition of compensatory dumps prior to the construction of a brickearth hearth. The dumps contained pottery dated 1050–1100. Again, no roof tile was recovered.

Building 8

The Roman masonry further north in TP14 may have been truncated about this time, and the east–west cross-wall at the south end of the trench was cut through locally at ground level, possibly for exploratory purposes (15.1). Three successive layers of brickearth datable to 1080–1150 were laid over the dark earth to the north of the wall to form the floors of a third cellared building (B8; see Fig 53). A deposit containing Roman mortar and *opus signinum* next to the wall possibly represents the weathering of the surviving exposed section (15.2). The final floor was sealed by deposits that may have been windblown, suggesting the abandonment of the building.

This deposit was cut in the small area observed by between 150–200 stakeholes and post pits (15.3) which varied in shape and depth, intercut frequently and formed no visible pattern (Fig 54). Two of the larger post pits contained pads of reused Roman brick fragments and a piece of ragstone. The fills of all the features were uniform, consisting of a soft lower fill of organic sandy silt – probably partly decayed wood – and an upper fill of intrusive silts similar to the overlying layer.

The function of the posts cannot be surmised, but is suggestive of a repeated craft or industrial activity, apparently after Building 8 had been abandoned.

The cellar was infilled by deposits of soil resembling dark earth, divided by a thin layer of burnt clay (15.4). The layers contained a high proportion of residual Roman building materials and artefacts, indicating reworking of earlier deposits during the formation of the soil, and this is reflected by the mixture of pottery datable from as early as 1000–1150 to 1240–70. The mixture of pottery could reflect the lengthy time period over which the material accumulated, although the later

Fig 54 Trench TP14. *View of part of the extensive group of early medieval postholes in Building 8 under excavation, from the south*

sherds could have been intrusive or related to the next phase of occupation. The artefacts included a London coarseware frying pan and a curfew, both of 12th-century date. Roof tiles of early type in fabric 2273 – which probably came into use in the 1130s – were also present, as well as glazed tiles in fabric 2587, dating certainly from before the 15th century, and presumably considerably earlier unless they were intrusive. Large numbers of terrestrial and freshwater molluscs were recovered from these deposits.

Building 9

The dark earth deposits were removed by the cut for a fourth sunken-floored building (B9; see Figs 53, 55) to the level of the underlying brickearth surfaces, leaving an undisturbed 1.0m strip at the south end of TP14 (16.1). The vertical south edge of the cut was lined with planking. The base of the cellared area was sealed by 0.1–0.15m of organic material, perhaps composed of decayed rush or straw floor covering (16.2), which contained pottery of 1050–1100, with some almost certainly intrusive material of 1350–1500. An iron arrowhead <40> was also recovered. The first surface was followed by a similar floor containing ragstone and ferruginous sandstone rubble, brick and tile, and a piece of laminated limestone paving or inlay, mainly if not all of Roman origin. Animal bones from this area

included the main domesticates, with evidence of pig butchery, as well as the remains of mouse or vole skulls, perhaps indicative of living conditions. The floor extended over most of the cellar, which was heated by a sunken brickearth hearth set in the north-east corner (16.3). A later replacement hearth in the same position was given a brickearth base roughly edged by ragstone rubble and brick, covered by ash layers from the hearth's use covered by levelling dumps (16.4).

The cellar area was then partially backfilled and a thin sand floor laid (16.5) containing a residual Roman coin of Constantius II (AD 355–65: <24>) and pottery dated 1140–50. Overlying this were the remains of several further floors of crushed mortar (16.6) containing oyster shells and small fragments of the bones of large domesticates, as well as the remains of rats, mice or voles, fish and eggshell. The deposits also contained charcoal and charred grains including bread wheat and barley, and elder, which together with the presence of the rodent bones indicate food storage or preparation. Rushes may have been used for flooring. The mortar surfaces were followed by scorched brickearth and two successive rammed chalk floors (16.7–8), which contained presumably residual pottery of 1050–1100 and roof tile dating from after the 1130s (fabric 2273). Charcoal and ash accumulated in the east suggesting the presence of a hearth beyond the limit of excavation.

Fig 55 Trench TP14. View of a chalk floor of the early medieval sunken-floored Building 9 from the south, with the cellar cut visible in the foreground. To the left, the area is cut by the arched foundation of the west wall of Building 15 (0.5m scale)

The area was cut by a line of post pits and a stakehole (16.9) supporting a partition at 90° to the original cellar wall. The southernmost post was set on a timber pad against the cellar side and may also have retained a new lining for the cellar cut itself, and possibly supported the load of the building's superstructure. The final dirty gravel floor (16.10) seems to have been laid after the partition went out of use.

Although the small amount of pottery recovered indicated a construction date of 1050–1150, this is probably residual material considering the potential early 13th-century date of the underlying infill of Building 8. The pottery and tile from the earliest floors suggest a date towards the end of the range, after c 1140. The cellar was finally infilled with mixed dumping (16.11) containing pottery dated 1180–1200/20 which was clearly later than the occupation.

Building 10

In MH3, thin organic deposits and brickearth floors (17.1) c 0.5m below the cellar level of Building 7 suggest the presence of a further sunken area (B10; see Fig 53), although the actual cellar cut was outside the limit of the excavation. Like Building 7, it was apparently affected by subsidence into earlier underlying pits, and a layer of ragstone and tile rubble, probably from Building 3, was laid to compensate for the subsidence and form the base for a second brickearth floor (17.2). As the cellar passed out of use it was infilled with layers of Roman building material and other debris which extended west of the former Building 3, where they were cut by a single rubbish pit (17.3–4).

Building 11

In the south-east (EN20) a levelling deposit for a brickearth surface dated 1080–1100 was laid over the earlier pit sequence (18.1). This may represent the floor of an early medieval building (B11; see Fig 53) fronting a forerunner of Ducksfoot Lane, although interpretation was made difficult by the limited area uncovered and extensive truncation. The only sign of use was a charcoal deposit (18.2), which was sealed by organic refuse and dumps of soil (18.3) dated to 1050–1150 (see Fig 6). The site of the structure was cut through, probably in the 12th century, by the chalk foundations of Building 13.

Building 12

In the west (TP13) the former area of Buildings 6–7 was raised by deposits of sandy silt datable to 1140–50 to form a level surface for a new structure (B12: 19.1; see Fig 53 for general location). The fact that a single building now replaced two indicates a change in property layout at this time. A substantial hearth constructed of brickearth and rubble included medieval roof tile, some of it glazed.

A series of thin charcoal deposits and mortar patching around the hearth show that it was well used, possibly over a long period (19.2). A little to the south, continual subsidence into the earlier cellared Building 6 was countered by a series of mortar and brickearth surfaces, and a dump of mortar and chalk rubble (19.3–4). A final brickearth surface was covered by deposits containing burnt debris which may well represent the destruction of the building (19.5–6). This event probably occurred in the early 13th century, since pottery of 1140–1220 was recovered from the occupation levels of the structure, and roof tile dating from no earlier than the 1130s (fabric 2273) was found among the burnt debris. Some glazed tile in fabric 2587 was also present; this came into use a little later, continuing in use until the 15th century, and may have been intrusive.

4.3 Later medieval and post-medieval periods: *c* AD 1150/1200–1700

The following period saw the construction of a series of masonry buildings, replacing the older pattern of development (Fig 56). The original tenement boundaries – at least those on the western half of the site – appear to have been replaced to make way for a number of larger properties which were to form the basis of the local topography until the 19th and, in some cases, 20th centuries.

Building 13 and Open Area 5

The earliest of the new buildings (B13) was constructed in the south-east on the site of Building 11, probably during the 12th century, at a time when the latest of the succession of timber-framed structures further west on Suffolk Lane were still occupied (see Fig 56).

Truncation of the surrounding area by modern basements ensured that the contemporary ground level had been removed, and the building was represented solely by several stretches of north–south mortared chalk foundation located some distance to the east of Ducksfoot Lane (Fig 57). The northernmost of these, in TP8 and immediately to its south, rested on a series of decayed horizontal beech timbers (21.1). A further section was observed continuing to the southern limit of excavation (EN20: 21.2) and, in contrast, was supported on cleft piles, although still of beech. At 72–75 Cheapside (CID90), a similar beech piled chalk foundation was dated by dendrochronology to 1090–1 (Hill & Woodger 1999, 43–4). In this instance, an actual date in the early 12th century is more likely, particularly as similar walls have now been found nearby at Bull Wharf and Vintry (Ayre & Wroe-Brown in prep). In EN20, the lowest course of the superstructure survived, consisting of irregular ragstone blocks which were slightly larger than the chalk used in the foundation (see Fig 6).

To the west of and respecting the foundation in EN20 was a large rubbish pit dated c 1140–50, cut in the south-west by a smaller cesspit after the first had gone out of use, between 1175–1230 (21.3–4). Glazed tile in fabric 2587 was recovered, although this type remained in use as late as the 15th century.

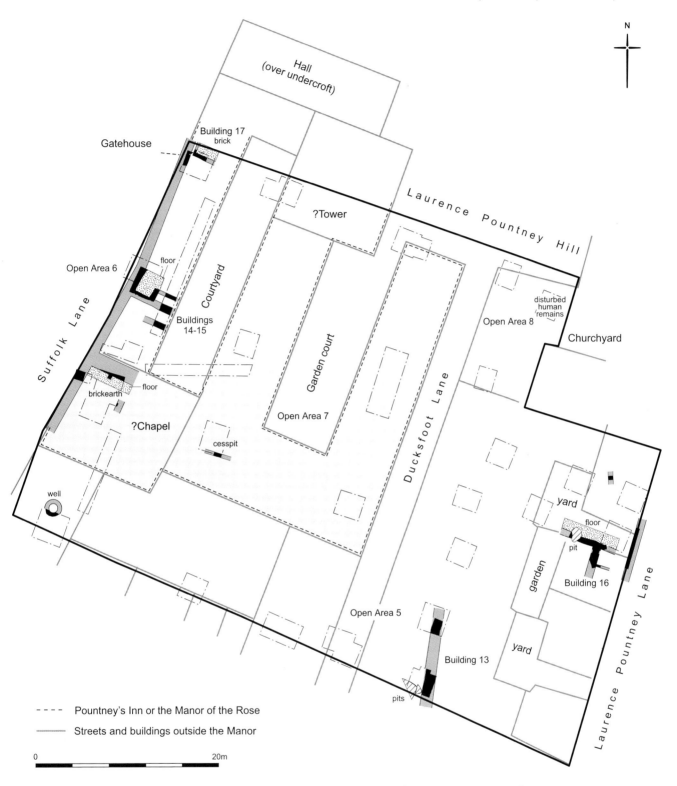

N

Fig 56 Plan of principal 13th- to 17th-century archaeological features: Buildings 13–17, with outlines of contemporary buildings known from cartographic evidence overlaid

A second much later pit filled with organic rubbish, wood ash and rubble (28.1) contained pottery which as a whole was probably datable to 1450–1500, including a funnel-necked Siegburg beaker and glazed peg tiles in fabric 2587. Post-medieval glass was also present.

The presence of these pits suggests that Building 13 fronted Laurence Pountney Lane, and that the area to the rear remained open until at least the latter half of the 15th century (OA5). This could imply that Ducksfoot Lane was not yet in place, or perhaps simply not developed until later.

Fig 57 Trench TP8.View of the north–south 12th-century chalk foundation of Building 13 under excavation from the north-east. The wall rested on foundations of beech piling

Building 14

Most of the evidence for Building 14 and its replacement, Building 15 (Pountney's Inn, later known as the Manor of the Rose), came from the western range fronting Suffolk Lane (see Fig 56). In the north-west (TP1), most of the area was covered by mixed make-ups (22.3) in preparation for the construction of Building 14 (Fig 58). Although the deposits contained residual pottery of 1080–1150, including a long-spouted Early Medieval Sandy ware (EMS) pitcher, and roof tile of a type dating from the 1130s at the earliest (fabric 2273), Building 14 was a substantially later structure with chalk foundations, including a pier 'mortared' with brickearth (24.1). Only the lower 0.36m of the base survived, but enough remained to suggest that it had probably carried an arched foundation supporting the west wall of Building 14, facing on to Suffolk Lane.

To the south were several further fragments of north–south mortared chalk foundation which were presumably part of a continuation of the Suffolk Lane frontage, although as none of these had related stratigraphy, it is unclear whether they were part of the original structure or the later Building 15 which was rebuilt on the same lines. These elements were recorded in MH3 (20.1), in a pipe trench heading to the west (20.2) and in an extension of TP13 beyond the existing street frontage (24.5).

Within the western range (TP14; AE1) a Roman wall belonging to Building 3 was reused as the foundation of an east–west mortared chalk wall (23.2, 23.8; see Fig 38), which formed a partition within the western range of Building 14. The wall was abutted by a 1.2m long chalk foundation (23.6) which returned eastwards across AE1, perhaps enclosing an installation such as a staircase. A third east–west wall observed in AE1 a little to the south of the main partition may have been later (perhaps part of B15), but could have supported the south

Fig 58 Trench TP1. View of the arched foundation for the west wall of Building 15 cutting the earlier pier of Building 14, the original version of Pountney's Inn, from the south-east. To the right of the arched masonry is the brickwork for a cellar wall, part of Building 17, the Merchant Taylors' School. Early medieval pits cutting later Roman deposits are visible in the foreground (0.5m scale)

side of a cross-passage. All three must have joined the east wall of the western range of the building, which probably passed immediately to the east of AE1 (see Fig 56).

Internal features to the north of the cross-wall in TP14 (not illustrated) are exclusively related to the construction process, the contemporary floor surfaces having been removed by modern truncation. These include a stone-packed post pit which may have held the base of a scaffold post, a rubbish pit to the north-east (23.3) which could have been cut by the builders for use during the early stages of construction, and later silt and mortar make-ups cut by a shallow slot presumably representing a further temporary installation (23.4–5).

Further south in TP13 an east–west mortared chalk foundation cut a trampled construction surface dated 1230–1300 (23.1), and incorporating roof tile which may have been left over from the demolition of the underlying Building 12, where the same type was present. The foundation can be identified as supporting the north wall of what was – in the 17th century at least – the chapel of Building 14. The base of the masonry was deeper in the west, which may suggest that the foundation had been arched, resting on piers at either end. An iron arrowhead <28> was found among the stonework.

Although make-ups of dark clayey soil were dumped internally, no floor levels of this structure survived. This was,

however, the only datable section of wall in Building 14, with pottery from the construction trench and associated make-ups placing its inception some time after 1250–70.

Building 15: Pountney's Inn and the Manor of the Rose

The subsequent structural history of Building 14 in the century following its construction is unclear, but – either in the 14th century, when it was rebuilt by Sir John de Pulteney, or in the 15th century when it passed to the de la Poles, dukes of Suffolk – it was substantially rebuilt (B15).

The west wall of the building was recorded in several places. In the north-west, a chalk arch (TP1: 25.1) cut through the existing pier of Building 14, curving down towards the presumed location of the pier at the northern limit of excavation (see Fig 58).

The new streetfront wall continued southwards (TP14) to cut the west end of the existing cross-wall of Building 14 (24.4) and enough survived of this section of foundation to determine the method of construction (Fig 59). The base of the construction trench for the arch consisted of a relatively level section separating the deeper cuts for the chalk piers. The higher intervening section was then built up with compacted soil to create a

Fig 59 Trench TP14. Detail of the arched foundation for the west wall of Building 15, from the east (1.0m scale)

Fig 60 Trench TP13. View of brickearth and mortar construction spreads contemporary with the buttress (left) attached to the earlier chapel wall of Building 15, from the west (0.5m scale)

curved former for the 2.94m long arched foundation of uncoursed chalk rubble bonded with pale grey ashy sandy mortar. Angled chalk and occasional ragstone blocks formed the facing of the arch itself. The points of the arches were generally a little below the contemporary floor, although alterations and later truncation of the foundations and surfaces themselves make these levels difficult to assess at Suffolk House. At the priory of St Mary Spital, the depth of make-up material above the tops of the arches was c 0.3m (Thomas et al 1997, 98). The adoption of arched foundations appears to have been an early 13th-century innovation, dating from perhaps the 1220s, and remaining in use until the mid 15th century (Schofield 1991, 5). Typologically they are therefore only broadly datable.

Further south in TP13, the existing chapel wall was demolished, and replaced with an arched chalk foundation on an almost identical alignment to its predecessor. Rough ragstone voussoirs formed the underside of the arch (24.2; Fig 60). A north–south foundation located immediately behind the eastern limit of excavation of TP13 was of quite different construction to both the arched foundation and its predecessor in Building 14, being constructed of ragstone set in off-white chalky mortar. It was probably a later addition, dividing the area into separate rooms. Horwood's map of 1813 shows a property boundary on this alignment, which perhaps made use of the earlier foundation, although this may be coincidental as no such division appears on the earlier 1676 survey by Ogilby and Morgan (see Fig 50).

A series of thin make-ups and surfaces, a small isolated stakehole and a 2.15m x 0.33m north–south slot formed internal features south of the wall. The slot was sealed by a series of general make-ups including a thick layer of sandy mortar, and its purpose is uncertain, unless it may have held the base board of scaffolding used in construction. The fact that all of these features were at a relatively low level within the building confirms that the area was used as a cellar or undercroft, quite probably excavated as part of the alterations, perhaps after this part of the building was converted to a chapel. If this were the case, it explains the absence of stratigraphic evidence for the construction of the first phase of the building. After the additional north–south wall had been completed, a substantial slab of brickearth, mortar and ragstone rubble (24.3) was laid to form the undercroft floor and combat subsidence in the south in the vicinity of the former Building 6 (see Fig 60). As well as residual pottery dated 1180–1270, the slab also contained more contemporary glazed roof tile of 14th- to 15th-century date in fabric 2587. Traces of occupation, particularly in the subsided area where it was protected from later truncation, included the edge of a temporary hearth of blackened sand at the southern limit of the trench. An isolated stake cut the truncated brickearth slab in the east (25.2).

Subsequently, a small square buttress of roughly coursed mortared ragstone and chalk was built against the north wall of the undercroft (25.3), with roof tiles, some of them in fabric 2587, formed a bonding course at the surviving top. The floor was resurfaced as the same time using the same mortar. The buttress quite possibly either supported the springer of a vaulted roof or a joist for the floor above, either of which would

suggest a major rebuild of the chapel. In the south of TP13 a final series of make-ups were deposited in an attempt to level the floor surface, which had continued to subside into the underlying cellared area of Building 6. A thin band of ash and charcoal in section was almost certainly the north edge of a second hearth (25.4). These final dumps were dated 1270–1350 and contained roof tiles of the same fabric as those used in the buttress, indicating a similar 14th- to 15th-century date.

A substantial oval hearth of brickearth on a sand base, again in the south of the trench, was sealed by laminated ash and silt representing the use of the feature (25.5). A similar hearth was set in the angle between the new buttress and main wall. The two were apparently closely contemporary, although it seems possible that one represents the old type of central hearth, and the second a fireplace set against the wall; the buttress may in fact have attained a secondary function as the jamb of a chimney breast.

The pottery recovered from several features in the area suggests that the latest activity could have occurred at any time between c 1270–1500. Several peg tiles in fabric 2276 were not manufactured until the late 15th century, however, and this is perhaps the most likely period for the final modifications. There were few artefacts apart from a fragment of horseshoe <375>. Animal bones recovered from the area of the hearths in the southern part of the trench indicate that the undercroft may have been used as a kitchen; these included small fragments of the main domesticates, chicken, wildfowl, rabbit, fish and shellfish, mainly oyster but also mussel. The presence of food had attracted mice and rats. The plant remains from among the charcoal in the hearth area included a few seeds of charred grass – possibly the remains of tinder – with fig, elder and Rubus species, sufficient also perhaps to indicate food preparation.

Both hearths and the rest of the room area were sealed by general make-ups, followed by a brickearth slab (25.6–7).

East of Building 15 was a late medieval chalk-lined cesspit (EN18: 26.4) which was originally considered to occupy part of Open Area 7, the garden court of the Manor of the Rose, but more probably lay within the range of buildings forming the west side of the court (see Fig 56). The cesspit was at least 2.2m deep, with a sloping well-dressed inner face covered by a very thin skim of hard brown mineralised cess. In the base of the pit was a deposit of charcoal (26.5), which may have been used for cleansing the interior of the cesspit, although it could have been burnt debris from the Great Fire of 1666. The bulk of the final fill of the cesspit consisted of brick, tile and mortar (26.6) probably of the same date. Among the debris was a curved ridge tile in fabric 2587, which may have been fitted originally with a decorative finial; the tile presumably came from a demolished medieval structure nearby, quite probably from Building 15 itself.

In the south-west corner of the site, almost certainly within a structure to the south of Building 15 (see Fig 56), was a chalk-lined well with an internal diameter of c 0.92m resting on a two-piece curved timber baseplate (EN11: 26.1; Fig 61). The inner face of the large chalk blocks forming the lining had apparently been dressed in situ leaving a layer of chippings near

W   E

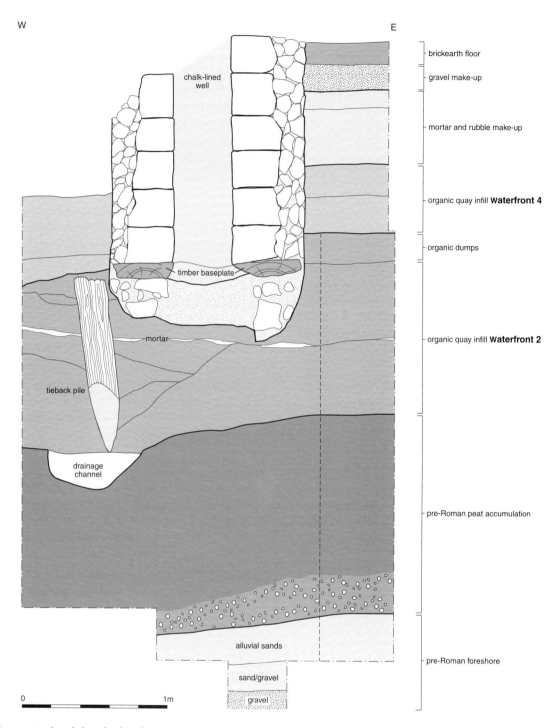

Fig 61 *South-facing section through the archaeological sequence in the south-western corner of the site (Trench EN11)*

the base of the cut, unless these were the remains of later damage. The original level of the surface from which the well was excavated cannot be estimated easily, although it was quite possibly located within a cellar rather than a ground-floor room. A 15th- to 16th-century construction date is likely on the evidence of a peg tile with diamond-shaped nail holes of the period.

The initial fill of coarse silt (26.2) was dated c 1480–1550, and contained an oblate wooden disc <389> which has been interpreted as the base or top of a bentwood box (see Fig 72), a scale tang knife <362> and a fragment of cloth <361>. Seeds

of aquatic and semi-aquatic species were present, mostly from waste or disturbed ground, as well as some fruit seeds, hops and hazelnut shells, although the assemblage was dominated by cereal bran. The animal bones in the fill were fragmentary, with evidence of cattle and sheep butchery. Chicken, dog and rat or mouse were all represented, as well as a variety of shellfish. Most of the bones were burned, and it is possible that the well was at least partly backfilled after the Great Fire of 1666. The primary fill was covered by brick and roof tile (26.3); the presence of slate indicates a probable 19th-century date for this final infill.

Building 16

Near Laurence Pountney Lane in the east were a number of features recorded during the watching brief phase of the excavation programme. These are largely undated, but their earliest phase was probably contemporary with Building 14 (see Fig 56).

A chalk and ragstone foundation at least 12m long beneath the modern site boundary formed the frontage of a substantial structure, Building 16 (29.1, 29.8). The lower courses contained Roman building materials disturbed from underlying structures, which is generally indicative of a 12th- or 13th-century date. The north end may have been arched, although it was apparently truncated below the level of the springing; if so, a 13th-century construction date is the most likely. At the south end of the foundation, further chalk masonry extended eastwards beneath the modern pavement, perhaps part of a buttress supporting the main frontage, or a cesspit extending under the lane. It was almost certainly added at a later date, an interpretation supported by differences in construction, including an absence of reused material. The presence of an integral vertical slot filled with sand containing pottery dated 1230–1400 marked the position of a timber upright, perhaps supporting the main superstructure, which could well have been timber-framed in this period (29.2). By the time of Ogilby and Morgan's survey of 1676, and probably considerably earlier, Building 16 was apparently bisected by an alley giving access to a yard to the rear. The short length of foundation beneath the alley may have become redundant unless it remained in use as the retaining wall of a cellar.

Behind the frontage, an east–west foundation, largely of chalk, ragstone, flint and tile (29.3), formed what was probably an internal wall of the original building, although it was in the same position as the south side of the yard referred to above. The masonry had been cut through by a later pit of uncertain date (29.7), but was presumably rebuilt at a higher level, as the yard and the later post-medieval successors of Building 16 survived until the construction of Norfolk House in the late 19th century. An area of pebbly mortar immediately to the north of the wall seems to have been a construction horizon, or possibly a cellar floor. A substantial ragstone and chalk internal wall abutted the south side of the yard frontage (29.5). The northern part of the wall was refaced in brick at some point, probably at the same time as part of a general late remodelling. A later east–west brick foundation adjoined the east face of this, almost certainly continuing eastwards to join the street frontage to form an enclosed cellar (29.6). The cellared area seems to have been given an initial surface of beaten brickearth, although this was often used as the make-up for brick floors in similar situations. Further north near the south side of Rectory House was a north–south chalk foundation (29.4), presumably within a building to the north of the yard, although no other part of this structure was found.

Building 17: the Merchant Taylors' School

Considerably later than most of the activity outlined above, Building 15 was replaced in or shortly after 1671 by purpose-built premises for the Merchant Taylors' School, Building 17. In the north-west of the site (TP1; see Fig 58), an east–west partition wall of unfrogged red brick with a chalk rubble core was cut into the west wall of Building 15 (30.1). The form of construction and materials suggest that the wall could well have been part of the original 17th-century structure. On the north side was a possible cellar floor of brick fragments covered with a deposit of cess and rubble, containing pottery dated 1640–1800 (30.2). Other later features representing parts of the later 18th- and 19th-century development of the site were observed, but are not included here in detail. These include a massive east–west wall in TP3/EN3 forming the north wall of the Merchant Taylors' School, and a second in TP4 with a typical coal cellar of the later period to the north under Laurence Pountney Hill entered through an arched doorway leading from a sunken 'area'. In TP9/EN9 was a substantial north–south wall with brick foundations containing horizontal timbers – a late 18th-century technique – which formed the east wall of a building facing on to Ducksfoot Lane to the south of the Merchant Taylors' School. Although not illustrated in this report, these three walls are in locations indicated by property boundaries shown on Fig 56.

Open Area 6, Suffolk Lane

A thick deposit of sandy silt observed 1.2m west of TP14 suggests the presence of an external area (OA6: 23.7). Although this was the site of *Wolsyeslane* or *Basyngeslane*, the forerunners of Suffolk Lane, at least as early as 1267–8, no metalling was observed and the date of the material is unknown, although it was probably late medieval or post-medieval.

Open Area 8

In the north-east (EN4: 27.1), close to the former junction of Laurence Pountney Hill and Ducksfoot Lane, dumped soil was used to fill a slumped area (OA8) overlying an early medieval cesspit (see Figs 53, 56). This deposit contained a substantial quantity of human skeletal remains, including at least two apparently articulated individuals, but the presence of other bones including c 100 unidentified midshaft fragments potentially increases the number represented substantially. These remains can only have originated in the neighbouring churchyard of St Laurence Pountney (Conheeney in Ainsley *et al* 1996), and although not reliably dated, pottery of 1140–1220 within the general fill may place their origin near the beginning of the documented history of the church. By the post-medieval period, the area appears to have been occupied by buildings, and one possibility is that the burials were disturbed when the boundary wall of the graveyard was removed for alterations to those buildings, although when this occurred is uncertain. Several bones had been splashed with concrete, perhaps during the construction of the 1969 building, although the original disturbance almost certainly occurred substantially earlier than that.

4.4 Period discussion

The 11th–12th centuries

General layout

Although the pottery recovered from the pits recorded in most areas and the first-known buildings implies that there was actually little difference in date between them, the pits were stratigraphically earlier in many instances. This suggests that the first phase of buildings either followed a different layout, or, perhaps more likely, were entirely ground-laid structures which have left no trace, whereas those which were recorded were without exception sunken-floored. The ceramic evidence supports a date between the late 10th and mid 11th centuries for the first activity, mainly on the basis of the presence of several early pottery fabrics, including a large proportion (20%) of Late Saxon Shelly ware (LSS), which was not produced after *c* 1050. Although most of this pottery came from later pits, and was therefore residual, it does suggest that there was intensive occupation in the area during the period 970–1050. This is not surprising given the proximity of the site to Queenhithe, with its evidence for late 9th- and 10th-century occupation (Ayre & Wroe-Brown in prep).

The few pits recorded did not, unfortunately, constitute a large enough sample to determine evidence for an early 11th-century property layout. As was suggested at the beginning of the chapter, however, it is likely from the evidence of other sites at this period that the pits formed groups or strips roughly marking out separate areas corresponding to burgage plots (*eg* Regis House (Brigham & Watson in prep) and the Cheapside area (Schofield *et al* 1990)). In the case of Suffolk House, these would probably have been aligned, for the most part, east–west, respecting the Suffolk Lane and Laurence Pountney Hill frontages assuming those streets to have been parts of the primary street grid. Thames Street, which was laid out in this period (Vince 1990, 40–1), lay too far to the south to have influenced developments at the south end of the site. To the north, the churchyard of St Laurence Pountney was probably not laid out until the mid 12th century or a little earlier (*Calendar of Charter Rolls*, iv 333), although it is not known what existed in the area previously. The presence of pits and a building (B11) in TP8 and EN20 do not necessarily support the early existence of Ducksfoot Lane, since burgage plots were often of considerable length, and ancillary buildings or dwellings could be sited well back from street frontages, in this case Laurence Pountney Lane.

The buildings

The earliest buildings in the area (Buildings 6–12; see Fig 53) were largely sunken-floored or cellared, a type that has been recorded elsewhere in the City. Until the late 1980s, the majority of structures recorded were located in two areas: east of London Bridge around Pudding Lane, and around Cheapside (Horsman *et al* 1988). Since then, buildings with surviving timbers and

wattlework have been revealed elsewhere, notably at Guildhall, 1 Poultry and Bull Wharf. The fragmentary remains of several sunken-floored buildings were also recorded at Regis House.

At Suffolk House and elsewhere the walls would have been timber-framed rather than constructed of masonry, although in most cases there was no evidence for either. It does appear, however, that some of the buildings, including Buildings 9 and 12, were roofed with tiles in fabric 2273 dated no earlier than the 1130s. Building 8 may also have been roofed with the same tiles, but it is more likely that they were imported with the backfill of the cellar at the time Building 9 was erected to replace it, along with 12th-century pottery and an assemblage of residual 11th-century material. The rest of the buildings were probably roofed with thatch or oak shingles which have not left any trace, but would be more in keeping with the insubstantial construction. Beyond the cellar cuts themselves there were few instances of surviving structural elements apart from a few fragments of burnt timber lining in Building 7 and the posts of a partition dividing the cellar of Building 9. In some instances, such as the first phase of Building 7, the sunken areas may have occupied only part of the building with the main support posts set outside the cellar perimeter.

In general, both surface-laid buildings, which generally occupied the street frontage of plots, and sunken-floored structures were between *c* 3–5m wide, and at least 10m in length. Sunken-floored buildings seem mainly to have been confined to the rear of properties, and were probably used for ancillary purposes, although some were almost certainly true cellars or storage areas beneath habitations, and are more likely to have been found along the street frontages. At Suffolk House, the presumption that Suffolk Lane and Laurence Pountney Lane were in existence from an early period would suggest that Buildings 6–10 were cellared domestic buildings of the second type as opposed to ancillary structures. Building 11 on the other hand could have been an ancillary building set back from Laurence Pountney Lane, since the area to the west remained partly open even after the construction of Building 13.

An important factor that appears to have determined their location was the existence of Roman walls belonging to Building 3. The west wall of the building may, for example, have acted as the streetfront element of the cellars of Buildings 8–10, as well as determining the line of Suffolk Lane. The cellared areas of Buildings 6 and 7 (TP13) were separated by a Roman wall, which although partly robbed, seems to have formed a boundary between the two structures. At this point, the west wall of Building 3 had also been robbed to a lower level, and Suffolk Lane deviates to the south-west, probably because it was not present to influence a more direct line by the time the street was laid out. This is probably reflected in the extension of the cellared portion of Building 7 to the west.

In summary, the evidence suggests the construction of a series of sunken-floored or cellared buildings from the second half of the 11th century which, with the exception of Building 11, occupied the Suffolk Lane frontage, representing intensive use of that thoroughfare. The absence of similar structures along Laurence Pountney Lane can be ascribed to the lack of comparable detailed excavation and recording work in the area rather than an indication that it was unoccupied. The buildings began to be replaced in the early 13th century by more extensive masonry structures, although there was an overlap, particularly with the construction of Building 13 in the 12th century.

The 13th–17th centuries

General layout

The replacement of the early pattern of properties in the west with a single messuage some time before the 14th century meant that there was no continuity between the earlier and later medieval periods. The main courtyard of Pountney's Inn was probably laid out over the backs of existing properties, and the garden court may similarly have been laid over the yards of buildings fronting Ducksfoot Lane, which could have come into existence about this time. To the east, Building 16 may have formed part of a row of houses or shops in single ownership, which also abolished a number of earlier burgage boundaries, although a similar pattern would eventually re-emerge as the property was subdivided.

The buildings

The length of the frontage of Building 16, assuming it was all one build, would suggest that a row of houses and probably shops was built for subletting by a single owner. This was a common practice, although by the time of the 1676 survey, the area had been divided into separate properties, and probably had been for some time. This again was a common fate, as larger properties became divided by bequests, and by normal transactions or exchanges of land. Building 13 appears to have been the earliest of the masonry structures on the site, with an open area to the rear. It is possible that it was originally, or became, part of an extended property with Building 16, but if so that arrangement had disappeared by the time of the earliest reliable cartographic evidence (see Fig 50); the history of these properties could probably be elucidated by further documentary research.

The most important medieval structures on the site are clearly Pountney's Inn and its successor, the Manor of the Rose (Buildings 14–15), which probably had their origins in a late 13th- or early 14th-century building which already existed before Pulteney became the owner, and received his licence to crenellate in 1341. This can be identified in the elements of Building 14, which was largely demolished to make way for its successor, excepting the undercroft beneath the hall, which was retained, and survived until 1894.

The courtyard house was a pattern adopted for a number of important buildings in the medieval period, including company livery halls, such as Goldsmiths' Hall, and private houses, many of which became inns. This was, of course, the pattern for the Manor of the Rose, and perhaps for its predecessor, although there is much less evidence for the appearance and layout of the original building. The excavated evidence for both phases of the house consists largely of walls and some internal features belonging to the west wing along the Suffolk Lane frontage,

including, significantly, the north wall of the chapel and a sequence of deposits and features within its presumed undercroft. The outline and location of this wing can now be determined with some confidence from a combination of the archaeological, documentary and early cartographic sources (see Fig 56), but less is known of the main house which was set back on the northern and eastern side of the yard. The post-Roman deposits in TP2 near the north end of the same court consisted entirely of recent 'garden soil' in the area of the tower, suggesting considerable later disturbance, although a deep irregular intrusive feature at the eastern side of the trench could have been cut in the 19th century to remove the east wall of the tower at the time the original Suffolk House was built.

Nothing of the domestic ranges around the garden court survived in the recorded areas, with the exception of a cesspit found under the modern double basement (EN18), but again, the locations of the various elements can broadly be determined, as they were 'fossilised' in the post-Fire reconstruction, and survived as part of the street and property layout which prevailed until the late 19th century (see Figs 49–52). These confirm that the back of the house around the garden court was accessible from Laurence Pountney Hill near the church, since Ogilby and Morgan's survey of 1676 shows an entrance existed at the north end of Laurence Pountney Place in the immediate post-Great Fire period, and it was still there in 1873.

Architecturally, although the 16th- and 17th-century panoramas give an idea of the appearance of the Manor of the Rose, with its tower and crenellated hall, there was little archaeological evidence to support this beyond the presence of glazed roof tile and a finial. The structure was probably faced with Kentish rag or Reigate stone, with finer limestone or greensand dressings for the doors, windows and quoins, none of which have survived.

Although well represented cartographically, the post-Great Fire rebuild of the manor, the Merchant Taylors' School, was only represented by an east–west wall and part of a cellar floor in TP1, although this is explicable, as the considerable continuity of layout and reuse of foundations reduced the need to construct new subfloor structures. As already mentioned, the replacement of the manor with a second large property seems to have effectively fossilised the internal boundaries of the site, where piecemeal redevelopment would have altered the pattern more rapidly. There is virtually no difference between Ogilby and Morgan's survey of 1676 or Horwood's of 1813. Drawings of the building before its demolition show the Suffolk Lane frontage of the school to have been a typical post-Fire building, in brick, with stone window dressings.

In summary, although relatively little remained of the buildings of the medieval and post-medieval periods, this was sufficient for comparison with the cartographic record. The correlation between the two confirmed the basic assumption that the property layout remained fairly static to the west of Ducksfoot Lane until the relatively recent demolition of the 19th-century Suffolk House and Norfolk House further east. This action, and the extinguishment of the lane, allowed more rapid change, so that the 1969 building and its successor, Governor's House, paid much less attention to the original layout.

5

Conclusions

5.1 Introduction

As a result of previous work in the area, particularly that of Peter Marsden, the significance of the Suffolk House site was evident from the outset of the project. As part of a Scheduled Ancient Monument, it was clear that preservation in situ of the remaining resource as it survived the 1969 redevelopment was the only acceptable option for the management of the site. Consequently, a mitigation strategy was designed as the result of negotiations between English Heritage, the Corporation of London and the developer's archaeological consultant, Richard Hughes at Arup. The proposed development was designed from an early stage to have the minimum impact on the archaeological remains which evaluation work demonstrated still survived to a remarkable degree. Discussion with the Corporation of London and English Heritage established that the programme of archaeological mitigation would be applicable not only to the Scheduled Ancient Monument but also to the remainder of the site, as its history was clearly intimately linked to that of the scheduled area.

As already described (see 1.1 above), the strategy involved the reuse of 16 of the 1969 pile locations, the insertion of five piles in areas thought to have little archaeological survival and a further four piles in areas previously undisturbed. The low level of loss to the archaeological resource which would result from the construction process would be offset by detailed excavation, recording and analysis. The need to maximise the information recovered from the excavated areas was clear. In order to ensure a coherent approach to the archaeology of a small and widely spaced sample the work was managed within a clearly defined research framework. During the 1994 evaluation several multi-period, multi-disciplinary research aims were formulated, which were updated as a result of the more extensive 1996–7 work (Brigham et al 1998).

As a result of the mitigation strategy the archaeological resource on the site remains largely undisturbed, and the design and implementation of the strategy itself can thus be seen as considerable achievements. Furthermore the archaeological site investigation has built on the work of Peter Marsden to provide a wealth of new material about the pre-urban topography and environment, the Roman waterfronts, reclamation, and riverside and associated activities, and the development of buildings from the Roman to the post-medieval periods. With hindsight, there are, however, several lessons that can be learned from the Suffolk House mitigation strategy. Its successes and failures are now considered together with the implications it has for the future management of the monument.

The mitigation strategy

The mitigation strategy had two principal elements. First, the foundations of Governor's House were designed by the project engineers to have minimum impact on the archaeological remains, and second, a research design was formulated by the Museum of London Archaeology Service to provide a frame of reference for archaeological excavation as work progressed.

Changes within the construction industry mean that a more flexible response to foundation design is now possible. Between the 1950s and 1970s large buildings – including Suffolk House – were commonly erected on foundations consisting of several hundred small diameter piles in densely packed clusters, linked by pile caps which were constructed below basement-floor level. Without statutory protection or planning restraints, this led to the wholesale destruction of archaeological deposits, often without record. There has been a trend on more recent projects to use relatively few piles of much larger diameter, of which Governor's House is an example. This serves to limit disturbance to a small number of pile locations which can be evaluated individually, and if found suitable, excavated. Flexibility of design also allows piles to be moved to a limited extent, or replaced on an individual basis by carefully sited smaller piles linked by ground beams to reduce impact on particularly sensitive areas. Existing piles can also be drilled out and replaced directly by new ones of larger diameter. This is an expensive option, but one which will be increasingly returned to by future generations as site footprints become crowded with piles of different eras of development, often occupying key locations.

A central element of the Suffolk House project was to attempt to locate new piles on Victorian foundations identified initially by cartographic analysis undertaken by the archaeological consultant, and then by evaluation. This was intended as an alternative to drilling through the softer but significant archaeological deposits expected to survive to either side. This proved to be a workable strategy in some instances, where earlier foundations could be located accurately enough and could be shown to continue to such a depth that there were no significant deposits or structures below. The main problem with a historic townscape that has developed organically over many centuries is that property boundaries can remain relatively static. Post-medieval walls were often simply constructed on earlier foundations or walls, and these may themselves be of sufficient importance to require in situ preservation. (In this instance, for example, the west wall foundations of the Manor of the Rose were reused by the Merchant Taylors' School, and these were largely left in situ. By contrast the west wall of the medieval Leadenhall, which remained intact to eaves level, was encountered during site clearance and archaeological excavation prior to the construction of the Leadenhall Court development in 1986 (Samuel in Milne 1992, 114–25). Had the current climate leaning towards preservation been in place at the time, this wall would almost undoubtedly have survived and been incorporated in the modern development; it was unfortunately demolished.) In a few cases, archaeological deposits survived beneath. In addition to the pile locations, consideration was given to the monitoring of temporary works, excavations for service runs and ground beams, which were largely designed to avoid sensitive areas and levels, and the reduction of the basement level in the western area.

The modus operandi for the excavation of the pile holes has already been discussed in some detail (see 1.1 above). It involved the clearance of the basement-floor slab or pavement over an area up to 3.0m x 3.0m to allow the machine or hand removal of modern deposits and features to the surface of archaeological remains. Once encountered, these were cleaned and a decision reached as to their significance and extent. In some instances, for example in the case of TP1 and TP4, the remains were not considered of sufficient significance to preserve in situ, and they were excavated. In other cases, such as TP2 and TP3, enough of the area was cleared to allow the pile to be inserted, although the upcast from the piling process was still monitored. In a few instances, notably EN11 and EN20, the archaeological remains were of very considerable importance, including a timber quay and a Roman wall, but there was little alternative to the placement of the piles, and these were consequently hand dug in their entirety. Where excavation was not proceeded with, as in the case of TP13 and TP14, hand-augering was undertaken to try and ascertain the depth and nature of the underlying deposits, and alternative pile locations identified.

The research design demanded that a number of key issues were addressed as the excavation and the watching brief were carried out. These can be summarised as follows:
• to model the natural topography;
• to model early development of the waterfront;
• to clarify the plan, and date the construction and disuse of the structures identified by Marsden, and to determine their relationship to the 'Governor's Palace' site;
• to determine the post-Roman history of the site.

The degree to which it proved possible to pursue these objectives was obviously considerably constrained by site logistics. Where the preservation of the archaeological resource in situ is a key aspect of a development, there are few alternatives to the use of small trenches in areas of proposed deep foundations and services. Some of the main logistical problems with this type of operation have already been outlined. Working in very small areas means that only a very localised perception of the development of a site can be achieved unless common strata or structures are identified which link the separate areas of intervention. In effect, most of the individual areas of investigation were smaller than 3.0m sq, and it has been estimated that only about 4% of the area of the site was examined in 1994–7, with perhaps two-thirds of this actually excavated. This is a very small sample with which to interpret a complex, deeply stratified urban excavation. Although this was understood and accepted from the outset as an inevitable aspect of projects where preservation is the key issue, it is nevertheless worth listing a few of the problems which arose.

The relationship between widely separated medieval and post-medieval structures – such as those forming part of the Manor of the Rose – may be identifiable from documentary or cartographic sources, but such evidence is obviously not available for the Roman period. Matters were clearly made easier by Peter Marsden's previous work in 1969, which enabled otherwise isolated areas to be linked together, but cross-correlation between trenches is largely limited to the west wing of the main Roman townhouse near the Suffolk Lane frontage, where the density of interventions was greater. Even there, problems with the alignment of walls have arisen. This is partly because of the hazards of accurately locating short lengths of masonry or other features at depth, and in confined situations. These circumstances form a barrier to even the best surveying equipment.

Apart from the problems of location and interpretation, such localised excavations often produce only very small finds assemblages that cannot be used confidently to establish a dated sequence. In several cases at Suffolk House, trenches were opened but proved to be unsuitable for use as pile locations and were not investigated further. While plans of surface features can be produced in such situations, neither the stratigraphic sequence can be understood nor datable artefacts collected. Augering can help to produce further information in such situations, but this is hampered where solid obstructions such as inclusions of building materials or metalled surfaces are present, and the exact nature and depth of underlying deposits often remain elusive. Ground Penetrating Radar surveys, such as one carried out on the site by the MoLAS's Clark Laboratory in 1996, can be used to try and define features between areas of intervention. This, however, requires optimum conditions that are rarely achievable in environments such as urban developments, and the results in the case of Suffolk House were inconclusive (Mackie & McCann 1997). Even assuming more accurate and reliable non-destructive techniques are developed further in the future, the problems of determining the stratigraphic sequence of events and producing hard dating evidence without excavation will remain.

The final drawbacks with this type of operation are procedural and financial. Operating in constricted spaces often at considerable depths is difficult, and can be dangerous. Everything that the archaeologist requires to work effectively must be lowered safely by hoist, and all spoil and artefacts must be retrieved by the same means. Photography is often difficult, and sometimes impossible because of inadequate working space, which limits the choice of angles and image area. The possibility of using overhead camera angles diminishes with depth, which can also lead to poor lighting conditions. The production of good images is therefore much more difficult to achieve than on open area excavations. Plans are of limited value, as they represent only a fraction of a given structure or deposit, and although large masonry buildings may be traced between trenches, structures such as clay-and-timber buildings are unlikely to be fairly represented. Under such circumstances, sections can become the crucial element of the site record, but access to the exposed stratigraphy can be affected by the type of shoring selected by the contractor and the need to maintain safe sides to the trench.

Despite all these difficulties, however, the growth in our understanding of the archaeology of the site and its surroundings as presented in the preceding chapters and summarised below have amply justified the mitigation strategy adopted. Of the areas singled out in the research design as particularly significant, the considerable additions to our knowledge include:

- the modelling of the underlying topography, and its effects on the subsequent development of the site, together with the identification and subsequent sampling of a prehistoric marsh;

- the discovery of several datable phases of Roman waterfront, notably Waterfront 2 with its implications for the 'palace' site, together with the small but important pottery and finds assemblage from subsequent waterfronts, which has been compared with those from other waterfront and non-waterfront sites;

- the increased understanding of the construction, layout, development and fate of the main townhouse, and to a lesser degree the buildings to the east, and the way these structures fit into the more general picture of development along the waterfront;

- a similar understanding of an important medieval and post-medieval townhouse, whose plan can now be reconstructed with some confidence, as well as some details of early medieval structures on Suffolk Lane.

In addition to these may be added a fair understanding of the quality, nature and extent of the surviving archaeological resource as a tool to aid the future management of the Scheduled Monument and its environs.

Lessons learned from this and similar field exercises suggest that working methods, and consequently data recovery, can be optimised by careful planning at an early stage. It is essential to ensure that where pile locations are under evaluation the trenches employed are large enough for safe and effective working, and also to allow a more extensive surface area to be examined once the archaeological level is reached. Where the archaeological resource is particularly sensitive, the use of larger trenches enables more flexibility in selecting the optimum position for the pile. A shoring system that enables cumulative sections to be recorded should also be specified, although this may be subject to overriding safety considerations as was the case in the deeper excavations at Suffolk House. The records of any previous investigations would naturally help to analyse the results of the exercise, but where these are absent, the new data produced can be treated as a valid sample for future use, or where, as was the case at Suffolk House, basement levels are reduced across large areas, or ground beams and service runs are planned as further stages of the same development. A similar approach to preservation was adopted, for example, at the Roman forum site, 168 Fenchurch Street in 1998–9. Here, although some open area excavation proved unavoidable to allow the insertion of deeper basements and goods lifts, damage to the archaeological resource elsewhere was limited by a combined programme of evaluation, selective removal and a flexible approach to the design of the foundations.

5.2 Summary of results and implications for future research

It was intended to produce as full as possible a picture of the underlying natural clay and pre-Roman gravel in order to reconstruct the topography of the area. The original 1994 evaluation had already shown how this affected the subsequent development of the site, although relatively little information was available from the eastern half of the site. A combination of pre-existing borehole data and observations made during the evaluation and piling operations has enabled the production of a contour plan of the underlying London Clay, which is retained in the site archive. In addition, further information has been gained about the levels of Thames Terrace gravels (chapter 2).

The evidence for a prehistoric marsh, which was also observed on the unpublished neighbouring Cannon Street Station excavation (Burch & Hill 1988), is of considerable interest, and has proved a very worthwhile addition to the understanding of the prehistoric river valley (chapter 2, and see 6.1 below). Its presence on the site was not previously suspected, and it did not therefore appear in the original research aims. The formation of the marsh has wider implications for sea level during the prehistoric period, suggesting that it rose considerably during the pre-Roman Iron Age; it was therefore particularly useful to extract a range of absolute dates from the peat. This confirms data collected from Southwark, which is the subject of a separate study (Sidell et al in prep). Another factor in this particular instance is that the presence of the marsh limited the development of the 'palace' site and Suffolk House until successive phases of reclamation had taken place. This was not properly appreciated previously, but does much to explain the various stages of 'palace' development noted by Marsden.

Although the line of a mid 1st-century or early Flavian timber waterfront (Waterfront 1) was not observed on the predicted line (see Fig 7), the presence of Waterfronts 2–4 was of great importance, particularly as they give termini post quem for the development of Buildings 3–5. Waterfronts 2 and 4 may be identified with timber structures noted beneath Thames Street in 1927 (RCHM 1928, 143), although the exact location of these is unknown. The structural carpentry of Waterfront 2 and reused timbers within Waterfront 3 have added detail to our understanding of Roman carpentry, adding, for example, a new joint to the known repertoire, and forming a prototype for the better-known later 1st-century quay at Pudding Lane and Peninsular House (Milne 1985). Most significantly, the date of Waterfront 2 suggests that the currently undated and unpublished quay at Cannon Street Station (Burch & Hill 1988) had also been built c AD 84, and that the two together formed a single development as extensive and impressive as those around the bridgehead. Their position directly in front of the 'Governor's Palace' also underlines the potential importance of that site and its cohesiveness as a single land division. Because it largely lies under Upper Thames Street, the Suffolk House/Cannon Street Station wharf can also be expected to survive relatively intact, and to be preserved for the foreseeable future.

In view of the importance of trade to the town, the imported pottery assemblages and artefacts associated with the quays are of national interest, particularly when set beside those from other waterfront sites. Their incidence in relation to their wider distribution in Roman London and Roman Britain provides a powerful insight into contemporary commercial organisation. In this instance (see 6.5 below), a higher proportion of imported wares, particularly 1st- and 2nd-century South Gaulish samian,

can be demonstrated at Suffolk House and Regis House than on sites in the town. These assemblages are of broader significance in view of the possible function of Roman London as a supply base or distribution point, particularly in this early period. The recent growth of pan-European ceramic studies has meant that port assemblages can become of increased international importance, especially when they can be set in their context by using powerful databases to compare sites and test assumptions (eg Symonds 1998).

In terms of the Roman buildings, the relationship between Building 1 and Building 3 could not be stratigraphically proven, and there remains an apparent hiatus between the construction date of Building 1 and that of its final floors. The relatively high-quality building materials found in those later surfaces and dumps do, however, suggest that the two structures were connected. The location of Building 1 on the upper terrace has therefore proved to be crucial to the understanding of the northern part of the main townhouse. By analogy, this was also of great significance in understanding the way the 'Governor's Palace' could have been extended southwards from an original core, regardless of the intervening terrace boundaries. The importance of Building 1 therefore belies the lack of details of its plan and development history. An apparently contemporary structure, Building 2, was identified to the east for the first time. Again, the relationship between this and the later building to the south (Building 4) is unclear. There is some evidence that Building 2 may have been the site of a goldworker's premises.

One of the main aims of the site investigation was to collect artefactual evidence to date the construction, use and disuse of the Roman buildings discovered in 1969 (Marsden 1975, 54–60). The 1969 watching brief produced no dating evidence with the exception of a 3rd-century coin from above the mortar floor of Room 59 (Marsden 1975, 63).

In this respect, the project was not universally successful. The construction sequences excavated within the area of Marsden's townhouse produced a limited amount of dating evidence apart from that in TP1, which was assigned to Building 1. Fortunately, the excavation of the waterfronts and associated dumps in EN11 and EN20 provided a terminus post quem for the date of construction of the townhouse, since the southern ranges could not have been built until after the construction of quays beneath modern Upper Thames Street. A drain dated AD 128 and pottery of AD 100–20 from this area seem to relate to a waterfront phase (Waterfront 4) predating the reclamation of the ground below the southern range of Building 3. Pottery obtained from the backfilled flue system in MH3 was sufficiently convincing to suggest a date between AD 200–400 for the disuse of Building 3, and final demolition in the 4th century (AD 300–400). This matches the date of the later dumps in Building 1 (AD 270–400).

The significance of Building 3 lies partly in its potential relationship to the 'Governor's Palace'. Although the 'palace' interpretation has been questioned since Marsden's original report (Perring 1991, 30–3; Milne 1985, 130; 1995, 91–3; 1996, 49–55), no convincing alternative interpretation of this massive high-quality complex has yet emerged. Evidence recorded in 1969 suggested that there were intervening mortar surfaces suggestive of a covered passageway (Marsden 1975, 73). The only trench situated in the crucial area in 1994–7 (EN11) failed to provide any significant information: however, the recording of a late Roman external metalled surface during a watching brief under Suffolk Lane did seem to suggest that the main monument and the townhouse were separated by a narrow road rather than a corridor. Whether or not the 'palace' complex was associated with either the provincial governor or the procurator, and regardless of any relationship between the two areas, Building 3 is still clearly a high-status residential structure, a rare and early example of an urban courtyard house.

Significant medieval sequences were recorded in seven of the hand-dug areas, accounting for quite a high proportion of the total number of contexts, although the remains were severely truncated by post-medieval or modern basements. Like the Roman remains, the medieval building on the western part of this site was part of a substantial structure, in this case Pountney's Inn or the Manor of the Rose; although little remained, some evidence of living conditions was recovered. The medieval and post-medieval layout of the area is better understood from the documentary and cartographic evidence available: some of the fragments of medieval walls on the eastern part of the site can be identified on maps and surveys of the 17th to 19th centuries, for example.

It should be clear from the contents of this volume that there remain outstanding questions about the site and the area in general, some of which may have a place in the development of a research agenda for London. Where further excavation or evaluation work is not possible, it may instead prove possible to pursue some of these questions through the analysis and reanalysis of existing archaeological sequences from excavations in and around the mouth of the Walbrook, including Cannon Street Station and Dowgate Hill House. (DGH86; a summary of the waterfront sequence appears in Brigham 1990a, 129–31.) From these sites, the extent of the prehistoric marsh could be determined, for example, to produce more detailed evidence of past environments and the tidal regime, and more precise dating evidence for the onset of marsh formation and its subsequent development.

For the Roman period, much remains to be revealed about the development of the early waterfront around the Walbrook and the environment of the early river, including the tidal regime and the river's salinity at different periods. Such evidence is elusive because the nature of the Thames and its management during the Roman occupation do not generally appear to have favoured the formation of organic deposits or the preservation of biological material along the foreshore, at least in the City of London.

More consideration to the nature and role of the 'palace' complex is still needed, and the Suffolk House evidence should be taken into account here. This could be undertaken as part of a survey of the development and status of buildings along the waterfront, but these aspects also need to be compared with similar structures in the town as a whole. There is some evidence to suggest that the waterfront was favoured by a concentration of masonry buildings in the 1st and early 2nd centuries, at a period when the use of stone was rare in London and largely confined to public works. It is possible that the waterfront area itself had some special status in the early period, but if so, further evidence is required to chart its later history, the evidence for which, admittedly, largely lies in an inaccessible location beneath modern Thames Street.

Little is yet known about the Anglo-Saxon occupation of the western waterfront area. Excavations at Bull Wharf suggest that Queenhithe was occupied before much of the rest of the town (Ayre & Wroe-Brown in prep), but large open areas of relatively untruncated ground would need to be examined to provide a worthwhile level of information about spatial patterning. The sunken-floored buildings along the Suffolk Lane frontage at Suffolk House contribute little to this, although it is a good example of how the development of 11th- and 12th-century properties was curtailed by more extensive later medieval structures, in this case Pountney's Inn. The inn itself was a fairly typical medieval townhouse, and although its archaeological remains have only been partially uncovered, it could form part of a study of such structures in London, which as the national capital was well endowed with large private domestic buildings between the 13th and 16th centuries.

For the future, the archaeological resource on the site, now Governor's House, remains largely undisturbed as the result of the mitigation strategy, and the 1994–7 programme of works should be seen as a considerable achievement. A framework has been provided against which any further work on the site can be tested: the presence, quality and nature of features and deposits can be predicted in most areas, together with the degree of damage caused by modern intrusions. This proved useful where new services were to be provided for Governor's House in 1998, and it was possible to determine from existing site records that there were no surviving archaeological features in the affected area without further evaluation being necessary. Clearly, in cases such as this, costs to future developers will be considerably reduced, and the heritage of this important site preserved.

6

Specialist appendices

6.1 The prehistoric marsh

Jane Sidell

Introduction

An integrated palaeoecological approach was considered the most suitable to reconstruct the ecological conditions prevailing within the prehistoric marsh deposits. Several samples were scanned to establish whether pollen was preserved, which proved to be the case, so a series of pollen samples were split. Several more samples were taken for diatom analysis, although these proved unsuitable. To provide information on the sedimentary sequence in addition to that provided by the descriptions, samples for magnetic susceptibility and loss-on-ignition were split. Magnetic susceptibility is a useful indicator of human activity as many anthropogenic activities such as burning and pottery manufacture lead to magnetic enhancement (see Thompson & Oldfield 1986). Thus in this study magnetic susceptibility data have been used to determine the presence or absence of human activity and impact during sediment accumulation. Loss-on-ignition was selected to characterise the organic sediments further by measuring the ratio of organic to inorganic components. Such measurements are particularly useful in examining sites where peats and largely inorganic mud are found interbedded, as closely spaced measurements can indicate the degree of conformity in sedimentary contacts and provide evidence of short-lived flood or stand-still events that are not visible in the lithological record.

Chronostratigraphy

Four samples were submitted for ^{14}C assay in the early stages of the project (Table 1), and calibrated using Oxcal version 3.3 and the 1998 curve of Stuiver *et al* 1988. The results confirmed that the peats were certainly pre-Roman, and even that formation in one location had begun in or before the Early Neolithic (3900–3350 BC). However, the dating raised several questions associated with the relative altitude of the dated horizons in the two sequences. Sequence 72 has the lowest and oldest sedimentation; however, the upper part of this sequence, dating to the Middle and Late Iron Age (360–280 BC or 260 BC–AD 10), corresponds in height with the base of sequence 56 which dates to the Middle Bronze Age (1500–1120 BC), continuing into the Late Bronze Age to Middle Iron Age (790–400 BC). It seems likely that a hiatus is present in sequence 72 and/or sedimentation occurred across the site asynchronously. A further possibility is that one or more of these dates is not a true date. This could be a result of several factors including contamination by younger roots or old wood. To this end, further samples were submitted (Table 2), ranging from the Neolithic (3100–2890) in sequence 72 to the Bronze Age (1750–1435 BC) in sequence 56.

Table 1 First suite of ^{14}C samples

Lab no.	Sequence	OD height (central point)	Result	Error	Calibrated result (95% confidence)
Beta 96089	Sample 56	+0.17m OD	2470	± 70	790–400 BC
Beta 96090	Sample 56	−0.23m OD	3070	± 70	1500–1120 BC
Beta 96091	Sample 72	−0.90m OD	2120	± 50	360–280 BC
					or 260 BC–AD 10
Beta 96092	Sample 72	−1.83m OD	4820	± 100	3900–3350 BC

Table 2 Second suite of ^{14}C samples

Lab no.	Sequence	OD height (central point)	Result	Error	Calibrated result (95% confidence)
Beta 129556	Sample 72	–	4360	± 50	3100–2890 BC
Beta 129557	Sample 56	–	4190	± 70	2910–2575 BC
Beta 129558	Sample 56	–	3320	± 70	1750–1435 BC

Lithostratigraphy

Two sections were examined, from sequences 56 and 72. The reason for considering two rather than one representative sequence was that the two sequences, although consistent in general appearance, were present at varying OD heights with anomalous ^{14}C dates. Several possible causes for this have been suggested above (Chronostratigraphy). Descriptions were made using the Troels-Smith system of sedimentary classification (1955).

Sequence 56

This was sampled from −0.46 OD where the underlying sand and gravel matrix was considered to be part of the Pleistocene river-terrace deposits, in this case the Shepperton Terrace. The lowest part of the sequence consisted of a group of minerogenic units with a tendency to fine upwards. At just above 0m OD, the onset of organic sedimentation took place with a gradual non-erosive contact between the two facies types. The lowest organic deposit was organic mud with extremely degraded plant material, and traces of roots indicating in situ formation. Some traces of gravel were present in the deposit, which may indicate that the sampling location was in the vicinity of the contemporary foreshore. The low levels of energy suggested by the fine mineral particles and in situ vegetation would preclude waterlain gravel being deposited here by natural fluvial processes. Alternatively, gravel may have been deposited by the human population. This is not unknown, although anthropogenically derived gravel spreads are rare in organic sequences. A Bronze Age gravel causeway at Hays Storage, Dagenham, penetrating the marshes adjacent to the Thames is an example of this type of activity (Meddens 1996). The organic mud continued to accrete to c +0.5m OD where there is a brief swing to a less organic mud. Again, contacts are gradual and non-erosional indicating

this may have marked a period of flooding across the site. At 0.55m OD the organic component increases, containing wood fragments and roots, again suggesting in situ growth. At c +0.8m OD the peat is mixed with domestic waste from the archaeological layers above.

Sequence 72

This was sampled from −2.0m OD. Unfortunately, owing to logistical constraints, it was not possible to sample the lowest sediment exposed, which was at c −2.1m OD and was visually noted as a grey clay/silt. The interface between the silt and the sampled deposits was at c −2.05m OD, but it was not noted whether this was a gradual contact or not. Organic mud was the lowest sample collected, with some fragments of wood present within the peat and subsequently, from −1.8m OD, root fragments, again suggesting in situ formation rather than detrital accumulation of organics within a fluvial system. The mineral component is consistent suggesting constant gentle inundation from a nearby channel, in this case likely to be the Thames or possibly the confluence of the Thames and the Walbrook stream. There are two periods where the minerogenic component is greater than the organic, again as with sequence 56 possibly suggesting floods or maybe migrations of the channel closer to the sampling site. These occur at c −1.9m OD and c −1.48m OD. During these events organic deposition continues, suggesting that the energy levels leading to sedimentation were not greatly increased. Towards the top of the sequence, c −1.3m OD, there is a final swing to more minerogenic sedimentation, but organic deposition apparently persists until the onset of Roman occupation.

In addition to the descriptions from which models of sedimentation may be proposed, subsamples were split from the cores for additional analyses. Unfortunately, several of these were irrevocably damaged during the analytical process.

X-radiography

The three monolith samples from EN20 were submitted for X-ray analysis in order to see if the sediments were finely laminated, which might indicate gradual, incremental sedimentation. In addition, it may have been possible to spot any hiatus in the sequence or any contamination through root penetration (see Barham 1990). The X-rays show no sign of fine laminae, nor an obvious hiatus. Also, there is no indication of root penetration from above, suggesting that there is no contamination from this source.

Magnetic susceptibility

The results from sequence 56 (Fig 62) show a clear increase in value at the upper levels within the profile which may reflect increased burning. This is consistent with the manifestation of human activity at the top of the organic sequence at c 0.8m OD and may indicate that in fact this was slightly earlier than evidenced by the physical record. There is one peak in the sequence prior to this, which may suggest that there was some local activity; this, however, is very isolated and may represent contamination. Otherwise, there is no evidence for local activity greatly before the settlement of the city. Sequence 72 (Fig 63) is greatly mixed; however, the results are very low, never greater than 5^{-8} m^{3}kg^{-1}, and do not present a pattern which can be interpreted.

Organic carbon content

The organic content was measured from sequence 56 and showed a steady increase up to c 0.6m OD, reaching 75% organic carbon. This was followed by a more rapid but still gradual decline in value, down to 25% at the top of the sequence, correlating well with the appearance of artefactual material within the sediments.

Discussion

The two sequences are intrinsically similar: it is the anomalous age/altitude which distinguishes them. Lithologically, they appear to represent organic mud forming over (in the case of sample 56) minerogenic waterlain deposits. The organic mud develops into more substantial organic facies, suggesting sedimentation processes are less directly associated with the river at this time. Towards the top of the profile, organic content drops, while magnetic susceptibility rises, in sample 56 (which appears the more consistent and possibly representative sequence) corresponding to the earliest observed human activity on the site.

Palynology

R G Scaife
Samples for pollen analysis were obtained from sample 56 by subsampling the monolith tins. These were subsampled for pollen at 40mm intervals and standard procedures were used to prepare slides. The pollen sequence is discussed below.

Pollen zonation

Four local pollen assemblage zones have been recognised in the analysis of this peat and sediment sequence, characterised from the base of the profile at −0.46m OD upwards.

ZONE 1 (BASAL ORGANIC SILT: −0.46M TO −0.28M OD)
This zone is delimited by higher values of *Pinus* (11%), *Corylus avellana* type (hazel) peaking to 80%, and spores of *Pteridium aquilinum* (bracken) and of *Dryopteris* type than found in the subsequent zones. Trees comprise *Pinus* (11%), *Tilia* (lime; to 20%) and *Alnus* (alder; 20%). There are few herbs with only occasional Poaceae and Cyperaceae.

ZONE 2 (PEAT: −0.28M TO +0.04M OD)
Pinus and *Ulmus* (elm) decline (to <5%) while *Quercus* (oak; c 35%), *Tilia* and *Alnus* expand. *Corylus avellana* type remains important but with reduced values, declining throughout to 20–30%.

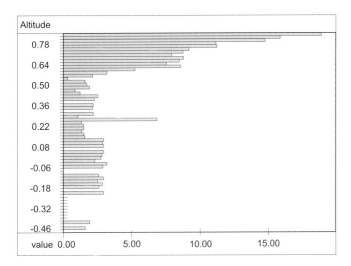

Fig 62 *Graph of magnetic susceptibility results: sequence 56*

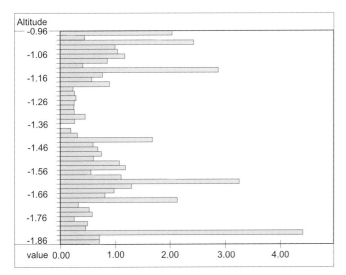

Fig 63 *Graph of magnetic susceptibility results: sequence 72*

75

There are reductions of Pteridium and Dryopteris type followed by expansion at the top of the zone and a peak of Polypodium vulgare (common polypody).

ZONE 3 (PEAT/ORGANIC SILT: +0.04M TO +0.44M OD)

Tree and shrub values decline sharply while herb totals and diversity increase markedly. Tilia declines to absence (from 40% in preceding zone) while Corylus avellana type is reduced (to 10%) and Quercus remains constant at 20%. Within the herbs, Poaceae (to 60%) is dominant with Lactucae (to 20%). There is a marked increase in herbaceous diversity including cereal and weed types, such as Chenopodium (goosefoots), Rumex (docks), Polygonum (knotgrass), Plantago lanceolata (plaintains) and Asteraceae types, along with expansions of marsh taxa (dominated by Cyperaceae). There are also significant expansions of spores; Pteridium aquilinum (to 30%) and Dryopteris type (average 25%).

ZONE 4 (ORGANIC SILT: +0.44M TO +0.72M OD)

Defined by further but smaller reduction in tree and shrub pollen with some additional increases in herbs. Quercus and Corylus avellana type decline to <5%. Herbs remain dominant and diverse with expansion of Sinapis type (8%), Rumex conglomeratus type (8%), Lactucae (20%) and Poaceae (maximum values of 65% at top of profile). Cyperaceae and spores (Pteridium and Dryopteris type) decline.

Development of the late prehistoric vegetation

Radiocarbon-dating of the lowest levels of peat in a nearby section (sample 72) indicates that accumulation started at or before 3900–3350 cal BC. As discussed above, the dates and altitudes between the two sequences do not directly correspond; however, the date obtained from the base of sequence 72 applies to the pollen profile examined from sequence 56. Data presented thus pertain to the Late Atlantic (Late Mesolithic) and sub-Boreal Neolithic and Bronze Age periods. It is possible therefore that a hiatus exists at the very lowest points of sequence 56. The pollen profile exhibits a number of important characteristics of the late prehistoric period.

Peat accumulation was initiated on basal organic silts due to allogenic factors such as regional eustatic changes in the Thames basin (sensu Thames stage III; Devoy 1979; 1980). Pollen assemblage zone 1 shows typical Middle Holocene dominance of woodland with a paucity of herbs present. Corylus avellana (hazel), Quercus (oak), Ulmus (elm) and Tilia (lime/lindens) were the most important tree taxa. Values of Tilia are significant given its usual under-representation in pollen assemblages (Andersen 1970; 1973) due to entomophily and flowering midsummer when woodland is in full leaf further negating dispersal. There is evidence that lime was dominant in southern England in the Middle Holocene (Birks et al 1975; Birks 1989) and in areas of London during the Middle and Late Holocene (Greig 1989; 1991; Sidell et al 2000). At these sites, values of up to 40% or more are known. Here it seems likely that mixed woodland was present in areas local to the site. Pinus (pine) (to 10%) is enigmatic; such values may result from long-distance transport, but given the dominance of woodland witnessed, it is possible that some localised growth

remained from its earlier Boreal dominance. A further alternative is over-representation in these basal fluvially lain sediments. Ulmus is similarly unusual, being absent in the lower sediment layers but present in the Middle Holocene in the top of the basal zone 1.

At the interface of zones 1 and 2 there is a change in both the pollen and lithostratigraphy, and while there may be a hiatus in deposition here between these units, this is not thought to be so since the pollen curves change smoothly over this level. Characteristically at this horizon, elm pollen declines to low values. This is mirrored by declines in Pinus and Corylus and immediately above by Tilia and Quercus. At the point of decline, however, Tilia and Quercus expand. Subsequently, in this zone Fraxinus (ash) and Hedera (ivy) also occur along with some herbs. This event appears to be the primary elm decline which is generally accepted as being a broadly synchronous phenomenon at c 3500–3000 BC (Smith & Pilcher 1973). Causation has in the past been attributed to a range of factors (Smith 1970; Simmons & Tooley 1981; Scaife 1987). It is now generally accepted that disease was more readily spread by elm bark beetle (Scolytus scolytus) with Neolithic disturbance and opening of the Atlantic (Middle Holocene) woodland (Girling & Greig 1985; Girling 1987). Such disturbance is also evidenced here by Fraxinus, Cornus (dogwood) and expansion of Hedera in zone 2 indicating growth of secondary woodland and expansion and flowering of ivy. However, values of these secondary colonisers are small and with absence of cereal pollen and typical weeds of disturbance and cultivation suggest that there was little Neolithic activity in close proximity to this site.

During zone 2 high percentages of Tilia with Quercus and Corylus suggest that woodland remained locally dominant. Whether this was mixed woodland or whether lime was dominant on better-drained soils with oak and hazel on heavier (valley-side) soils is unclear. However, change at +0.17m to +0.21m OD marks a major phase of vegetation and/or environmental change in proximity to this site. The high percentages of Tilia decline very sharply, along with reductions of Corylus. Quercus remains constant while herbs, including the first occurrence of cereals in this profile, increase sharply. This is a typical 'lime decline' which is now evidenced from a substantial number of (as yet unpublished) London sites. Declines of hazel and lime together suggest that these were growing in association, while oak, which remains more or less constant, may have remained unchanged or was further afield and also unaffected.

It is clear that these changes from zones 2–3 suggest a major phase of woodland clearance and ensuing agriculture. Originally thought to be caused by climatic change at the sub-Boreal to sub-Atlantic transition (Godwin 1940), it has become clear since Turner (1962) that human causes were responsible. This is clearly the case here with sharp reductions of lime associated with a clear increase in cereal pollen and many weed taxa (Chenopodiaceae, Rumex spp, Polygonum spp, Plantago lanceolata, Asteraceae types and Pteridium aquilinum). This event is, however, further complicated because of the clear expansion of sedge fen at the expense of Alnus, which correspondingly declines between +0.52m to +0.72m OD. This may suggest that removal of local woodland caused local hydrological changes through reduction in evapotranspiration, higher ground water table, increased surface run-off and corresponding change in the mire/floodplain habitat to a wetter sedge fen habitat. This lime event has not yet been dated here and recourse must be made to data existing from other London sites. Dates for the lime decline span the Neolithic at Union Street and Joan Street (Sidell *et al* 2000) to as late as the Saxon period in Epping Forest (Baker *et al* 1978). However, there are a substantial number of dates from London and southern England as a whole which suggest a Middle Bronze Age date of between *c* 1500–1000 BC (Scaife 1980; Sidell *et al* 2000). It seems likely that the Suffolk House event is attributed to woodland clearance and intensified agriculture of that period. This pattern of deforestation and agricultural intensification continued into the subsequent zone 4 which has been dated to the Iron Age (790–400 cal BC). However, ^{14}C dating of the 1st millennium BC is fraught with difficulty.

Summary

Sedimentation commences in the testpits with waterlain silts which could not be examined, but are assumed to be freshwater on account of likely date and altitude. Organic mud indicates that the minerogenic component derived from the nearby channel decreases in tandem with the beginnings of organic sedimentation. It is uncertain what caused this; however, several possibilities exist, such as the migration of the channel away from the sampling site, or a decline in the rate of river-level rise which could have tipped the balance to let vegetation get a hold on the sampling location.

Peat formation appears to have persisted up until the pre-Roman Iron Age (although as mentioned above, ^{14}C dating of this period is notoriously difficult), when artefactual debris starts appearing in the sequences. This is likely to have been pressed down from the first Roman occupation of the site. Certainly no obvious hiatus was observed in the sedimentary sequence, or from the X-rays; neither does the pollen record suggest any breaks in sedimentation. This suggests that the results of this site provide a reasonably accurate picture of the sedimentary and vegetational history of the sequences studied from Suffolk House. In view of the paucity of such data from north bank sites in comparison to Southwark or Westminster, for example (Sidell *et al* 2000), this analysis has provided important new information on the prehistory of the City and the appearance of the area prior to the construction of Londinium.

6.2 The pre-Roman plant remains

Lisa Gray

Introduction

A number of botanical samples were taken from the marsh (Table 3), and these produced evidence, as might be expected, for the presence of aquatic or semi-aquatic plant species as well as alder. A note of caution should be sounded, however: the

marsh was contaminated with Roman artefacts, and some of the seeds may therefore be intrusive, particularly those which represent the presence of exotic imports, such as fig and grape. For this reason, the species present in the pre-Roman and Roman periods are included together in a single table for comparison (see Table 18).

Table 3 Provenance of the pre-Roman environmental samples in OA2 (1.5)

Context no.	Sample no.	Feature type
19	1	peat
18	2	peat
569	57	peat
569	60	peat
693	73	marsh deposit 0–100mm
693	75	marsh deposit 200–300mm
693	77	marsh deposit 400–500mm
693	79	marsh deposit 600–700mm
693	81	marsh deposit 800–900mm

Results

The prehistoric marsh

{2} [18]; {1} [19]; {57} {60} [569]; {73} {75} {77} {79} {81} [693] (1.5) OA2
Waterlogging preserved most of these remains. Charred remains were few and probably intrusive.

HABITAT

Of the nine samples recovered from these deposits, the two from [569] contained the greatest number of different plant taxa, 32 taxa in each. In these samples the greatest range of species for a particular habitat was from damp/marsh and woodland/scrub/hedgerow habitats. The remaining species had habitat preferences for waste and disturbed ground and grassland. A similar pattern is apparent in the habitat preference of the plants represented in the remaining samples.

Aquatic/semi-aquatic plant seeds were present in six of the nine samples. These were pondweed (*Potamogeton* sp), celery-leaved crowfoot (*Ranunculus scleratus* L), gipsy-wort (*Lycopus europaeus* L), bur-reed (*Sparganium erectum* L), fine-leaved water dropwort (*Oenanthe aquatica* L), spike-rush (*Eleocharis* sp), yellow flag/iris (*Iris pseudacorus* L), marshwort (*Apium* sp) and lesser spearwort (*Ranunculus flammula* L) seeds. Also present were seeds and catkins of alder (*Alnus glutinosa* L). Samples [693] {75} {79} and {81} (sample depths 200–900mm) contained no seeds from these habitats.

No trends were apparent in the habitat preferences for the monolith samples [693] {73} {75} {77} {79} {81}. Although bedstraw (*Galium* sp) and woundwort (*Stachys* sp) occur for the first time in the sequence in sample {79} (sample depth 600–700mm). These are plants with cosmopolitan habitat ranges.

One sample, [569] {60}, contained remains of a plant found growing in cultivated and rough ground (Stace 1991, 342), a wild radish/charlock (*Raphanus raphanistrum* L) siliqua.

ECONOMIC USES

The archaeological evidence for this phase does not include evidence for human activity but it is useful to consider the possible economic resources available.

A hazelnut shell (*Corylus avellana* L) fragment was present in one sample [693] {77} (400–500mm) and a small number of sloe/cherry (*Prunus avium/cerasus*) stones [569] {57} {60}. Stinging nettle (*Urtica dioica* L) seeds were present in seven of the nine samples, particularly in [18] {2}. Other edible plant remains included the seeds of blackberry/raspberry (*Rubus fruticosus/idaeus*). Seeds of rush (*Juncus* sp) and sedge (*Carex* sp) plants were present. These have possible uses for thatching, floor covering or bedding but also grow naturally in wetland habitats and could be part of the local flora.

A charred spike-rush (*Eleocharis* sp) seed and four charred barley (*Hordeum* sp) grains were recovered. Charred seeds or grains were absent from all other samples in this phase. Barley grains were present in Roman deposits, for example the dark earth sample, and the only other grains present at the site were spelt grains and chaff from the Roman ditch and dark earth samples. This suggests that the contexts from which these remains were recovered may have been disturbed and mixing with later deposits occurred. The presence of two exotic fruit seeds – a fig seed (*Ficus carica* L) and a charred grape (*Vitis vinifera* L) seed – were present in samples [569] {57} {60}, and the sloe/cherry stones in samples {57} and {60} seem to confirm that this context has been disturbed and that these remains are intrusive.

Discussion

These samples produced a similar range of plant remains to those recovered from other floodplain prehistoric deposits. For example, the analysis of the environmental remains for the archaeological sites along the course of the upper Walbrook Valley situated within the site of the City of London, produced a range of ruderal and semi-aquatic plant seeds plus two aquatic species – stonewort (*Chara* sp) and horned pondweed (*Zanichella palustris* L) (de Moulins 1990, 89). The Walbrook Valley work presented a picture of a clean fairly slow-flowing stream passing through marshy areas.

The Suffolk House samples also produced a range of aquatic and semi-aquatic taxa which, when considered along with the variety of scrub, woodland and disturbed ground taxa recovered, complements the information already gathered about the pre-Roman environment in London which is one of marsh, alder carr, waterfilled channels and patches of open standing water. The species present support the image of nutrient-rich wetland habitats. For example, species of pondweed tend to grow in eutrophic environments with slow-moving water (Grime *et al* 1990, 266–8); celery-leaved crowfoot has been noted as an effective coloniser of disturbed and fertile wetlands, and lesser

spearwort was found in shaded mire habitats (Grime *et al* 1990, 284, 279).

As already mentioned, it is the possible resource environment that is considered here rather than evidence for use of plants during this phase. Seeds of economically useful plants were recovered. Fragments of hazelnut shell and cherry stones were found and may have come from trees growing locally. Stinging nettle leaves and blackberry/raspberry fruits are edible and would have been thriving in such a nutrient-rich environment. Rushes and sedge were used for thatching, floor covering or bedding, but these seeds were not present in numbers high enough to suggest that they were gathered for use.

6.3 The pre-Roman animal bone

Unlike the overlying deposits of Roman date, the marsh deposits of Open Area 2 proved to contain only a complete woodcock skull (1.5: [569]). If not intrusive, this may suggest the importance of fowling in the pre-Roman period, although the bird may have died of other causes.

6.4 The Roman and post-Roman timber technology

Damian Goodburn

Introduction

The preservation of waterlogged woodwork on both a large and small scale is well known from many sites in the City of London and Southwark. Such material survives from prehistoric times to the 18th century. A large and important part of the corpus of recorded material dates to the Roman period, and the work at Suffolk House significantly adds to the sum of knowledge of Roman woodworking in the London region. Several detailed studies of the woodwork of the period have appeared (Goodburn 1991a; 1996; in prep), and post-excavation work is in progress or nearing completion on a large quantity of material from other recent excavations, such as Regis House and Poultry. This large body of varied, well-recorded evidence, the multi-disciplinary study of it and some insights gained through systematic experimental woodworking are drawn upon for the selective discussion below.

This report deals with an analysis of the woodworking and closely related fields such as evidence for woodland history, rather than stratigraphic, topographic and more general issues covered in the main body of the report.

A few very brief comments on the nature of the work on site are, however, essential for understanding the character of the woodworking evidence. The confinement of the excavation work on site to deep, narrow trial pits and 'enabling trenches' as opposed to an open area excavation presented some problems of access to the structural woodwork found. Some of this consisted of large baulks which could not be easily moved and were only partially investigated as a result. Additionally, part of the woodwork found was fragmentary and damaged by essential shoring work, and this is not considered in detail here: for example, the broken remains of part of a jointed elm well-frame of late or post-medieval date were excavated in EN11 and could not be coherently reassembled. For these reasons, a full description and discussion of all the woodwork found unconditional on its information value would be of little use here: the full record is held with the site archive. Only three of the enabling trenches yielded significant woodwork: EN5, EN11 and EN20 (see Fig 3). A total of 71 worked timbers or pieces of roundwood were recorded and sampled following standard MoL procedure, which is in line with the updated English Heritage Guidelines on dealing with early waterlogged woodwork (Brunning 1996).

The remains in EN5 consisted of one oak plank laid on face which may have been either the base of a drain or the baseplate for a robbed-out wall. The sequences of woodwork found in EN11 and EN20 were more complex and the structures themselves are described in some detail in the main report,

simply summarised below. In EN11, the remains of the quay, Waterfront 2 (2.2), lay directly below the post-medieval well base (see Fig 61). Of the quay timbers, only the southernmost land-tie structure could be extensively recorded (Figs 64, 65): the northern structure was in the side of the trench and had been partly dismantled in antiquity. In EN20, the east–west pile-and-plank revetment, Waterfront 3 (4.2), lay beneath a truncated complex of partially preserved Roman oak plank drain timbers and stakes (Fig 66).

Waterfront 2

General description

As has been seen, the southernmost of the two recorded land-tie or tieback assemblies appeared to be largely intact and consisted of a stack of five horizontal baulks of oak which varied in scantling and length (see Figs 8, 9, 64, 65). Special housings for locking bars were cut in baulks [584], [582] and [589] (see below). Two oak locking bars remained in place and it was clear that these and their anchor stakes functioned both to prevent movement towards the quay frontage further east, and to help keep the baulks vertically above each other. The form of the

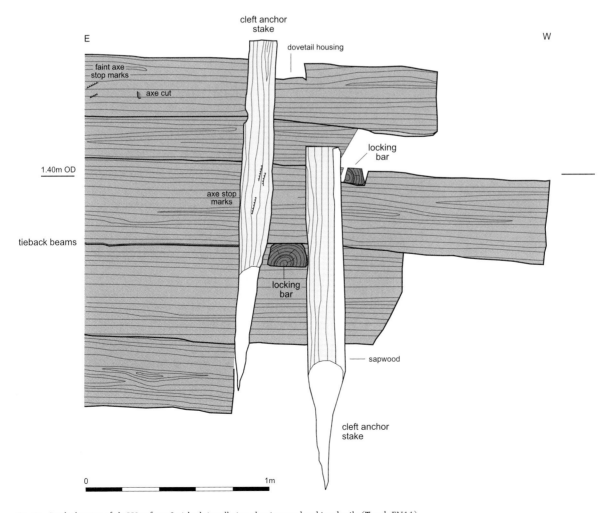

Fig 64 South elevation of the Waterfront 2 tieback installation, showing woodworking details (Trench EN11)

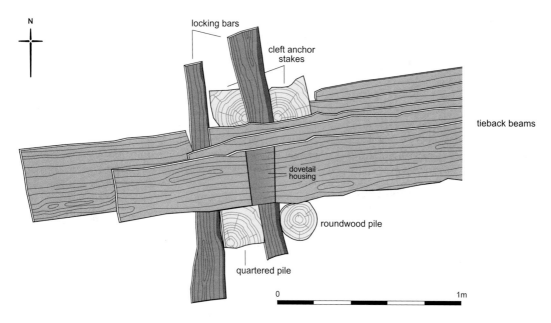

Fig 65 Plan of the Waterfront 2 tieback installation (Trench EN11)

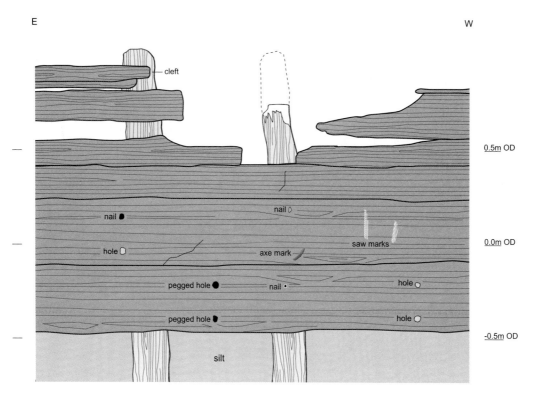

Fig 66 North elevation of the early 2nd-century post-and-plank revetment, Waterfront 3 (Trench EN20)

assembly is a little different to that used for other Roman quays investigated in London, most closely resembling the post-AD 95 structure at Pudding Lane (Milne 1985, 60–2).

Tree-ring analysis has shown that the land-tie baulk [594] retained its 'waney' or 'bark' edge with the latest tree ring preserved. Measurement and ring-sequence matching showed that it was felled in the spring of AD 84 and the estimates for the other timbers are compatible with this date. As there was no evidence of previous use of the timber or any appreciable seasoning 'shakes' (splits along the medullary rays in large oak

timbers caused by uneven shrinkage) in the baulks we might suggest that this part of the quay was built shortly after felling. The late March equinoctial low spring tides may have been used to allow the most favourable conditions possible for access to the foreshore.

Detailed recording both in situ and after partial dismantling of the structure provided evidence of several features of interest from the point of view of the study of woodworking techniques and the reconstruction of past woodland, and these are presented in outline below.

Evidence of the nature of the trees used

The reconstruction of ancient trees, treescapes and management practices in this country from what have been called the 'Dark ages of woodland' (Rackham 1976, 49) has become a key area of research (Goodburn 1991a; 1991b; 1996; 1998; Brunning 1996, 14; O'Sullivan 1998), although space only permits a brief analysis of this aspect of the Suffolk House evidence. Recent work in London has shown that many forms of oak tree were harvested for building purposes, each with its own particular 'tree-land' setting, from dense high wildwoods, to hedgerow or open field situations.

Although the land-tie assemblies were not fully exposed, the evidence – principally the grain form, scantling, tree-ring width and 'parent tree' ages – is sufficient to show that the oaks used grew in two different treescapes. Some timber was of typically old, slow-grown, straight-grained, wildwood type, for example land-tie baulk [594] and cleft stake [585], each with over 230 annual rings. The parent tree for [594] must have had a diameter at chest height of 1.0m or more, allowing for tapering (Fig 67). The second type of timber, however, came from much younger oaks of medium growth rate, which must have been harvested from more open secondary or managed woodland, for example baulk [589] with well under 200 annual rings and a basal diameter of around 650mm. This small sample of material mirrors the pattern of parent tree types found in the more completely investigated timbers of the Regis House quay.

Evidence for felling methods

All of the accessible baulk ends were cross-cut with axes, but some were more or less flat, while others had two angled flats. This was particularly the case for baulk [589]. The two facets appear to have been the minimally trimmed, felled, butt end of the tree, with the characteristic 'gob' and 'backcut' (Fig 68). Although not absolutely clear, it appears that the builders made an effort to alternate the often larger butt ends of the baulks with the smaller top ends, possibly to maintain a roughly level upper face.

No trace of baulk-end inscriptions, such as those recently found at the Guildhall Yard and Regis House sites, were found (Hassall & Tomblin 1996, 449). Neither was any trace of the use of saws for felling found.

Evidence for methods of bucking (cross-cutting)

After a tree is felled for timber, the unwanted top and side branches have to be removed and the main stem cross-cut or 'bucked' where necessary. For these timbers it was accomplished with axes rather than cross-cut saws (see Fig 68). The bucked end of baulk [584] had particularly clear axe 'stop marks' (lines or small steps left where the blade stopped cutting). None provided complete negative impressions of the axe blade used but the widest was about 80mm wide and slightly curved, which implies the use of an axe about 90–100mm wide or possibly more. The form of marks is very similar to those found on the

ends of the quay baulks at Regis House (Goodburn in Brigham & Watson in prep). The axes clearly had relatively thin blades, and may have been similar to the Roman army *dolabra* axes which were often of the right size and form (Bishop & Coulston 1993, fig 63). Just such an axe was found with part of its fruitwood handle at a site in Cheapside (CID90; Hill & Woodger 1999, 10), City of London, in a context dated to the AD 50s.

The conversion methods used

After topping, lopping and bucking, larger logs usually pass through a further stage or stages of processing termed 'conversion', to produce items such as beams, planks, boards and battens. It is increasingly clear that this work had many period-specific characteristics. Several methods used by the Romans, such as various methods of sawing out planks, or hewing beams square and true, represent revolutionary new steps in woodworking technology, unknown from Iron Age Britain.

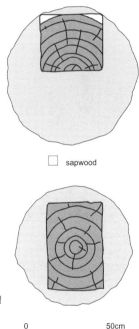

sapwood

Fig 67 Reconstruction of the hypothetical parent logs for Roman tieback timbers [594] and [589]

0   50cm

Three approaches to conversion are evinced by study of the timbers in the land-tie assemblies. The baulk faces were slightly abraded, but faint traces of conversion by careful 'notch and chop hewing' (Goodburn 1992, 113; Brigham & Watson in prep) were found. This took the form of a few surviving 'incuts' left where notches were cut out for chopping off the bulk of the waste. Incomplete slightly curved stop marks from an axe worked along the baulk at about 45–50° were recorded on baulk [582]. These marks were 70mm wide, essentially the same as those on the bucked ends. This probably implies that one general-purpose medium-sized form of axe was used for felling, bucking and hewing the baulks. This contrasts with other documented approaches to hewing oak beams – medieval evidence from London suggests that two separate axes were typically used: a narrow- and a broad-bladed tool. Hewing with

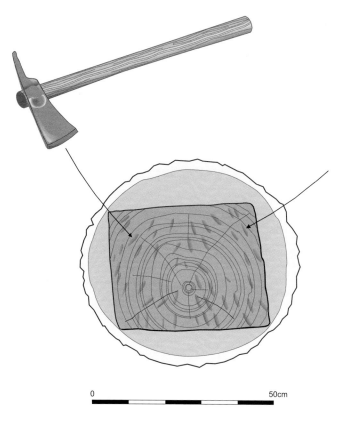

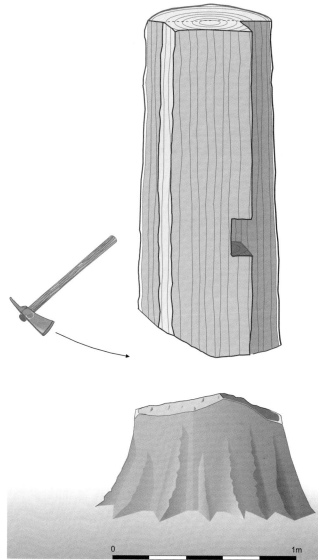

Fig 68 *Reconstruction of felling and bucking methods (cross-cutting with an axe) used in the production of timbers [589] and [584]*

one form of medium-sized axe seems to be characteristic of nearly all Roman structural woodwork from London that has been recorded in detail.

Most of the baulks were hewn from whole logs (boxed heart), but baulks [594] and [583] were made from half-log sections. How this halving was achieved could not be investigated due to access problems. The radially split anchor stake [585] was hewn to a regular blunt wedge cross-section, and the lock bars were also cleft. Several almost straight incomplete axe stop marks 110mm wide were recorded on this stake. The nature of the marks implies the use of a wider axe than used elsewhere, with a blade at least 120mm wide. This is still within the range of the *dolabra* types, although the marks could also represent a quite different form of axe, as a variety of forms are known (Manning 1985, 15–16). Whatever the form of axe, two work teams may be implied.

The dovetail housings

The tapered dovetail housings cut in the upper faces of baulks [582], [584] and [589] are an addition to the known repertoire of structural woodworking techniques in Roman London. They were neatly made and held suitably shaped lock bars (Fig 69). The joint required no extra fastenings once the lock bar was driven tight. The tapers were arranged so that the lock bars could be driven alternately from the north or south, which implies that the main east–west river wall must have passed more than 1.0m to the south of the trench to allow for the driving of

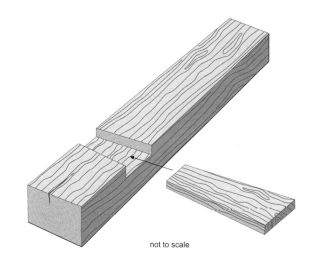

not to scale

Fig 69 *Evidence of a new joint type from Roman London: detail of the dovetail joint used to retain the locking bars of the tiebacks of Waterfront 2*

the lock bars; this is in any case probable because of the absence within the excavated area of tieback assemblies retaining the main frontage; a distance of at least 3.0m has been suggested above.

The comparative status of the work

In comparative terms the land-tie assemblies were solidly and carefully built out of new timber apparently cut for the purpose, a large investment. A number of skilled artisans, labourers and woodsmen must have worked on the project. Even though we can only review part of the structure, the status of the quay must have been relatively high, contrasting greatly with the later revetment (Waterfront 3) described below.

Waterfront 3

General description

This simple but robust pile-and-plank revetment (see Fig 66) appears to have functioned as a river wall and could have been built by a largely unskilled workforce. Even a structure such as this, however, would have required a work gang of perhaps a minimum of 10 people to manoeuvre the timbers and operate and move a pile driver, if one were used. Three squared piles were exposed, and parts of five courses of planking, only the bottom two of which were reasonably intact. The lower three courses of planking were nailed to the landward faces of the piles, and none could be lifted intact for very detailed recording, but it is clear that the lower two planks were sawn out in some way, while others were radially cleft.

The discovery of relict peg holes in the planking and joints in the piles indicated that much or possibly all of the timbers found were second-hand. There was no evidence that the structure was braced or tied to the land in any way: the fact that it was found in a state of collapse suggests braces and ties were absent. Clearly the revetment was not built to impress and must have been comparatively cheap to build, and the principal interest lies in the relict features of the second-hand building timbers reworked for the revetment piles, especially timbers [684] and [685] (discussed below). Clear axe marks did survive on the rehewn pile tips, the best preserved of which was slightly curved and 90mm wide.

The tree-ring analysis suggests a felling date range for the latest second-hand timbers between AD 90–121. The building post [685] discussed below (see Fig 70) had many sapwood rings surviving and was given a felling date range of AD 56–92. The presence of the bark edge appeared clear where the timber was sampled, however, and this may have been lost or damaged prior to dating. Thus a felling date in the late AD 50s seems probable. The last heartwood ring dates of the similar second-hand post [684] were well before the Roman invasion, which is not incompatible with the above suggestion.

The second-hand building timbers [684] and [685]

Clearly, in most situations, Roman building timbers do not survive as more than stains in the ground, thus any such elements which do remain assume considerable importance. In many cases the reuse of such timbers in totally waterlogged situations

is required for their preservation, as in this case. Relatively few detailed accounts of the construction of Roman buildings of timber or timber and earthen materials have been published (for exceptions see Perring & Roskams 1991, 73–95; Goodburn 1991a; Brigham *et al* 1995). This is despite the fact that they were clearly far more common than structures of masonry at most Romano-British sites. Therefore two reused timbers ([684] and [685]) are worthy of published presentation.

A third pile from the revetment, the easternmost squared oak upright [651], was broken *in situ*, and no detailed records of the complete timber could be made. However, it was about 200mm sq, containing at least four closely set small blind mortices in one face. The mortices might possibly have been for window bars or 'mullions' indicating that it had been a window sill or lintel.

The two more fully recorded timbers exhibited traces of three phases of use. The evidence for their final use in Waterfront 3 has been outlined above; the previous two are described below in relative chronological order.

Primary use in a building wall and evidence for the modification of the building

Recent and ongoing work in London has shown that a very common system of building in the 1st and 2nd centuries AD involved the use of prefabricated frames of squared straight oak timber (Goodburn 1991a) with ground sills (baseplates) and wall plates. The space between the studs and posts was commonly infilled with a distinctive form of wattle and daub. This required the cutting of sloping recesses in the sides of the uprights for sliding short cross-staves into position, around which vertical roundwood was woven. The fact that the sloping recesses were always deepest at the lowest end is fortuitous, as it allows the original head and foot ends of reused and *ex situ* Roman studs and posts to be determined. The infill was covered with locally produced daub, sometimes sheathed in timber or keyed for plaster by roller-stamping deeply embossed patterns. The studs were often exposed inside (Goodburn 1991a), but were also rendered over, as shown by the presence of secondary axe-cut peckmarks for keying plaster (Fig 70).

The two Suffolk House wall timbers were both hewn to shape but clear axe stop marks up to 90mm wide only survived on the rehewn pile tips. Timber [684] was hewn from roughly a quarter of a large log around 200 years old, while [685] was converted from a slow-grown whole log of around the same age. The slope of the knots in timber [685] showed that it had been used with the crown end uppermost unlike later medieval carpentry where it was usually placed downwards.

The cross-section of *c* 200mm x 190mm is substantially larger than the corresponding sections of typical reused Roman studs found elsewhere in London. This scantling, together with a minimum original length of about 3.0m for timber [685], implies an origin in a fairly large building, or possibly in a gable end.

Both timbers had the typical chiselled sloping recesses for the infill staves set at 0.6m, two Roman feet (*pedes monetales*) apart, a common unit in Roman structural woodwork from London

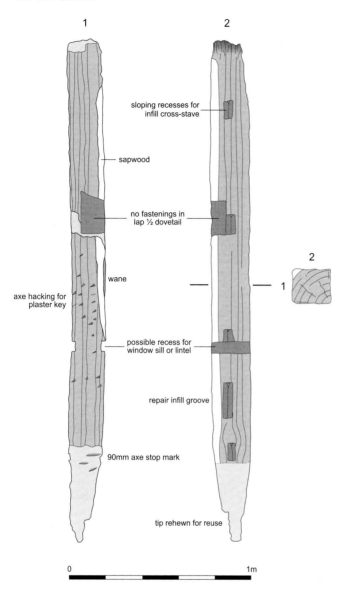

Fig 70 *The 1st-century house stud [685] reused as a pile in Waterfront 3. Several phases of relict joints, recesses for infill battens and axe nicks for keying plaster are shown*

(Goodburn 1991a, 197). Timber [685] also had two faces keyed for plaster, but this feature was not found on [684]. Thus in one case the vertical was rendered over while in the other it does not appear to have been. Indeed some 4mm sq iron nails in two faces of [684] might indicate that it was boarded over originally.

An interesting feature of the two posts is that they both had pairs of narrow housing joints cutting through earlier sloping recesses. These secondary joints appear to indicate evidence of the modification of a standing wall, possibly for the insertion of small windows. The wall may have been patched with mudbricks or some other form of infill above and below the openings as there would probably not have been space for the common form of wattle infill. Early Roman mudbrick and pisé walls recorded in 1995 a little to the east at Regis House had thin plank 'string courses' in them, as speculatively shown in Fig 71.

Evidence for a second phase of use

A further series of joints were found in both timbers which appear to imply a use as horizontal beams in an unknown structure. The joints were single unpinned lap half-dovetails, which could only have functioned with the timbers in a horizontal position.

Summary

While the quantity of early woodwork recorded at Suffolk House was relatively small by the standards of some London excavations, detailed recording, sampling and analysis have yielded significant new information in several areas. An additional form of Roman land-tie assembly is now known, together with an addition to the known corpus of Roman joints. Further information on the nature of 'tree-land' in the hinterland of Roman London was also gained, and of the methods and tools of timber conversion.

Fig 71 *Conjectural reconstruction of a section of Roman timber-framed wall using timber studs similar to [685]. The diagram also shows a possible interpretation of the function of secondary joints for housing small horizontal trimming timbers to form window openings*

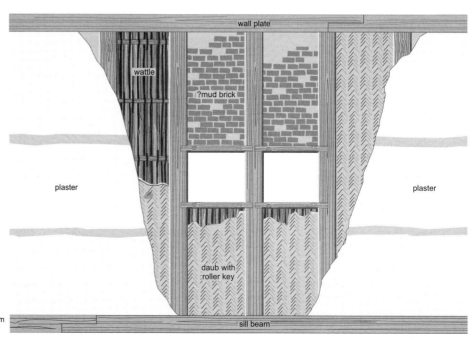

Medieval and post-medieval timber technology

The site produced comparatively little post-Roman woodwork. However, there were several significant items.

The backfill of a late medieval to 16th-century well in the southern part of Building 15 (26.1) contained several small oak offcuts; one appeared to have traces of a knife-cut Roman numeral III, presumably an indicator of carpentry work nearby during the period when the well was being backfilled.

A much rarer find for London was a radially cleft and hewn oak base or top to a bentwood box about 310mm in diameter from the fill of the same well (26.2: [532]; Fig 72). The diagnostic features included a notch cut out to accommodate the overlapping pieces of the sides, and 5mm sq cleft oak pegs in the edges. Small incised lines marked the location of the pegs, and they had to be precisely located in the base as it was only a maximum of 15mm thick. Such bentwood box elements have been found on sites in a number of north European medieval towns such as Viking Coppergate, York where they are on display. In London the only known parallel to date was found in a c 16th- to 17th-century cesspit backfill at the City site of Thames Exchange

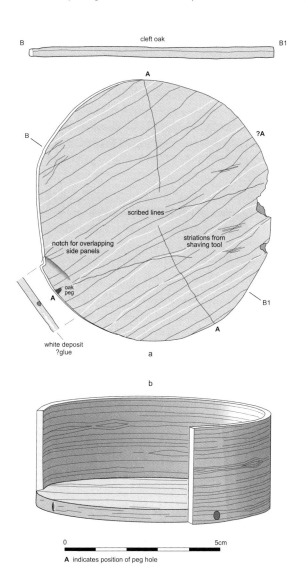

Fig 72 *The bentwood box base or top [532] from the 16th-century fill of a well, and a conjectural reconstruction of the box*

in 1989, and is currently unpublished. The original container would have probably resembled the well-known Shaker 'hat boxes'.

The use of radially cleft beech logs similar to those found under a chalk rubble foundation of Building 13 (21.1) is now recognised as a classic feature of foundation construction in waterfront buildings in London from the late 1090s through the 12th century. Similar examples are known from Thames Exchange, Bull Wharf and Vintry, all sites in the vicinity of Suffolk House, but to the south of Thames Street.

6.5 The Roman pottery

Robin Symonds

Introduction

Before discussing the pottery from the site in detail, it would be useful to explore briefly the context of the site and its pottery. Suffolk House is the westernmost of a substantial number of sites along the waterfront of the Roman City of London, many of which have furnished evidence for the importation of pottery and other goods into both the City and Britain as a province. A recent publication (Symonds 1998) has attempted to summarise the pottery evidence from a total of 14 waterfront sites: 12 on the north bank of the Thames and two in the northern part of Southwark near London Bridge. Table 4 shows a summary of those sites and the character of the pottery found in them.

Although the list in Table 4 is not exhaustive, it does illustrate the current state of knowledge of London's Roman port. Suffolk House is the westernmost and the northernmost of these sites, and it has several distinctive elements. The first of these is that this is the latest of early waterfront sites, starting to function in the early 80s AD, although naturally there is a certain amount of earlier pottery which may have been dumped into the site during construction of the first quay. Interestingly, however, the earlier residual pottery includes no Lyon ware, no other early fine wares apart from samian, and a handful of early coarse wares. Yet, by contrast, the samian forms which would normally be thought to be falling out of circulation by the Flavian period – particularly 4DR29, 4RT12, 5DR15/17, 6DR24/25 and 6RT8 (see Table 10) – make up about 10% of the samian present, including unidentifiable forms. Even though it contains no substantial dumps of samian ware, Suffolk House has furnished one of the highest percentages of samian ware – 22–23% – of any larger individual site or group of sites in London (see Table 5b), although clearly this high percentage is partly due to the fact that the site is unusually lacking in large late Roman assemblages, in which samian would be rare. Just 13 out of the 76 contexts with Roman pottery contain types which can be dated to AD 200 or later, and just 4% of the pottery types (2.1% of the sherds) present in the site can be dated to AD 200 or later. These aspects need to be included in any consideration of the data presented in Tables 5–8, wherein the data for this site as a whole are compared with other sites in London.

Table 4 Summary of recently excavated Roman waterfront sites, and the associated pottery (derived from Symonds 1998)

Site	Code	Comments and dating	Imported pottery types
Billingsgate Buildings	TR74	Mainly AD 70–160; with the character of occupation rather than portuary activity	Despite the nature of the site, the percentages of samian are relatively high, especially in the 3rd century
Billingsgate Lorry Park	BIG82	Quays contemporary with Swan Lane, Seal House and St Magnus/New Fresh Wharf, but no 4th-century material	Similar material to New Fresh Wharf (below), but without the 4th-century types
Custom House	CUS73	Late 2nd- to 3rd-century quays	Occupation-like pottery, not analysed
Jubilee Line Extension, London Bridge site I (Southwark)	LBI95	Neronian to early 2nd century (warehouses)	Similar range of early amphorae to Regis House
Miles Lane	ILA79	Quays, mainly Flavian and early 2nd century	Despite the portuary nature of the quays, the pottery is that of an unexceptional occupation site
New Fresh Wharf and St Magnus House	NFW74 & SM75	Quays dated mainly to the early 3rd century, but including later material	'New' Central and East Gaulish samian, fine wares and a range of other imported wares including late amphorae
Peninsular House	PEN79	Includes a 1st-century quay, but most notable for late material	Most notable for a range of late Roman amphorae and other imported wares
Pudding Lane	PDN81	Activity similar to that at Regis House in the 1st century, then a break, Central and East Gaulish samian up to the end of the 2nd century	Mainly early amphorae and 2nd-century samian
Regis House	KWS94	Intensive portuary activity c AD 50–130; occupation from 130 to end of 2nd century; further occupation in 4th century	Amphorae, especially pre-AD 70, South Gaulish samian, Les Martres de Veyre samian, Pompeian Red ware 3
Seal House	SH74	Much disturbed late material	Similar material to New Fresh Wharf (above)
Suffolk House	SUF94	Quay, and 'Governor's Palace' buildings, mainly AD 80–120, with some later occupation	High imports, especially South Gaulish samian, but also Romano-British oxidised flagons
Swan Lane	SWA81	Quays from the 2nd to 4th centuries	Similar material to New Fresh Wharf (above)
Three Quays House	LTS95	Late 2nd-century waterfronts	Wholly dominated by Central Gaulish samian
Toppings and Sun Wharves (Southwark)	TW70	Neronian to mid 2nd century, some 3rd to 4th century	Occupation-like pottery, not analysed

Key to Tables 5–8

BB	Black-burnished	JLE	Jubilee Line Extension sites: site codes BGH95, LBA95, LBI95, REW92 and TOM95
City	A group of smaller sites in the City: site codes BAX95, ETA89, FCC95, IRL95, NST94 and OBL97	KWS94	Regis House
		ONE94	I Poultry
EH S'k	English Heritage-funded backlog sites: site codes 107BHS81, 11STS77, 120BHS89, 170BHS79, 175BHS76, 179BHS89, 213BHS77, 2SSBS85, 4STS82, AB78, CH75, CW83, GDV96, GHL89, HIB79, SB76, SCC77, SKS88, STE95, STS88, USA88 and USB88	R-B	Romano-British
		SUF94	Suffolk House

Table 5a A comparison of pottery ware types between portuary, City and Southwark sites: numbers of rows and sherds. (*The apparent anomaly of having more rows than sherds in the miscellaneous category of SUF94 is due to the recording of a small amount of pottery recorded from sieving without sherd-count)

	ROWS						SHERDS					
	Portuary sites		City		Southwark		Portuary sites		City		Southwark	
Fabric type	SUF94	KWS94	ONE94	City	EH S'k	JLE	SUF94	KWS94	ONE94	City	EH S'k	JLE
Amphorae	99	1429	2014	1341	2681	1578	326	4984	6248	4112	8229	4627
Samian	246	2445	3246	1781	4102	1982	635	5762	5916	2845	7360	3252
Imported fine wares	10	169	303	190	657	140	21	444	766	253	1281	260
R-B fine wares	60	302	1188	624	1514	483	103	549	1682	1025	2625	744
BB-type wares	49	755	1544	1858	3263	984	76	1862	2335	3585	8683	1769
Fine reduced wares	72	509	629	539	1541	634	132	991	1087	1082	3368	1207
Reduced wares	260	2408	4046	3223	6971	3260	699	5599	8826	8560	22759	8113
Tempered wares	49	470	1049	628	2059	880	58	1056	2470	1292	4912	1905
Oxidised wares	203	2266	3349	2730	6221	2461	780	6775	8740	6689	19845	5883
Miscellaneous	6*	29	116	100	136	35	1	31	131	162	217	38
Total	1054	10782	17484	13014	29145	12437	2831	28053	38201	29605	79279	27798

Table 5b A comparison of pottery ware types between portuary, City and Southwark sites: percentages of rows and sherds

| | ROWS | | | | | | SHERDS | | | | | |
| | Portuary sites | | City | | Southwark | | Portuary sites | | City | | Southwark | |
Fabric type	SUF94	KWS94	ONE94	City	EH S'k	JLE	SUF94	KWS94	ONE94	City	EH S'k	JLE
Amphorae	9.4%	13.3%	11.5%	10.3%	9.2%	12.7%	11.5%	17.8%	16.4%	13.9%	10.4%	16.6%
Samian	23.3%	22.7%	18.6%	13.7%	14.1%	15.9%	22.4%	20.5%	15.5%	9.6%	9.3%	11.7%
Imported fine wares	0.9%	1.6%	1.7%	1.5%	2.3%	1.1%	0.7%	1.6%	2.0%	0.9%	1.6%	0.9%
R-B fine wares	5.7%	2.8%	6.8%	4.8%	5.2%	3.9%	3.6%	2.0%	4.4%	3.5%	3.3%	2.7%
BB-type wares	4.6%	7.0%	8.8%	14.3%	11.2%	7.9%	2.7%	6.6%	6.1%	12.1%	11.0%	6.4%
Fine reduced wares	6.8%	4.7%	3.6%	4.1%	5.3%	5.1%	4.7%	3.5%	2.8%	3.7%	4.2%	4.3%
Reduced wares	24.7%	22.3%	23.1%	24.8%	23.9%	26.2%	24.7%	20.0%	23.1%	28.9%	28.7%	29.2%
Tempered wares	4.6%	4.4%	6.0%	4.8%	7.1%	7.1%	2.0%	3.8%	6.5%	4.4%	6.2%	6.9%
Oxidised wares	19.3%	21.0%	19.2%	21.0%	21.3%	19.8%	27.6%	24.2%	22.9%	22.6%	25.0%	21.2%
Miscellaneous	0.6%	0.3%	0.7%	0.8%	0.5%	0.3%	0.0%	0.1%	0.3%	0.5%	0.3%	0.1%
Total	100.0%	100.0%	100.0%	100.0%	100.0%	100.0%	100.0%	100.0%	100.0%	100.0%	100.0%	100.0%

Table 6a A comparison of the origins of pottery types between portuary, City and Southwark sites: numbers of rows and sherds

| | ROWS | | | | | | SHERDS | | | | | |
| | Portuary sites | | City | | Southwark | | Portuary sites | | City | | Southwark | |
Origin	SUF94	KWS94	ONE94	City	EH S'k	JLE	SUF94	KWS94	ONE94	City	EH S'k	JLE
Britain	678	6516	11581	9443	21282	8568	1829	16506	24687	21977	61666	19426
Central Gaul	63	687	1019	903	1574	503	94	1692	1675	1358	2831	893
East Gaul	7	85	474	256	693	164	9	184	653	381	1227	239
Gaul	3	13	40	45	100	15	5	14	45	54	180	19
Italy	4	55	33	36	82	37	5	84	57	49	138	84
Mediterranean	9	114	97	72	124	95	26	191	262	554	220	206
North Gaul	13	161	134	118	177	92	17	291	277	194	386	135
Rhône Valley	23	402	492	370	736	428	82	1132	1270	953	1976	1155
South Gaul	181	1804	2037	771	2350	1429	538	4278	4331	1317	4270	2357
Iberian Peninsula	36	619	1002	609	1236	738	143	3114	4124	2097	4829	2676
Unknown	37	326	575	391	791	368	83	567	820	671	1556	608
Total	1054	10782	17484	13014	29145	12437	2831	28053	38201	29605	79279	27798

Table 6b A comparison of the origins of pottery types between portuary, City and Southwark sites: percentages of rows and sherds, including Romano-British wares

| | ROWS | | | | | | SHERDS | | | | | |
| | Portuary sites | | City | | Southwark | | Portuary sites | | City | | Southwark | |
Origin	SUF94	KWS94	ONE94	City	EH S'k	JLE	SUF94	KWS94	ONE94	City	EH S'k	JLE
Britain	64.3%	60.4%	66.2%	72.6%	73.0%	68.9%	64.6%	58.8%	64.6%	74.2%	77.8%	69.9%
Central Gaul	6.0%	6.4%	5.8%	6.9%	5.4%	4.0%	3.3%	6.0%	4.4%	4.6%	3.6%	3.2%
East Gaul	0.7%	0.8%	2.7%	2.0%	2.4%	1.3%	0.3%	0.7%	1.7%	1.3%	1.5%	0.9%
Gaul	0.3%	0.1%	0.2%	0.3%	0.3%	0.1%	0.2%	0.0%	0.1%	0.2%	0.2%	0.1%
Italy	0.4%	0.5%	0.2%	0.3%	0.3%	0.3%	0.2%	0.3%	0.1%	0.2%	0.2%	0.3%
Mediterranean	0.9%	1.1%	0.6%	0.6%	0.4%	0.8%	0.9%	0.7%	0.7%	1.9%	0.3%	0.7%
North Gaul	1.2%	1.5%	0.8%	0.9%	0.6%	0.7%	0.6%	1.0%	0.7%	0.7%	0.5%	0.5%
Rhône Valley	2.2%	3.7%	2.8%	2.8%	2.5%	3.4%	2.9%	4.0%	3.3%	3.2%	2.5%	4.2%
South Gaul	17.2%	16.7%	11.7%	5.9%	8.1%	11.5%	19.0%	15.2%	11.3%	4.4%	5.4%	8.5%
Iberian Peninsula	3.4%	5.7%	5.7%	4.7%	4.2%	5.9%	5.1%	11.1%	10.8%	7.1%	6.1%	9.6%
Unknown	3.6%	3.1%	3.4%	3.1%	2.8%	3.0%	3.0%	2.1%	2.2%	2.3%	2.0%	2.2%
Total	100.0%	100.0%	100.0%	100.0%	100.0%	100.0%	100.0%	100.0%	100.0%	100.0%	100.0%	100.0%
% Imported wares	35.7%	39.6%	33.8%	27.4%	27.0%	31.1%	35.4%	41.2%	35.4%	25.8%	22.2%	30.1%

Table 6c A comparison of the origins of pottery types between portuary, City and Southwark sites: percentages of rows and sherds, excluding Romano-British wares

| | ROWS | | | | | | SHERDS | | | | | |
| | Portuary sites | | City | | Southwark | | Portuary sites | | City | | Southwark | |
Origin	SUF94	KWS94	ONE94	City	EH S'k	JLE	SUF94	KWS94	ONE94	City	EH S'k	JLE
Central Gaul	16.8%	16.1%	17.3%	25.3%	20.0%	13.0%	9.4%	14.7%	12.4%	17.8%	16.1%	10.7%
East Gaul	1.9%	2.0%	8.0%	7.2%	8.8%	4.2%	0.9%	1.6%	4.8%	5.0%	7.0%	2.9%
Gaul	0.8%	0.3%	0.7%	1.3%	1.3%	0.4%	0.5%	0.1%	0.3%	0.7%	1.0%	0.2%
Italy	1.1%	1.3%	0.6%	1.0%	1.0%	1.0%	0.5%	0.7%	0.4%	0.6%	0.8%	1.0%
Mediterranean	2.4%	2.7%	1.6%	2.0%	1.6%	2.5%	2.6%	1.7%	1.9%	7.3%	1.2%	2.5%
North Gaul	3.5%	3.8%	2.3%	3.3%	2.3%	2.4%	1.7%	2.5%	2.0%	2.5%	2.2%	1.6%
Rhône Valley	6.1%	9.4%	8.3%	10.4%	9.4%	11.1%	8.2%	9.8%	9.4%	12.5%	11.2%	13.8%
South Gaul	48.1%	42.3%	34.5%	21.6%	29.9%	36.9%	53.7%	37.0%	32.0%	17.3%	24.2%	28.2%
Iberian Peninsula	9.6%	14.5%	17.0%	17.1%	15.7%	19.1%	14.3%	27.0%	30.5%	27.5%	27.4%	32.0%
Unknown	9.8%	7.6%	9.7%	10.9%	10.1%	9.5%	8.3%	4.9%	6.1%	8.8%	8.8%	7.3%
Total	100.0%	100.0%	100.0%	100.0%	100.0%	100.0%	100.0%	100.0%	100.0%	100.0%	100.0%	100.0%

Table 7a A comparison of pottery forms between portuary, City and Southwark sites: numbers of rows and sherds

| | ROWS | | | | | | SHERDS | | | | | |
| | Portuary sites | | City | | Southwark | | Portuary sites | | City | | Southwark | |
Form types	SUF94	KWS94	ONE94	City	EH S'k	JLE	SUF94	KWS94	ONE94	City	EH S'k	JLE
Amphorae	100	1463	1902	1337	2682	1613	338	5084	6254	4111	8471	4708
Beakers	62	532	857	674	1626	712	115	1125	1508	1307	3844	1306
Bowls	122	1121	1832	1264	2810	1309	227	2652	3185	2539	6135	2425
Bowls/dishes	24	229	634	711	967	370	35	481	952	1220	2102	616
Cups	67	607	654	465	876	436	171	1214	1178	747	1520	696
Dishes	114	981	1332	786	1724	816	283	2091	2341	1343	2993	1429
Flagons	42	387	504	400	1103	412	80	1611	1552	949	4161	844
Flagons/amphorae	2	10	10	2	10	31	3	11	46	4	28	44
Jars	203	2523	3298	2793	5853	2998	481	6320	7645	6682	16953	7499
Lids	40	274	228	321	757	320	79	451	351	646	1204	616
Mortaria	46	332	814	479	898	399	88	654	1198	748	1362	565
Other forms	14	112	122	82	247	99	22	165	142	117	467	152
Unidentified	218	2211	5297	3700	9592	2922	909	6194	11849	9192	30039	6898
Total	1054	10782	17484	13014	29145	12437	2831	28053	38201	29605	79279	27798

Table 7b A comparison of pottery forms between portuary, City and Southwark sites: percentages of rows and sherds

| | ROWS | | | | | | SHERDS | | | | | |
| | Portuary sites | | City | | Southwark | | Portuary sites | | City | | Southwark | |
Form types	SUF94	KWS94	ONE94	City	EH S'k	JLE	SUF94	KWS94	ONE94	City	EH S'k	JLE
Amphorae	9.5%	13.6%	10.9%	10.3%	9.2%	13.0%	11.9%	18.1%	16.4%	13.9%	10.7%	16.9%
Beakers	5.9%	4.9%	4.9%	5.2%	5.6%	5.7%	4.1%	4.0%	3.9%	4.4%	4.8%	4.7%
Bowls	11.6%	10.4%	10.5%	9.7%	9.6%	10.5%	8.0%	9.5%	8.3%	8.6%	7.7%	8.7%
Bowls/dishes	2.3%	2.1%	3.6%	5.5%	3.3%	3.0%	1.2%	1.7%	2.5%	4.1%	2.7%	2.2%
Cups	6.4%	5.6%	3.7%	3.6%	3.0%	3.5%	6.0%	4.3%	3.1%	2.5%	1.9%	2.5%
Dishes	10.8%	9.1%	7.6%	6.0%	5.9%	6.6%	10.0%	7.5%	6.1%	4.5%	3.8%	5.1%
Flagons	4.0%	3.6%	2.9%	3.1%	3.8%	3.3%	2.8%	5.7%	4.1%	3.2%	5.2%	3.0%
Flagons/amphorae	0.2%	0.1%	0.1%	0.0%	0.0%	0.2%	0.1%	0.0%	0.1%	0.0%	0.0%	0.2%
Jars	19.3%	23.4%	18.9%	21.5%	20.1%	24.1%	17.0%	22.5%	20.0%	22.6%	21.4%	27.0%
Lids	3.8%	2.5%	1.3%	2.5%	2.6%	2.6%	2.8%	1.6%	0.9%	2.2%	1.5%	2.2%
Mortaria	4.4%	3.1%	4.7%	3.7%	3.1%	3.2%	3.1%	2.3%	3.1%	2.5%	1.7%	2.0%
Other forms	1.3%	1.0%	0.7%	0.6%	0.8%	0.8%	0.8%	0.6%	0.4%	0.4%	0.6%	0.5%
Unidentified	20.7%	20.5%	30.3%	28.4%	32.9%	23.5%	32.1%	22.1%	31.0%	31.0%	37.9%	24.8%
Total	100.0%	100.0%	100.0%	100.0%	100.0%	100.0%	100.0%	100.0%	100.0%	100.0%	100.0%	100.0%

Table 8a A comparison of pottery functions between portuary, City and Southwark sites: numbers of rows and sherds

| | ROWS | | | | | | SHERDS | | | | | |
| | Portuary sites | | City | | Southwark | | Portuary sites | | City | | Southwark | |
Pottery functions	SUF94	KWS94	ONE94	City	EH S'k	JLE	SUF94	KWS94	ONE94	City	EH S'k	JLE
Drinking	129	1139	1511	1139	2502	1148	286	2339	2686	2054	5364	2002
Liquid container	45	432	526	411	1146	453	84	1678	1720	964	4240	929
Table	92	1017	1163	470	1288	870	265	2715	2637	949	2282	1708
Kitchen/table	133	1016	2211	1774	3073	1271	216	1886	3198	2882	5341	2059
Kitchen	232	2259	3605	3015	6311	2812	541	5547	7376	7136	17250	6376
Kitchen/storage	88	1049	986	975	2067	1090	165	2026	1729	1867	3907	2536
Storage	5	85	172	103	196	161	13	424	631	322	957	439
Transport	103	1474	1912	1344	2717	1626	341	5108	6264	4125	8525	4723
Ritual/transport	0	2	15	7	15	7	0	2	19	10	17	8
Ritual	2	62	54	56	193	51	2	78	59	70	1264	86
Lighting	3	14	12	4	24	14	3	31	20	14	61	20
Writing	1	15	5	6	9	7	1	16	10	7	10	9
Unknown	221	2218	5312	3710	9604	2927	914	6203	11852	9205	30061	6903
Total	1054	10782	17484	13014	29145	12437	2831	28053	38201	29605	79279	27798

Table 8b A comparison of pottery functions between portuary, City and Southwark sites: percentages of rows and sherds

| | ROWS | | | | | | SHERDS | | | | | |
| | Portuary sites | | City | | Southwark | | Portuary sites | | City | | Southwark | |
Pottery functions	SUF94	KWS94	ONE94	City	EH S'k	JLE	SUF94	KWS94	ONE94	City	EH S'k	JLE
Drinking	12.2%	10.6%	8.6%	8.8%	8.6%	9.2%	10.1%	8.3%	7.0%	6.9%	6.8%	7.2%
Liquid container	4.3%	4.0%	3.0%	3.2%	3.9%	3.6%	3.0%	6.0%	4.5%	3.3%	5.3%	3.3%
Table	8.7%	9.4%	6.7%	3.6%	4.4%	7.0%	9.4%	9.7%	6.9%	3.2%	2.9%	6.1%
Kitchen/table	12.6%	9.4%	12.6%	13.6%	10.5%	10.2%	7.6%	6.7%	8.4%	9.7%	6.7%	7.4%
Kitchen	22.0%	21.0%	20.6%	23.2%	21.7%	22.6%	19.1%	19.8%	19.3%	24.1%	21.8%	22.9%
Kitchen/storage	8.3%	9.7%	5.6%	7.5%	7.1%	8.8%	5.8%	7.2%	4.5%	6.3%	4.9%	9.1%
Storage	0.5%	0.8%	1.0%	0.8%	0.7%	1.3%	0.5%	1.5%	1.7%	1.1%	1.2%	1.6%
Transport	9.8%	13.7%	10.9%	10.3%	9.3%	13.1%	12.0%	18.2%	16.4%	13.9%	10.8%	17.0%
Ritual/transport	0.0%	0.0%	0.1%	0.1%	0.1%	0.1%	0.0%	0.0%	0.0%	0.0%	0.0%	0.0%
Ritual	0.2%	0.6%	0.3%	0.4%	0.7%	0.4%	0.1%	0.3%	0.2%	0.2%	1.6%	0.3%
Lighting	0.3%	0.1%	0.1%	0.0%	0.1%	0.1%	0.1%	0.1%	0.1%	0.0%	0.1%	0.1%
Writing	0.1%	0.1%	0.0%	0.0%	0.0%	0.1%	0.0%	0.1%	0.0%	0.0%	0.0%	0.0%
Unknown	21.0%	20.6%	30.4%	28.5%	33.0%	23.5%	32.3%	22.1%	31.0%	31.1%	37.9%	24.8%
Total	100.0%	100.0%	100.0%	100.0%	100.0%	100.0%	100.0%	100.0%	100.0%	100.0%	100.0%	100.0%

Discussion of Tables 5–8

The sites

All the data in Tables 5–8 are derived from the Museum of London Specialist Services/MoLAS Oracle database, which means that they are derived mainly from sites excavated by MoLAS and spot-dated since the autumn of 1995. Some sites are included which were excavated long before that date but have only been recently spot-dated, but conversely many sites which were spot-dated in the 1970s, 1980s and the early 1990s cannot yet be included because they have not been transferred from the previous Unix system into the Oracle database. Most of the sites spot-dated before 1995 do not include sherd-count; only a few such sites have been transferred, and in those cases quantification is possible only by rows (see below). The first column represents the pottery from Suffolk House (SUF94); the second column represents pottery from recent excavations at Regis House (KWS94), a waterfront site adjacent to the north end of the Roman bridge across the Thames, and the third column represents pottery from the recent site at 1 Poultry (ONE94), on the western bank of the Walbrook just south of the Roman forum. The fourth column represents a group of recently excavated sites in the City of London. The last two columns represent two groupings of sites in Southwark, EH S'k and JLE, which form part of two major joint MoLAS/MoL Specialist Services projects, the first being a forthcoming English Heritage-funded project on Roman Southwark (Cowan in prep), and the second a project on the Southwark sites of the Jubilee Line Extension, funded by London Underground (Sidell et al in prep).

Quantification

Rows can be defined as the number of records in the MoLAS/MoLSS Oracle database, each of which contains all examples of each unique fabric, form and decoration combination (Tables 9–11 expand the abbreviations used in the catalogue below). Discussions of the use of rows as a means of quantification occur in a number of recent MoLAS/MoLSS publications, most notably in Rauxloh and Symonds (in prep). In practice, rows function in a very similar manner to 'minimum numbers of vessels', or the measurement most commonly used in francophone countries, 'minimum numbers of individuals' (NMIs).

Anomalies

Tables 5–8 show immediately that the two port sites, Suffolk House (SUF94) and Regis House (KWS94), are exceptional. For example, Table 5b shows that both sites have the highest overall percentages (more than 20%) of samian ware, and Regis House has the highest overall percentage of amphorae. Curiously, Suffolk House also has the highest percentage of oxidised wares by *sherd-count*, although the percentage of oxidised wares by *rows* is not exceptional. This seems likely to derive from a group of near complete flagons, although it could also represent a larger number of broken flagons, whose key characteristics of fabric, form and decoration are identical. This latter possibility might seem more logical at a portuary site, if one accepts the idea that coarse Romano-British pottery may have been brought into London by riverine transport to the same quays at which wares arrived from the Continent. Table 6b shows that the two portuary sites also have the highest percentages of imported wares (by sherd-count SUF94 and ONE94 appear to be identical at 35.4%, but the difference is 0.018% in favour of Suffolk House). Table 6c shows that the largest proportion of these wares are from south Gaul, which means essentially samian ware from La Graufesenque. Undoubtedly a significant factor in these percentages is the fact that both of these particular portuary sites are early – that is, 1st and 2nd centuries – whereas many of the other sites included, in particular 1 Poultry, have important contexts belonging to the late Roman period, when both samian wares and amphorae are less abundant not only in Britain but throughout the northern provinces of the Empire. Among the form types shown in Table 7, there are relatively few differences between the various sites that appear to be significant, with the possible exception of dishes and cups, which are both higher at the portuary sites, probably because of the high levels of samian ware at both sites. A similar explanation probably pertains to the functions of vessels, shown in Table 8, where drinking vessels and table vessels are both higher at the portuary sites than elsewhere.

In spite of the apparent importance of the anomalies visible in the above data, it is important to recognise the limitations of this kind of analysis, particularly when applied to portuary sites, where pottery itself may be among the most important commodities passing through the site. Although the high percentages of certain types seem to offer a window on the commerce involved, it remains more or less impossible to know in what quantities various types may have been passing through, unbroken. Also, it is not easy to know how the regionally produced Romano-British types arrived at the site, in other words whether these types arrived with the dockworkers, or in the material dumped in the quays as fill, or by boat as pottery to be redistributed in the same manner as the wares imported from the Continent. All the same, when one encounters large groups of samian wares, as at Regis House and Three Quays House, and when one looks at the cumulative evidence provided by all the sites described above, or at least those situated on the north bank of the Thames, one can easily imagine a portuary industry which might it some ways have been equally as important as the sites from which the various imported wares emanated.

All the above aspects add up to a rather unusual site.

Table 9 Roman pottery fabric codes

Code	Description
Amphorae	
AMPH	Miscellaneous amphora fabric type
BAETE	Baetican Dressel 20/Haltern 70 amphora fabric, early
C189	Camulodunum type 189 amphora fabric
F148	Fishbourne type 148.3 amphora fabric
GAUL	Miscellaneous Gaulish amphora fabric
GAUL1	Pélichet 47/Dressel 30 amphora fabric
LIPR	Lipari (Richborough 527) amphora fabric
Imported fine wares	
CCIMP	Miscellaneous imported colour-coated ware
KOLN	Cologne Colour-coated ware
Romano-British fine wares	
LOMA	London Marbled
NVCC	Nene Valley Colour-coated ware
OXRC	Oxfordshire Red/Brown Colour-coated ware
VRMI	?Verulamium Region Mica-dusted ware
Fine reduced wares	
FMIC	Fine Micaceous Black/Grey ware
Reduced wares	
AHSU	Alice Holt/Surrey ware
HWC	Highgate 'C' Sand-tempered ware
SAND	Miscellaneous sand-tempered ware
VRG	Verulamium Region Grey ware
Tempered wares	
GROG	Grog-tempered ware
HWB	Highgate 'B' Grog-tempered ware
SHEL	Miscellaneous shell-tempered ware
Oxidised wares	
EIFL	Eifelkeramik
NFSE	North French/South-east English Oxidised ware
PORD	Portchester 'D' ware
RHWW	Rhineland White ware
VRW	Verulamium Region White ware

Table 10 Roman pottery form codes

Code	Description
1A	Collared (or Hofheim-type) flagon
1B2	Ring-necked flagon with flaring mouth
1B4	Ring-necked flagon with everted neck; prominent rim
1B5	Ring-necked flagon with very prominent rounded rim
1C	Pinch-mouthed flagon
2	Miscellaneous or otherwise unidentifiable jar
2A16	Lid seated bead-rim jar
2U	Narrow-necked globular jar
3	Miscellaneous or otherwise unidentifiable beaker
3B	Ovoid beaker
4	Miscellaneous or otherwise unidentifiable bowl
4A	Reeded-rim bowl
4DR29	Dragendorff form 29 bowl
4F	Bowl with flat, hooked or folded-over rims
4F4	Bowl with folded-down rim; constriction below rim
4F6	Bowl with flat square profile rim
4K	'Surrey bowl'
4M	Black-burnished-type flanged bowl
4RT12	Ritterling form 12 bowl
5	Miscellaneous or otherwise unidentifiable plate
5DR15/17	Dragendorff form 15/17 dish
6DR24/25	Dragendorff form 24/25 cup
6RT8	Ritterling form 8 cup
7	Miscellaneous or otherwise unidentified mortarium
7BEF	Bead and flange mortarium
7DR45	Dragendorff form 45 mortarium
7G238	Hartley group ii mortarium
7HOF	Hooked flange mortarium
8	Miscellaneous amphorae
8C189	Camulodunum form 189 amphora
8DR2–4	Dressel form 2–4 amphora
8DR20	Dressel form 20 amphora
8DR20PW18	Dressel form 20 amphora (Peacock & Williams, 1986, fig 65.18)
8F148	Fishbourne type 148.3 amphora
8G4	Gauloise type 4 amphora
8R527	Richborough form 527 (Lipari amphora)
9A	Lid (usually post-70)
9GL	Castor box lid

Table 11 Roman pottery decoration codes

Code	Description
AL	Black-burnished-type acute-lattice decoration
BAD	Barbotine decoration
RCD1	Sand/quartz roughcast decoration
ROD	Rouletted decoration
SPT	Spout
WBAD	White barbotine decoration

Catalogue of illustrated pottery

[788] (2.4) W4 (AD 50–140)
<P1> (Fig 22)
AHSU 4K, 2 sherds, AD 50–140
Probably an early version of a 'Surrey bowl' in Alice Holt Surrey ware.

[528] (3.3) W4 (AD 100–20)
<P2> (Fig 22)
SAND 4, 4 sherds, AD 50–400
Profile unusual form.

<P3> (Fig 22)
VRM1 5, 1 sherd, AD 70–120

[624] (4.2) W3 (AD 100–20)
<P4> (Fig 13)
BAETE 8DR20PW18 <262>, burnt, 2 sherds, AD 70–170
Stamp. Reads OCR but probably QCR (Callender 1965, 1442) dated AD 60–110 by Callender.

<P5> (Fig 13)
GAUL1 8G4, 2 sherds, AD 50–250
Intact rim and neck.

[689] (4.4) W4 (AD 100–20)
<P6> (Fig 22)
AHSU 4K, burnt and sooted, 1 sherd, AD 50–140

<P7> (Fig 22)
AMPH 8DR2–4, burnt, 2 sherds, AD 50–150
Handle and rim. Two fabrics.

<P8> (Fig 22)
C189 8C189, residue present, 16 sherds, AD 50–150
100% of rim.

<P9> (Fig 22)
FMIC 2, 4 sherds, AD 50–120
Heavy cordons below neck. Pedestal base. Narrow neck.

<P10> (Fig 22)
HWC 4F, burnt and sooted, 3 sherds, AD 70–140

<P11> (Fig 22)
HWC 4F4, burnt and sooted, 3 sherds, AD 70–140

<P12> (Fig 22)
KOLN 3B RCD1, 2 sherds, AD 100–20
Indented.

<P13> (Fig 22)
NFSE 7G238, burnt and sooted, 1 sherd, AD 50–100
Spout.

<P14> (Fig 22)
SAND 4F6?, burnt and sooted, 2 sherds, AD 100–60
Girth grooves like 4A type reeded-rim bowl.

<P15> (Fig 22)
VRW 1B2, burnt, 1 sherd, AD 70–120

<P16> (Fig 22)
VRW 1B4, burnt, 2 sherds, AD 100–50
1 burnt.

<P17> (Fig 22)
VRW 1C, burnt, 1 sherd, AD 60–160

<P18> (Fig 22)
VRW 7HOF <226>, burnt and worn, 4 sherds, AD 50–140
Profile. Two stamps. Read SOLLUSF. Over 50% of vessel present. Slightly burnt.

<P19> (Fig 22)
VRW 7HOF <260>, 1 sherd, AD 50–140
Stamp MARINVS.

<P20> (Fig 22)
VRW 7HOF <261>, abraded and burnt, 1 sherd, AD 50–140
Stamp. Reads –VII?

<P21> (Fig 22)
VRW 9A, burnt, 2 sherds, AD 50–160
Profile.

[623] (5.1) W4 (AD 120–60)
<P22> (Fig 28)
LIPR 8R527, burnt, 1 sherd, AD 50–150

<P23> (Fig 28)
VRW 1A, 1 sherd, AD 50–100
Variant form with two handles and square rim.

[600] (5.1) W4 (AD 120–60)
<P24> (Fig 28)
LOMA 4, 1 sherd, AD 70–120
Unusual form.

<P25> (Fig 28)
VRW 1B4?, burnt, 1 sherd, AD 100–50
Not a large vessel but has a slightly prominent top rim – intermediate between a 1B2 and a 1B5.

[698] (5.1) W4 (AD 120–60)
<P26> (Fig 28)
GAUL1 8G4, burnt, 5 sherds, AD
50–250
Burnt around entire rim top.

<P27> (Fig 28)
VRW 4?, 1 sherd, AD 50–160
Red paint residue, very unusual.

<P28> (Fig 28)
VRW 7HOF <277>, burnt, 1 sherd,
AD 50–140
Stamp ..VGVD

[688] (5.12) W4 (AD 70–100)
<P29> (Fig 22)
VRG 2A16, 1 sherd, AD 50–100
Variant with short neck.

[711] (7.1) B2 (AD 120–60)
<P30> (Fig 34)
GROG 2 AL, 7 sherds, AD 120–250
HWB-like unusual Black-burnished-
like jar.

[678] (7.2) B2 (AD 60–100)
<P31> (Fig 34)
AHSU 2U, 10 sherds, AD 50–160
Good example large sherds.

[676] (7.3) B2 (AD 70–120)
<P32> (Fig 34)
BAETE 8DR20 <228>, 1 sherd,
AD 50–170
Stamp SATVRNI on handle.

[677] (7.3) B2 (AD 120–40)
<P33> (Fig 34)
GROG 4K, 1 sherd, AD 50–140
HWB-like.

[904] (8.4) B3 (AD 120–400)
<P34> (Fig 42)
NVCC 3 WBAD ROD, 6 sherds,
AD 180–300
No rim so uncertain whether necked
(Howe et al 1980, fig 5, nos 47–50, and
see their discussion on dating, p 20).

<P35> (Fig 42)
NVCC 9GL ROD, 7 sherds,
AD 200–400
Two-thirds of vessel (cf Howe et al
1980, fig 7, no. 89. Probably 3rd
century; see their discussion on
dating, p 24). Profile.

[899] (8.15) B3 (AD 300–400)
<P36> (Fig 42)
RHWW?, 7 SPT, 1 sherd,
AD 50–300
Very large diameter.

[503] (10.3) S1 (AD 140–250)
<P37> (Fig 44)
CCIMP 4 BAD, 1 sherd,
AD 50–400
Unusual decor and form;
unknown source.

<P38> (Fig 44)
GAUL 8, 2 sherds, AD 50–250
Rim; micaceous fabric. Gaulish
source?

[547] (10.7) B5 (AD 140–200)
<P39> (Fig 47)
RHWW 7BEF SPT, 1 sherd,
AD 140–200
Abundant red siltstone
inclusions.

[494] (10.9) B5 (AD 270–400)
<P40> (Fig 47)
OXRC 7DR45 SPT, 1 sherd,
AD 270–300
Ear of spout and incised lines.

<P41> (Fig 47)
SHEL 4M, 1 sherd, AD 250–400
Flanged bowl in form more
common in PORD and EIFL.

[17] (1.5) OA2 (AD 50–400)
<P42> (Fig 10)
F148 8F148, 1 sherd
Fishbourne Type 148.3 amphora
rim.

6.6 The Roman finds

Angela Wardle

Introduction

The site produced some 350 accessioned finds, mostly of
Roman date. Much of the metalwork was especially well preserved
in the anaerobic waterfront deposits, and organic remains,

wood and leather, also survived; the wooden objects, shoe
and non-shoe leather are dealt with separately. Away from the
waterfronts, in the quarry pits of Open Area 3 or in the buildings,
for example, preservation was less good, with burial conditions
more akin to those found on inland areas.

The objects are discussed here by stratigraphic group and
within each group in accordance with their perceived function.
The catalogue is also arranged by function and not by material
using the broad classification devised by Nina Crummy for
Colchester (1983). In a relatively small assemblage this is
thought to give a good general overview.

Open Area 2

This marshy area contained several objects of Roman date,
including some of the earliest material from the site, with a coin
of Antonia (AD 41–5). The metalwork, as in other waterlogged
contexts, was generally well preserved, but there was some
contamination from later deposits as demonstrated by the
presence of a medieval spangle. A one-piece copper-alloy brooch
of the type known as a Nauheim derivative <141> dates from
the early to mid 1st century, and although they are too small
for the exact type to be distinguished three fragments of mirror
are likely to be dated well within the 1st century. Three well-
preserved iron styli are of the more common simple types,
often, although not exclusively, found in 1st- and 2nd-century
contexts in London. Other finds comprise a copper-alloy spoon
with round bowl, the sides flattened perhaps deliberately to
form a scoop, miscellaneous fittings, studs and nails, also of
copper alloy, and several fragments that could be waste from
non-ferrous metalworking. There is a little glassware, and one
bottle <220> may be an import from the Mediterranean (see
The Roman glass, below). With the notable exception of leather
objects, the general character of this material is identical to that
found in the later waterfronts and it is highly likely that it
derived from the same source or sources.

Open Area 3 quarry pits

A coin of Valentinian [74] <8> (AD 364–78) is intrusive. There
are no other finds of any significance from this area: the copper-
alloy and iron is fragmentary and unrecognisable.

The buildings

As is very frequently the case in London, few objects were
found in the buildings themselves, and many of these were in
construction deposits. The finds, which are of mixed date, are
in general indistinguishable in character from those in the
waterfront dumps and, as waterfronts cannot be linked to specific
buildings, it is not possible to draw any conclusions about function
and status from the building assemblages. Although there is no
direct stratigraphic link, it is however possible that Waterfronts 1
and 2 could have functioned with Buildings 1 and 2, and
Waterfronts 3 and 4 with Buildings 3–5, although on balance,
Waterfront 3 was probably an interim extension of Waterfront 2.

Most of the objects from the buildings were personal or domestic items dating broadly from the 1st or 2nd century, for example part of a simple one-piece brooch from Building 1. An exception, also from Building 1, is a fragment of engraved glass vessel. A fragment of crucible <440> with gold residue adhering came from Building 2, while a complete crucible <243> (see Fig 73: <S28>) with gold residue was found in Building 4, further evidence of the working of precious metals in the area. A coin of Vespasian (AD 71) came from Building 2. The 'townhouse', Building 3, produced no accessioned finds. Contexts associated with Building 5 yielded a domestic group, comprising personal items, a needle and glassware.

The waterfront dumps

Most of the Roman objects from this site came from the waterfront dumps, with by far the largest quantity from deposits associated with Waterfront 4. The coins from Waterfronts 3 and 4 are all of 1st- to 2nd-century date or earlier, the latest an issue of Trajan, but the groups include a rare native Iron Age coin of Eppillus (AD 5–10) and a coin of Augustus (30 BC–AD 6).

Table 12 shows the number of identified Roman objects from each successive waterfront, listed by functional category. It is immediately obvious that there are more shoes and leather artefacts (Category 17) than any other type of object, preserved in the waterlogged conditions. Similarly several wooden objects were recovered, a wooden comb from Waterfront 4 <72> (see Fig 17: <S11>) (Category 2) and part of a writing tablet <70> (see Fig 18: <S21>) (Category 7). A second fragment of writing

tablet came from Open Area 2, where similar burial conditions prevailed, and from where the assemblage shows marked similarities to the waterfront material, both in content and in preservation.

Fixtures, fastenings and fittings (Category 11) generally constitute a major component of Roman urban groups and in a relatively small collection they form one of the most numerous categories, closely followed by personal ornament and dress accessories (Category 1). Among the latter are an exceptionally fine 2nd-century enamelled disc brooch <140> (see Fig 24: <S2>), a copper-alloy wire bracelet with twisted expanding clasp <173> (see Fig 23: <S3>) and copper-alloy hairpins <182> <104> (see Fig 15: <S7> <S8>), all from Waterfront 4. Other personal items are well represented (Category 2), comprising a nail cleaner <101> (see Fig 23: <S9>), tweezers <124> (see Fig 14: <S10>), an iron razor of classic Roman form <5> and fragmentary mirrors <85> <127> <178>. Fragments of simple rectangular and disc mirrors are relatively common finds in London, and are characterised by their distinctive alloy and sharp fracture. They were luxury items and the general pattern of distribution in south-east Britain probably reflects trading patterns with the Continent (Lloyd-Morgan 1977, 239).

Needles (Category 3) were found in a variety of materials, including iron, of which there were three examples from the waterfronts <131> (see Fig 14: <S13>) <192> <202>. Iron needles were undoubtedly in common use and may have been both less expensive than their copper-alloy counterparts and more effective for finer and indeed tougher materials than

Table 12 Registered finds by category and land use

Category	1	2	3	4	5	6	7	8	9	10	11	12	13	14	15	16	17	18
Open Area 2	2	3					5				3				6			
Waterfront 2																	4	
Waterfront 3				1							1							
Waterfront 4	8	7	6	5	2		1			4	21		2	1	18		61	1
Open Area 4	2																	
Building 1	1																	
Building 2	1														1			
Building 4															1			
Building 5	3		1															
Road 1				1														
Residual				1							1				7			
Total	17	10	7	8	2	0	6	0	0	4	26	0	2	1	33	0	65	1

Key to Table 12

1 Personal ornament and dress accessories
2 Cosmetic and medical implements
3 Textile production and working
4 Domestic utensils and furniture
5 Recreation and leisure
6 Weights and measures

7 Writing materials and associated objects
8 Objects associated with transport
9 Buildings and services
10 Tools
11 Fasteners and fittings
12 Agricultural implements

13 Military equipment
14 Objects associated with religious beliefs and practice
15 Metalworking waste
16 Boneworking waste
17 Shoes and leatherworking waste
18 Objects of uncertain function

bone, but they rarely survive in recognisable form in the archaeological record because of their fragility and the nature of the material. Most other iron needles of Roman date known from London come from similar waterlogged deposits, notably the collection from the Walbrook bed and banks (*eg* Bucklersbury House: Wilmott 1991, 131, nos 481–3; Roach Smith Collection: Manning 1985, 35).

The waterfront groups produced a few domestic items, notably a superbly preserved copper-alloy drop handle <138> (see Fig 14: <S15>), which still retains the double spiked loops by means of which it was secured to a chest or drawer. A flagon lid <143> is not an unusual find: metal vessels are well represented in London during the 1st and 2nd centuries, although being both expensive and recyclable they are rare in contrast to ceramic vessels of similar function. Three fragmentary lamps are basic utilitarian forms, two products of the Verulamium industries outside London, the other an imported *Firmalampe*, probably of Italian manufacture (<263> <272> <280>).

There are only two items from the dumps which have any association with leisure activity (Category 5), but one of the two bone counters <233> (see Fig 16: <S16>) is unusual in bearing an inscription 'A D'. Among the writing implements from the site (Category 7), a stylus with decorative mouldings <174> (see Fig 11: <S20>) of Manning Type 4 came from Open Area 2, together with three other well-preserved styli of plain form.

A limited number of other iron objects from the waterfront dumps are also in extremely good condition, although the knives are not complete. The most interesting tool is a chisel <132> (see Fig 29: <S22>) with a spatulate blade, perhaps used by a stone mason, an addition to the types known from London.

After leather shoes, the largest group from the waterfronts was the general category of fasteners and miscellaneous fittings, nails, studs and the like. All items are common Roman forms. Two fittings <128> <107> (see Fig 23: <S25>) come from armour (Category 13), a reminder of the undoubted military presence in London in the 1st and 2nd centuries. The decorative stud is typical of those found on 1st-century belts or aprons, although coming from Waterfront 4 it is clearly residual in its context.

One object with religious association (Category 14), an incomplete Venus figurine <244> (see Fig 25: <S26>), is of greater interest as it appears to be a waster, or at least a 'second', having suffered damage to its base during manufacture. The moulding is generally blurred and of poor quality. It is interesting to observe that it was thought worth importing such second-rate items to London, where there was, presumably, a market. The object could also, of course have been brought from Gaul as a personal possession.

A distinctive feature of these dumps is further evidence for the working of precious metals, in the form of two fragmentary crucibles. One of these and the examples from Buildings 2 and 4 have a bright yellow metallic residue adhering to the rim or inner surface. Analysis at the Ancient Monuments Laboratory has confirmed this to be gold, and that the crucibles provide evidence of cupellation, parting and melting of gold. Unlike the previous discoveries, the crucibles found in the recent excavations have no clay luting, but the form of the complete crucible is

similar to those found during earlier excavations in the area at Bush Lane (Marsden 1975, 100). One reasonable assumption is that they may all have derived ultimately from the same workshop or group of workshops, although one fragment was found in Building 2, the complete crucible in Building 4, and the other fragments in waterfront dumps. These were all on the east side of the site, the opposite side to Bush Lane, which implies the presence of a second goldworking centre on or near Suffolk House, possibly in Building 2. Either interpretation, however, strengthens the argument for a local source for the waterfront groups as a whole. Analysis of other industrial debris produced evidence for the working of other metals but this is not associated with any specific area or building.

Comparison with other waterfront groups

Other waterlogged deposits from London with well-preserved metalwork show a similar range of material, although in areas such as the Walbrook Valley this has been found in far greater quantities. More recent groups from the waterfront site at Regis House and the lower Walbrook site at 1 Poultry await publication. The significance of the finds from the Walbrook has already been the subject of several studies and merit further research. The finds from Suffolk House, which superficially at least resemble the Poultry material in general range, if not quantity, will provide useful comparison.

Catalogue

Category 1 Personal ornament and dress accessories

BROOCHES

<141> [569] (1.5) OA2 <S1> (Fig 10)
Complete: length 50mm. Copper-alloy one-piece brooch known as a Nauheim derivative. Stout plain wire bow with circular section, sharply angled below the head; plain catchplate. The type dates from the early to mid 1st century.

<140> [600] (5.1) W4 <S2> (Fig 24)
Complete: length 37mm. Copper-alloy enamelled disc brooch with peripheral lugs. Conical centre with a small knob divided into eight radial champlevé cells, the enamel colour now appearing ?red and green. A deep channel separates the centre from the rim which also had a series of triangular cells containing enamel of which only slight traces remain, colour indeterminate. A lug containing a circular field conceals the catchplate for the hinged pin, and on the

opposite side is a chain loop; on each side are three small lugs, spaced at equidistant intervals. The general type dates from the 2nd century.

<99> [623] (5.1) W4
Copper alloy. Fragment of pierced catchplate.

<446> [46] (6.9) B1
Copper alloy. Fragments of spring, very corroded, but possibly from a one-piece brooch.

BRACELETS

<173> [698] (5.1) W4 <S3> (Fig 23)
Complete: diameter 58mm. Copper alloy. Plain wire bracelet with a twisted expanding clasp. There are many examples of this type, as Crummy 1983, 39, fig 41, 1601, from Colchester.

<73> [496] (1.9) B5 <S4> (Fig 47)
Incomplete: approximate external diameter 80mm; shale armlet internal 63mm. Rectangular

section with radial notched decoration on the outer edge of both faces.

<75> [676] (7.3) B2 <S5> (Fig 34)
Incomplete: approximate external diameter 93mm; internal 73mm. Heavy shale armlet with ribbed outer face; the inside has the characteristic V-section, caused by cutting the circle from both sides of the parent block.

FINGER-RINGS

<190> [698] (5.1) W4
Incomplete: diameter 16mm. Copper-alloy ring made from a thin sheet, with wide front tapering sharply until there is only a thin strip of metal at the back. This is now broken and it is possible that the terminals were never joined, making the object either an expanding finger-ring, or possibly an earring. The metal is very pitted, but there may have been a punched design on the face, now irretrievable.

<108> [698] (5.1) W4
Nearly complete: length (distorted) 24mm. Copper-alloy ring key, now flattened; part of the pierced rectangular ward remains.

HAIRPINS

<231> [502] (10.3) B5 <S6> (Fig 44)
Complete: length 82.5mm. Bone. Spherical head, Crummy Type 3, with type A head.

<199> [502] (10.3) B5
Incomplete: length 56.5mm. Bone. Spherical head, Crummy Type 3, with type B head. Broken towards the bottom of the shaft.

<182> [527] (3.4) W4 <S7> (Fig 15)
Complete: length 99mm. Copper alloy. Knob head, below which are two cordons. Cool Type 6 (1991), which dates c AD 50–150.

<104> [623] (5.1) W4 <S8> (Fig 15)
Complete: length 92mm. Copper alloy. Knob head with single groove below. Cool Type 6 (1991), dating as above.

<371> [310] (12.1) OA4
Incomplete: length 32.5mm. Dark blue glass; part of stem with

swelling at centre, broken at each end. Late Roman form.

SHOENAILS

Hobnails from leather shoes or sandals came from the following areas:

<166> [569] (1.5) OA2
<180> [527] (3.4) W4
<56> [306] (11.2) OA4

Category 2 Cosmetic and medical implements

NAIL CLEANER

<101> [623] (5.1) W4 <S9> (Fig 23)
Complete: length 39.5mm. Copper alloy. Leaf-shaped, with engraved linear decoration along the edge and suspension loop at right angles to the blade. Mid to late 1st-century type, continuing into the 2nd century.

TWEEZERS

<124> [689] (4.4) W4 <S10> (Fig 14)
Complete: length 42.5mm. Copper alloy. Flared blades each with a bevelled inner edge and single groove along the outside edges.

MIRRORS

<85> [623] (5.1) W4
Incomplete: dimensions 21mm x 19mm x 0.8mm. Copper alloy. Fragment from circular mirror, with dot and circle decoration on the reflecting surface. The piece comes from near the edge, but the edge itself is not preserved. The reverse has turning marks.

<210> [692] (4.1) OA2
Incomplete: dimensions 13mm x 1.5mm x 0.9mm. Copper alloy. Rectangular fragment, plain, with roughened back.

<211> [692] (4.1) OA2
Incomplete: dimensions 15mm x 10mm x 0.7mm. Copper alloy. Fragment from the edge of a circular mirror; bevelled edge with turning marks on the reflective surface.

<209> [692] (4.1) OA2
Incomplete: dimensions 23mm x 13mm x 1.3mm. Copper alloy. Fragment, encrusted, but recognised as a mirror by the sharp fracture of the metal.

<127> [689] (4.4) W4
Incomplete: dimensions 27mm x 15mm x 1.5mm. Copper alloy. Fragment from the edge of a rectangular mirror with bevelled edge. Plain reflecting surface with characteristically rough reverse.

<178> [698] (5.1) W4
Incomplete: dimensions 17mm x 11mm x 0.5mm. Copper alloy. Fragment, trace of decorative turning mark visible on one surface.

RAZOR

<5> [160] (5.6) W4
Nearly complete: the blade is now bent and the handle loop incomplete; approximate length 140mm: width of blade 6.5mm. Iron. Long parallel-sided blade, the edge longer than the back, with an integral rod-like hexagonal handle ending with a loop. This is a typical example of Manning knife Type 4 (1985, 108–10), which was probably used as a razor. The type is well known from London in 1st- and 2nd-century contexts.

COMB

<72> [528] (3.3) W4 <S11> (Fig 17)
Almost complete: length 490mm. Boxwood (*Buxus sempervirens*). One-piece double-sided comb, with coarse and fine teeth on opposing sides of the central bar.

Category 3 Textile production and working

NEEDLES

<257> [543] (10.1) S1 <S12> (Fig 44)
Incomplete: surviving length 68mm. Bone needle, Type 1 with pointed head; the large eye has been made by drilling two adjacent holes, giving a slight figure of eight effect. Incomplete; broken at approximately the mid point of the shaft.

<196> [689] (4.4) W4
Incomplete: bone. Fragment of stout shaft, broken at both ends; one end is flattened for the beginning of the eye.

<136> [527] (3.4) W4
Complete, but bent and with damage to the head: approximate length 75mm. Copper alloy, Type 2,

with spatulate head and long rectangular eye.

<131> [689] (4.4) W4 <S13> (Fig 14)
Complete: length 73mm. Iron. Slender head, squared at the top, but equivalent to Crummy Type 1, with a long eye, now encrusted.

<192> [689] (4.4) W4
Complete: length 86mm. Iron. Similar in form to <131> above.

<202> [689] (4.4) W4
Surviving length 48mm. Iron. Similar in form to <131> above, but broken above the point and just below the eye.

<203> [689] (4.4) W4
Incomplete: bone needle or pin; lower part of shaft.

Category 4 Domestic utensils and furniture

VESSEL

<143> [623] (5.1) W4
Incomplete: width 44.5mm. Copper-alloy flagon lid. Trefoil-shaped with stout projection in the centre as Crummy 1983, 73, no. 2049. There are traces of a differently coloured alloy on the top above the projection. Terminal and hinge broken.

SPOONS

<142> [691] (4.2) W3 <S14> (Fig 13)
Almost complete: length 73mm; length of bowl 24mm. Copper alloy. This is a typical round-bowled form, with plain rod handle, now broken, but the spoon bowl has been bent on both sides to form a scoop or shovel-shape. While this could be pre- or post-burial damage, the distortion appears to be so regular that it was probably deliberate and the standard form was adapted for a specific use.

<138> [689] (4.4) W4 <S15> (Fig 14)
Complete: length 86mm. Drop handle with decoratively moulded terminals. The loop of the handle is lozenge-shaped in section, becoming circular at the terminals. The handle was fastened to a box or drawer by means of the double-spiked loops which still survive. This example is very similar to

one from Colchester (Crummy 1983, 81, no. 2134).

LAMPS

<280> [698] (5.1) W4
Incomplete: approximate diameter 72mm. Ceramic *Firmalampe*, top of discus with central filling hole and smaller air hole; one lug remains (of an original pair), crisply moulded with a small decorative circle on its upper surface; the lamp is broken at the junction with the nozzle. Loeschcke Type IX. Import, ?north Italian fabric.

<263> [689] (4.4) W4
Incomplete: diameter 100mm. Ceramic open lamp; shallow lamp, part of the base and side wall remaining, with stub of an applied handle; nozzle missing. Verulamiam Region White ware.

<272> [689] (4.4) W4
Incomplete. Ceramic open lamp; part of nozzle, burnt. Alice Holt/Surrey ware.

QUERNS

<450> [893] (8.12) R1
Incomplete. Fragment of lava quern; no original surfaces remaining.

<47> [198] (21.1) B14 (residual)
Incomplete. Lava quern; indeterminate fragment.

Category 5 Recreation and leisure

COUNTERS

<233> [528] (3.3) W4 <S16> (Fig 16)
Complete: diameter 20mm. Bone. Plain (Crummy Type 1) with bevelled edges. A hole has been drilled through the centre, worked from both sides. One face bears an inscription, the letters A and L clearly visible at either end, but ?two central letters have been damaged by the drilling of the hole; possibly I to the right of the hole and only a horizontal mark on the left.

<198> [549] (5.4) W4
Complete: diameter 21mm. Plain, Type 1, with sharply bevelled side, the edge placed off-centre and central lathe indentation on one face.

Category 7 Writing materials and associated objects

STYLI

<165> [569] (1.5) OA2 <S17> (Fig 11)
Complete: length 97mm; width of eraser 4.5mm. Iron. Manning Type 1, with plain stem tapering to a point and no marked shoulder between stem and eraser. The eraser is carefully made and has a small projection or spur on one side, a feature frequently seen on well-preserved styli. This may be a manufacturing rather than a functional feature and could indicate that the object has seen little or no use. Stem bent.

<137> [691] (4.1) OA2 <S18> (Fig 11)
Complete: length 116mm; width of eraser 6mm; length of eraser 8.8mm. Iron. Manning Type 2 with plain stem tapering to the point; well-made straight-sided eraser, carefully finished (no projecting spur or rough edges), with straight top. There is a very slight ridge at the junction of stem and point, probably caused by the manufacturing process but the distinction is clear enough to place this stylus in Type 2. The appearance of 'reeding' along the stem is also likely to have been produced by tooling.

<216> [692] (4.1) OA2 <S19> (Fig 11)
Complete: length 131mm; width eraser 5.5mm. Iron. Type I with carefully made point, no clear shoulder between seam and point. Relatively long eraser with angled top (unlikely to have been caused by wear); projecting spur at side of eraser (on side where top is lower). Tool marks (reeding) visible on stem.

<174> [698] (1.5) OA2 <S20> (Fig 11)
Complete: length 122.5mm; width of eraser 9mm. Iron. Type 4, with mouldings below the eraser and at the junction of stem and point. The mouldings are unclear due to some corrosion but appear to be grouped in bands of three. The eraser is slender and well formed (U-shaped) – the stem tapers towards the eraser which is the same thickness as the stem.

WRITING TABLETS

<74> [569] (1.5) OA2
Incomplete. Silver fir. Small fragment of outer leaf with recessed area for the wax on one side.

<70> [689] (4.4) W4 <S21> (Fig 18)
Incomplete. Silver fir. Small fragment.

Category 10 Tools

TOOLS

<230> [689] (4.4) W4
Incomplete: length 90mm. Bone ?handle. Fragment of long bone, roughly squared and polished ?with use. One end is notched on both sides, possibly for the insertion of a tanged blade.

<132> [549] (5.4) W4 <S22> (Fig 29)
Complete: length 146.5mm; width of blade 39mm. Iron chisel with flat rectangular spatulate blade and a relatively short stout handle which terminates in a knob. The blade is comparatively wide and blunt and does not appear to be suitable for use as a woodworking or a metalworking tool. The closest parallel is the modern stonemason's mallet-headed chisel and the size of this implement makes it suitable for use as a finishing chisel.

KNIVES

<147> [689] (4.4) W4
Nearly complete: length of blade 52.5mm. Iron knife blade, with part of tang; a small example of Manning Type 13 (1985, 114).

<148> [689] (4.4) W4
Incomplete: length 70mm. Fragment of knife blade.

Category 11 Fasteners and fittings

?CLASP

<181> [527] (3.4) W4 <S23> (Fig 14)
Complete: length 22mm, width 14mm. Copper alloy. Cast rectangular frame set on a narrow rectangular-sectioned shank with a T-bar terminal. This appears to be a clasp, perhaps for fastening clothing, with the loop sewn to

cloth or leather. It appears to be functionally similar to a fastener with a ring head from South Shields, thought to be a development of Wild's Type 1X button and loop fastener (Allason-Jones & Miket 1984, 222, no. 3.762; Wild 1970).

MOUNTS

<119> [624] (4.2) W3
Incomplete: length 32.5mm; width 17mm. Copper alloy. Rectangular sheet pierced with five neatly made circular holes, two of them broken across the mid point, each outlined with a single inscribed circle. Possibly a beltplate.

<114> [689] (4.4) W4
Complete: length 53mm. Copper alloy. Triangular sheet, at the centre of which is a single circular hole, with a hemispherical terminal at the narrower end, also pierced with a hole.

<122> [698] (5.1) W4
Incomplete: length 29mm; width 17mm. Copper alloy. Narrow strip with two circular holes, one broken across the centre.

<115> [689] (4.4) W4 <S24> (Fig 14)
Complete: width 30.5mm. Copper alloy. Cast pelta-shaped plate with bevelled edges, probably a mount, but with no obvious method of attachment.

<160> [623] (5.1) W4
Complete: length 44mm. Iron. Rectangular plate with two holes, one containing a dome-headed rivet *in situ*.

<4> [160] (5.6) W4
Complete: length 46mm. Copper alloy. Rectangular plate made from copper-alloy sheeting, pierced with three nail holes. Possibly a patch.

RINGS

<162> [692] (4.1) OA2
Complete: internal diameter 11.5mm. Copper alloy. Plain ring with faceted outer surface and irregular triangular inner section. The irregularity of the inner face and the small size of the ring makes it more likely to have been a fitting than a finger-ring. Such rings could have had a wide variety of possible uses.

<105> [698] (5.1) W4
Complete: internal diameter
18mm. Copper alloy. Plain ring,
with an irregular lozenge-shaped
section; slight wear on one side.
Probably a fitting, but its size is
suitable for a finger-ring.

<111> [689] (4.4) W4
Complete: internal diameter
14mm. Copper alloy. Plain hoop
with D-shaped section, slightly
worn on one side. This is of a
suitable size to be classified as a
finger-ring, but is undecorated
and it could equally well have
functioned as a fitting.

NAILS

<125> [689] (4.4) W4
Complete: length 29.5mm; width
of head 17.5mm. Copper alloy.
Globular head, as <156>.

<156> [569] (5.1) OA2
Complete: length 21.5mm; length
of shank 16mm; width of head
17mm. Copper alloy. Globular
head with square-sectioned shank;
well made. Such nails were used
on furniture or other items where
a decorative finish was required.

<103> [623] (5.1) W4
Complete: length 19.5mm; width
of head 15mm. Copper alloy.
Small globular head.

STUDS

<215> [692] (4.1) OA2
Incomplete: diameter 14mm.
Copper alloy. Domed head with
flat rim; shank missing.

<113> [689] (4.4) W4
Incomplete: diameter 15mm.
Copper alloy. Domed head with
carinated rim; encrusted; shank
missing.

<126> [689] (4.4) W4
Incomplete: diameter of head
c 20mm. Copper alloy. Flat head
with decorative groove at edge;
shank fractured.

<201> [689] (4.4) W4
Incomplete: approximate diameter
11mm. Copper alloy. Flat head,
plain, now incomplete; shank
broken.

<88> [696] (4.4) W4
Incomplete: diameter 10mm.
Copper alloy. Small domed head;
shank fractured.

<90> [696] (4.4) W4
Incomplete: diameter 11.5mm.
Copper alloy. Flat head with down-
turned edge; square-sectioned
tapering shank.

<102> [623] (5.1) W4
Incomplete. Diameter of head
c 15mm; length 3mm. Strap fitting.
Copper alloy. Flat head, probably
plain, but now incomplete; the
reverse has a very short riveted
shank suitable for attachment to
leather.

<349> [623] (5.1) W4
Incomplete: diameter of head
8.5mm. Copper alloy. Small
domed head, suitable for using in
furnishing; shank broken.

<179> [698] (5.1) W4
Complete: diameter 18mm;
overall length 34.5mm; length
of shank 27.5mm. Copper alloy.
Domed head with flat rim; heavy
?lead-alloy infill; square-sectioned
tapering shank.

<191> [698] (5.1) W4
Incomplete: diameter 12mm.
Copper alloy. Small domed head;
shank fractured.

<354> [599] (5.4) W4
Incomplete: diameter 25.5mm.
Copper alloy. Domed head, with
lead solder infill; encrusted; shank
missing.

<144> unstratified
Complete: diameter of head
22mm; length of shank 10mm.
Copper alloy. Flat head with single
decorative groove 3mm from the
edge; square-sectioned tapering
shank, possibly military type.

RIVETS

<94> [696] (4.4) W4
Complete: diameter 13.5mm.
Lead. Circular rivet for the repair
of a ceramic vessel.

Category 13 Military equipment

ARMOUR

<128> [689] (4.4) W4
Incomplete: length 34mm; width
15mm. Copper-alloy hinged strap
fitting from *lorica segmentata*; one
plate with two rivet holes and
part of the broken hinge. There
are many examples of this type of

fitting from London; for other
examples, which date from the
1st–2nd centuries, see Bishop &
Coulston 1993, 89, fig 52.

<107> [698] (5.1) W4 <S25>
(Fig 23)
Complete: diameter 19.5mm;
length of shank, now bent,
c 17mm. Copper-alloy stud with
dot and circle around the edge,
surrounding an inner circle
composed of a series of triangles,
filled with radial line decoration.
The lines may originally have held
niello; square-sectioned tapering
shank. The form and style of
decoration is typical of 1st-century
belt or apron fittings.

Category 14 Objects associated with religious beliefs and practice

FIGURINE

<244> [698] (5.1) W4 <S26>
(Fig 25)
Incomplete: diameter of base
45mm. Ceramic (pipeclay) Venus
figurine; base and lower part of
legs with drapery to one side. The
hemispherical base is misshapen,
with a distinct knife-cut at the
front, the damage having occurred
during manufacture, making this
a waster. Apart from the misfiring
the modelling on the surviving
fragment is blurred. It is interesting
that it was thought worthwhile to
import such second-rate objects to
Britain from their manufacturing
centres in Gaul.

Category 15 Metalworking waste

The crucibles were submitted for
analysis at the Ancient
Monuments Laboratory (AML)
and are reported in section 6.12
below.

CRUCIBLES

<232> [623] (5.1) W4 <S27>
(Fig 73)
Incomplete: diameter 65mm;
height 31mm; thickness of wall
c 5mm. Ceramic. Shallow circular
crucible with a lip on one side;
sooting and vitrified material on
the interior with bright yellow
metallic residue on the rim
identified by the AML as gold
droplets. The form is typical of

crucibles used for the working of
precious metals. Verulamium
Region White ware.

<243> [660] (9.1) B4 <S28>
(Fig 73)
Complete: diameter 38.5mm;
height 19.5mm; thickness of wall
6mm. Ceramic. Flat base, straight
sides, plain rim. There is a
yellow/orange residue on the
interior containing specks of gold,
which is thicker in the area which
surrounded a solidified gold
droplet produced in the crucible.

<443> [549] (5.4) W4
Incomplete. Ceramic. Fragment
of base and small part of rim.
Verulamium Region White ware.

<440> [673] (7.4) B2
Incomplete. Ceramic. The inner
surface is covered in a thin vitrified
layer in which gold droplets are
visible.

FOIL SHEET

<157> [569] (1.5) OA2
Incomplete: length 20mm. Brass
(identification by the AML).
Fragment with repoussé decoration,
a lozenge filled with raised circles.

<212> [692] (4.1) OA2
Incomplete. Copper-alloy ?waste;
fragment of sheet, possibly offcut.

<89> [696] (4.4) W4
Incomplete: length 18mm.
Copper-alloy ?waste. Fragment of
folded sheet.

<83> [623] (5.1) W4
Incomplete: maximum length
27mm. Tin bronze (identification
by the AML). Thin sheet and folded
strip, ?waste (offcut).

<161> [623] (5.1) W4
Incomplete: length 25mm;
thickness 0.2mm. Tin foil
(identified by the AML), with
repoussé decoration in the form
of straight ?radial lines; small
fragment of thin sheet.

<87> [698] (5.1) W4
Incomplete: length 24mm. Copper
alloy. Irregularly shaped folded
fragments of sheeting, offcuts.

<109> [698] (5.1) W4
Incomplete; length 30mm.
Copper alloy. Triangular fragment
of sheeting, probably an offcut.

COPPER-ALLOY WASTE

Waste came from the following contexts:

<207> [692] (4.1) OA2
Droplet; possibly a melted object or residue from casting. Brass (identification by the AML).

<380> [301] (12.7) OA4
Residual waste fragment.

<27> [214] (19.4) B12
Residual.

LEAD WASTE

Some fragments of lead or lead-alloy waste or scrap could be associated with industrial processes, but there are no major concentrations or diagnostic fragments and they are as likely to be debris from structural demolition. They were found in the following areas:

<153> [528] (3.3) W4
Sheet, burnt.

<186> [528] (3.3) W4
Sheet.

<151> [527] (3.4) W4
Sheet.

<158> [569] (1.5) OA2
Twisted sheet, scrap.

<150> [692] (4.1) OA2
Small fragments.

<213> [692] (4.1) OA2
Small fragments.

<187> [689] (4.4) W4
Indeterminate fragments.

<91> [696] (4.4) W4
Fragments, some burnt.

<92> [696] (4.4) W4
Sheet.

<364> [600] (5.1) W4
Indeterminate burnt fragments.

The Roman glass

John Shepherd and Sasha Smith

The excavations on this site produced 70 fragments of glass vessels, eight fragments of window glass and one bead. In general the assemblage is very fragmentary making it difficult to be precise about the identifications of the forms of a number of the diagnostic fragments.

Twenty-seven of the vessel fragments come from the ubiquitous square-sectioned prismatic bottle of the 1st to 3rd centuries, and a further 27 are body fragments from vessels whose precise forms cannot be deduced.

<110> [623] (5.1) W4
Sheet, circular; pewter (high tin content identified by the AML).

<79> [623] (5.1) W4
Sheet, ?offcuts.

<163> [623] (5.1) W4
Sheet.

<98> [698] (5.1) W4
Sheet and fragments.

<46> [204] (12.1) OA4
Lump.

<387> [204] (12.1) OA4
Indeterminate fragment.

<388> [204] (12.1) OA4
Sheet.

<50> [315] (12.4) OA4
Molten scrap.

<49> [358] (12.13) OA4
Offcut – sheet.

Category 18 Objects of uncertain function

?MOUNT

<133> [698] (5.1) W4 <S29>
(Fig 23)
Complete: length 55mm; width of each arm 13mm. Copper-alloy ?mount. Two identical arms, each consisting of two parallel strips joined by a linking bar just above the mid point and at the top, where the bar extends beyond the line of the frame to form a curved terminal; one closed and one open hole are set into each terminal. At the other end the two arms are joined and were apparently not intended to swivel as there is a solid moulding at the base. The function of this object is uncertain but it may be a form of chape.

The remaining 16 vessel fragments come from a variety of bowl, jar and jug forms which are well attested not only across London but in the provinces of the northern Empire in general (eg the pillar-moulded bowl <187>, the cracked-off beaker <238>, the bulbous-bodied jars, and jars or jugs with similar body shapes. All of these vessels are common in assemblages dating from the second half of the 1st and the first half of the 2nd century.

The assemblage also includes fragments from the later Roman period, in particular <17> and <350>. Both fragments have been decorated by cutting, the first by incising and abrading, the other by wheel-cutting. The former, though small, is an exceptional piece of glassware. It is not possible to determine precisely the form but it is likely that it came from a bowl (eg Isings 1957, form 116; see also Cool 1995 for a discussion of these and other 4th- to 5th-century bowls). The decoration that survives shows the lower part of the face and neck of, probably, a youth or man. This style of decoration, both in design and technique, is not common but examples are known in Britain – for example an almost complete bowl showing a hunt scene came from Banwell, Wint Hill, Somerset (Harden 1960, 47–51, figs 2, 4–7) and fragments of similarly decorated bowls, together with many plain examples of this form, came from late 3rd- and 4th-century contexts at Shakenoak villa, Oxfordshire (Harden 1973, 102–3, nos 209–13, fig 52).

Catalogue

YELLOW/BROWN GLASS
<255> [529] (2.3) W2
Body fragment from a ribbed vessel of indeterminate form, possibly a jug or jar (eg Isings 1957, form 67c or 52b). Dark yellow-brown glass. Part of one narrow pinched-up rib.

COLOURLESS GLASS
<17> [34] (6.10) B1 <G6>
(Fig 31)
Body fragment from a vessel of uncertain form, probably a bowl (eg Isings 1957, form 116). Colourless glass. Decorated with an incised decoration of which part of the shoulders, neck and lower part of the face of a youth or man survives. This probably formed part of a hunting scene (see above for parallels). Late 3rd or 4th century.

<360> [675] (7.4) B2
Rim fragment from a vessel of uncertain form, possibly a cup or bowl. Out-bent rim with fire-rounded edge. The surface may have been ground and polished as it is heavily pitted.

<22> [196] (28.1) OA5
Three base fragments (not joining) from a vessel of unknown form. Colourless glass. The base is slightly concave. AD 60–100.

<350> [473] (11.1) OA4
Body fragment from a cup or beaker. Decorated with part of two wheel-cut oval designs. AD 300–50.

<372> [300] (12.1) OA4 <G7>
(Fig 47)
Base fragment from a vessel of uncertain form. Colourless glass. Tubular pushed-in base-ring. AD 60–170.

NATURALLY COLOURED GLASS
<187> [529] (2.3) W2
Rim fragment of a pillar-moulded bowl. Natural blue-green glass. Part of one rib remains. Evidence of shallow tooling marks is present on the interior of the fire-polished zone.

<256> [529] (2.3) W2 <G5>
(Fig 13)
Body fragment. Natural blue-green glass. Fragment has part of an oval ring below a horizontal ridge. AD ?170–230.

<238> [689] (4.4) W4 <G3>
(Fig 14)
Rim fragment and body fragment (not joining) of a beaker or cup (eg Isings 1957, form 12 or 29). Natural blue-green glass. Curved

rim, edge cracked off and ground; vertical straight side. One narrow abraded band beneath rim. AD 60–100.

<239> [689] (4.4) W4
Handle fragment from a vessel of unknown form. Natural blue-green glass. Straight ribbon handle, with one central vertical rib.

<240> [689] (4.4) W4
Handle from a small jug of unknown form, possibly from the type of trefoil mouth jug (eg Isings 1957, form ?56). Natural blue-green glass. Curved D-sectioned rod handle; folded upper attachment, simple lower attachment with two pinched ridges. AD 60–170.

<250> [623] (5.1) W4
Body fragment from a jug or jar with vertical rib decoration (eg Isings 1957, form 52 or 67c). One rib remains. AD 60–170.

<271> [698] (5.1) W4
Base fragment from a jar or jug (eg Isings 1957, form 52, 55 or 67c). Convex-curved body, open pushed-in base-ring, concave base. AD 60–100.

<16> [65] (5.5) OA2 <G1> (Fig 30)
Rim fragment from a collared jar (eg Isings 1957, form 67b or c). Natural blue-green glass. The vertical rim edge is bent out and down and tooled horizontally. AD 60–100.

<355> [671] (7.4) B2
Neck fragment from a small flask or unguent bottle (eg Isings 1957, form 26 or 82). Natural blue-green glass. AD 60–230.

<245> [672] (7.4) B2
Base fragment from a bottle (eg Isings 1957, form 89). Natural green glass. AD 100–70.

<344> [503] (10.3) OA3
Base fragment from a vessel of uncertain form, possibly a jar (eg Isings 1957, form 67c). The base is pushed in to form a tubular ring which has broken off. AD 60–170.

<370> [149] (15.4) B8
Handle fragment from a vessel of unknown form, possibly a jug or bottle (eg Isings 1957, form 50, 51, 55, 127 or 128). AD 60–170.

BOTTLES
<369> [527] (3.4) W4
Base fragment from a mould-blown prismatic bottle (eg Isings 1957, form 50). Natural blue glass. One circular moulded rib from the pattern remains.

<236> [689] (4.4) W4 <G2> (Fig 14)
Base and lower body fragment from a square-sided bottle. Natural blue-green glass. Base design: at least two concentric circular mouldings. AD 60–170.

<237> [689] (4.4) W4
Lower body and base fragment from a small mould-blown square bottle (eg Isings 1957, form 50). Natural blue-green glass. Base design: three concentric circles. AD 60–170.

<248> [689] (4.4) W4
Rim fragment from a bottle (eg Isings 1957, form 50, 51, 89 or 90). Natural blue-green glass. Rim edge is bent out, up, in and flattened. Small trail from handle attachment remains. Too fragmentary to measure diameter. AD 60–200.

<345> [600] (5.1) W4
Body and base fragment of a square bottle (eg Isings 1957, form 50). Natural blue-green glass. Base is slightly concave.

<251> [623] (5.1) W4
Handle and shoulder fragment from a bottle of uncertain form. Natural blue-green glass. Horizontal shoulder of bottle curving over to straight side. Reeded handle with simple lower sticking-point.

<259> [698] (5.1) W4
Handle fragment from a bottle (eg Isings 1957, form 50, 51, 89 or 90). Natural blue-green glass. Upper section of an angular reeded handle joining neck and underside of rim. Five ribs. AD 60–170.

<270> [698] (5.1) W4 <G4> (Fig 23)
Lower body and base fragment from a mould-blown square bottle (eg Isings 1957, form 50 or 90). Natural blue-green glass. Base design: at least four concentric circular mouldings. AD 60–170.

<217> [543] (10.1) S1
Handle fragment from a bottle (eg Isings 1957, form 50, 51). Natural

blue-green glass. The handle fragment forms the upper sticking-point. AD 60–170.

<224> [502] (10.6) B5
Rim and neck fragment from a bottle. Natural blue-green glass. Rim bent out, up, in and flattened; cylindrical neck. AD 60–170.

<247> [689] (4.4) W4; <225> [509] (10.2) S1
Bottle (Isings form 50)

<220> [569] (1.5) OA2; <242> [528] (3.3) W4; <258> [526] (3.5) W4
Bottle (Isings form 51)

<193> <194> <195> [510] (10.1) S1; <217> (x3), <218> <219> <252> <253> [543] (10.1) S1
Bottle (Isings form 50/51)

INDETERMINATE FORMS
<353> [528] (3.3) W4
Colourless with wheel-cut lines.

<373> [309] (11.2) OA4
Natural blue-green glass with wheel-cut lines.

<221> <222> <223> [569] (1.5) OA2; <254> [529] (2.3) W2; <353> [528] (3.3) W4 (x4); <346> [600] (5.1) W4; <343> [623] (5.1) W4; <351> [610] (5.3) W4 (x3); <249> [671] (7.4) B2; <357> [672] (7.4) B2; <359> [673] (7.4) B2 (x4); <275> [472] (11.2) OA4
Natural blue-green glass.

<246> [689] (4.4) W4; <18> [34] (6.10) B1; <358> [672] (7.4) B2; <348> [494] (10.9) B5; <37> [310] (11.2) OA4
Natural green glass.

WINDOW GLASS
<352> [528] (2.3) W4
Edge fragment of cast window glass. Natural blue-green glass.

<235> [689] (4.4) W4
Fragment of cast window glass. Natural blue-green glass.

<20> [41] (6.9) B1
Edge fragment of cast window glass. Natural blue-green glass.

<234> [714] (6.26) OA3
Fragment of free-blown window glass. Natural blue-green glass.

<448> [903] (8.15) B3
Two fragments (joining), one edged, of cast window glass. Natural blue-green glass.

<342> [510] (10.1) S1
Edge fragment of cast window glass.

<445> [309] (11.2) OA4
Fragment of window glass. Natural blue-green glass.

<347> [469] (12.10) OA4
Edge fragment of cast window glass. Natural blue-green glass. Two of the edges are grozed.

OBJECTS
<444> [528] (3.3) W4
Bead. Opaque blue and white glass. Square section cube-shaped (eg Guido 1978, 92, fig 37, no. 7). Beads of this type were found at Lankhills which were dated to the 4th century, although Guido states that others found elsewhere in Britain for the most part date to the 3rd and 4th centuries.

6.7 The Roman leather shoes

Penny MacConnoran

Introduction

A total of 49 different shoes was identified from the fragmented pieces of leather recovered from the waterfront dumps dating to the first half of the 2nd century. There are no discernible differences in style or construction between the footwear from the various waterfront contexts and it is therefore treated as a single assemblage. In terms of appearance and the relative proportions of the different shoe types present, this small collection of shoes compares favourably with the larger one found nearby on the Billingsgate Buildings site (Miller & Rhodes 1980, 99–108). The shoes all came from dumps which were probably associated with the construction of Waterfront 4 (Table 13), including a small group from the south-west (EN11) over the earlier quay Waterfront 2 (3.3–4) and two larger groups from the south-east (EN20) in front and over Waterfront 3 (4.4, 5.1). The pottery in these dumps implies that the leather was probably deposited some time after c AD 120, and can be dated as a group to the early 2nd century.

The condition of the Suffolk House leather is not so good: a number of the pieces are somewhat overdry and crumbly. Much of the footwear is represented by torn and broken fragments suggesting that it had been subject to much movement after it was discarded. There are no complete or nearly complete shoes. The majority are represented by a single bottom-unit layer or more usually a portion thereof. Four distinct shoe types are present: nailed shoes (*calcei*), sandals (*soleae*), stitched shoes (*socci*) and one-piece shoes (*carbatinae*). The constructional details of these shoe types have been covered at length elsewhere (van Driel-Murray 1998, 291–5; Hoevenberg 1993, 219–39; Miller & Rhodes 1980, 103–28).

As at the Billingsgate Buildings site, but with two fragmentary exceptions, the uppers of the nailed shoes, sandals and stitched shoes have entirely disappeared. The absence of shoe uppers is a common occurrence among excavated assemblages of Roman shoes and may be due to the uppers being made from less robust leather than that of the bottom units (van Driel-Murray 1998, 291) although other reasons may also be possible (Miller & Rhodes 1980, 100–1).

Table 13 *Provenance of shoes by type and land use*

Land use/ subgroup	Nailed shoes (*calcei*)	Sandals (*soleae*)	One-piece shoes (*carbatinae*)	Stitched shoes (*socci*)
W4 (3.3–4)	2			
W4 (4.4)	10	5	4	4
W4 (5.1)	13	4	6	1

Size categorisation

A comparison of the measurements of the Suffolk House conserved shoes with those of the pre-conservation drawings held in the archive shows that the conserved shoes have shrunk by around 10%. Post-conservation shrinkage has been noted among other Roman footwear assemblages, such as Castleford (van Driel-Murray 1998, 295) and Billingsgate Buildings (Miller & Rhodes 1980, 101–2), together with the difficulties associated with ascertaining accurate shoe sizes. For this reason

and in order to provide some indication of the status of the wearers of the Suffolk House shoes, the more measurable examples have been assigned broadly to an adult, small adult or child size in the catalogue rather than to a specific shoe size. The English shoe-size scale has been used as a guide whereby an adult size 1 sole measures 222mm (with each additional size being added in steps of 8.55mm). Small adult sizes fall in the range of English shoe sizes 1–5.

In the catalogue the measurements of the bottom unit parts are given as length, width of tread and width of waist. Incomplete dimensions are enclosed in brackets. The drawing conventions (see Figs 19, 20 and 26) are akin to those employed at Castleford using flat pattern drawings without shading (van Driel-Murray 1998, 286). The terms used to describe the various shoe parts are to be found in Thornton's glossary of shoes (Goodfellow & Thornton 1966).

Nailed shoes

At Suffolk House, nailed shoes are the most numerous category of footwear with 25 examples representing 51% of the total. This compares well with the ratio at Billingsgate Buildings where nailed shoes formed 54% of the total. The specific type of nailed shoe present at Suffolk House is the *calceus*: this had a bottom unit of one or more layers of leather and a closed, separately cut, upper which was attached to the bottom unit by means of a lasting margin sandwiched between the sole layers. Both van Driel-Murray (1998, 291) and Hoevenberg (1993, 219) have commented that this is the commonest Roman shoe construction to be found on archaeological sites generally: at Valkenburg, Netherlands, 83% of the total number of shoes were *calcei*.

Sizes

The Suffolk House nailed shoes range from child size to adult male size. The two largest shoes are <421> and <306> (see Fig 26: <L3>) and were probably worn by men. The bulk of the remainder fall into the smaller adult sizes while <396> is definitely a child's size. Toe shape, where it has survived, is gently pointed in most cases such as <396> <419> (see Fig 19: <L1>) and <398>, while <306> is blunt.

Nailing

The bottom unit layers, which consist of an insole and sole and in some cases a middle sole, were held together in nearly all cases by a single row of nails set around the edge of the unit together with some further internally placed nails. Two of the largest adult shoes, <421> and <306> (see Fig 26: <L3>), each have a double row of nails along the outer edge. The ornamental nailing patterns noted at Billingsgate Buildings (Miller & Rhodes 1980, 105–6 and fig 59) and other sites such as Carlisle (Padley 1991, 228–9 and figs 210–11) are absent here but this may be due in part to the incompleteness of the bottoms. Only a relatively small proportion of nails have survived and they are useful in showing up wear patterns on the soles. On <306> the nails towards the outside edge are worn flat while three conical ones positioned at the inside waist have escaped wear. Shoe <305> (see Fig 26: <L2>) has six nails at the toes end of the sole that are smaller and more closely spaced than the rest, and which were probably intended to better withstand wear at this point.

Uppers

Only one Suffolk House nailed shoe (<306>) (see Fig 26: <L3>) has part of the upper surviving. This is formed of robust bovine leather and is still joined to the bottom unit by a lasting margin held between the insole and sole. The upper is solid but there is no further clue to its design. Numerous insoles (<408> <398> <419>) (see Fig 19: <L1>) have tunnel stitch holes running around the edge of the flesh surface indicating how the upper lasting margin was first attached to the bottom unit prior to nailing.

Bottoms

There are several examples of surviving middle layers. Shoe <306> has a slender middle sole sandwiched between the insole and sole; this lies within the edges of the lasting margin. Both the insole and middle sole have six corresponding pairs of thong slots whereby these two layers were first joined by thonging. Another adult shoe <421> has a similar slender middle sole with centrally placed thong slots corresponding to those on the insole. There are other examples of insoles with central thong slots such as <430> and <424>. Goodfellow and Thornton have remarked that the main purpose of the thonging was likely to have been ease of handling while the upper and sole were being attached (1966, 15).

There are four probable wedges or repair pieces from nailed shoes. Five examples of wedges were noted from Billingsgate Buildings (Miller & Rhodes 1980, 103–5). Both <413> and <411> are tunnel-stitched on their flesh surfaces indicating that they were first stitched to the underside of the soles prior to nailing. Both <404> and <334> are seat wedges and both are chamfered at the inside edge for a smoother fit between sole and insole. Shoe <422> has a repair piece held in place by nails on the sole at the inside seat.

Sandals

There are nine examples of sandals (*soleae*), forming 18% of the total footwear assemblage. At Billingsgate Buildings, sandals represented 12% of the total. The Suffolk House sandals consist of two or more layers of leather forming the bottom unit which would probably have been held on to the foot by a between-toes strap and a cross-ankle strap. When worn in Roman London, the sandal is likely to have been a summer shoe.

Sizes

The sandals are without exception all small indicating that the wearers were children, women/young people. Hoevenberg (1993, 233) has produced a graph of sandal sizes from the

north-western provinces which demonstrates that larger men's sizes of sandal do not appear until towards the end of the 2nd century. At Billingsgate Buildings smaller sizes of sandal also dominated (Miller & Rhodes 1980, 117). The sole shapes that have survived intact are slender and have one or more of the toes marked out by scalloping, such as <414> (see Fig 19: <L4>) and <329> (see Fig 26: <L6>). This slender style which closely follows the foot shape is typical of the first half of the 2nd century (Miller & Rhodes 1980, fig 66).

Bottoms

In most cases the bottom unit layers are joined together both by marginal thong slots set in pairs at right angles to the edge of the sole and by a single row of marginal nails. There is one example of an unnailed thonged sandal <329> (see Fig 26: <L6>) which has an insole and sole that are still joined together by 3mm wide very fine thonging (probably goatskin) around the edge of the bottom unit. Four unnailed sandals were found at Billingsgate Buildings (Miller & Rhodes 1980, 120, figs 66 and 67). One other Suffolk House sandal <418> (see Fig 20: <L5>) which has a bottom unit composed of insole, middle layer and sole is essentially also a thonged sandal but it is nailed at the heel.

Four sandals have one or two middle layers of the cut-and-expanded type: <418> <333> <414> (see Fig 19: <L4>) and <339>. During their examination of Roman footwear from London's former Guildhall Museum, Goodfellow and Thornton found 10 examples of women's and children's sandals with this type of middle which they referred to as a 'skeleton through' (1966, 16–18). There are two examples from Billingsgate Buildings (Miller & Rhodes 1980, 117 and fig 66). In some cases, the leaf-shaped cavities of the Suffolk House middle layers are each still filled with a small loose piece of leather roughly corresponding to the shape of the cavity as in the case of <418> and <414>. The main aim behind this constructional feature was flexibility as the amount of solid leather to be bent in walking was reduced. The feature is seldom found outside London. There is one sandal from Valkenburg with this type of middle (Hoevenberg 1993, 235 and fig 60).

Rather surprisingly, one sandal <329> (see Fig 26: <L6>) has a surviving fragment of upper strapwork. The creased end was originally in place between the sole and insole at the waist/lower forepart junction; the other end with the single thong hole would have been connected to a between-toes strap arising from the slot at the toe end of the insole. The strap, which is of very thin leather (probably goat), is very irregular in shape and it is difficult to see it as part of the original construction of the sandal. It is more likely to be a home-produced repair.

Stamps

Some of the Suffolk House sandal insoles have stamped motifs. This is a common occurrence on excavated sandals (Hoevenberg 1993, 230). The repeated ring-and-dot motifs around the insole edges on <418> (see Fig 20: <L5>) and the concentric circles on <338> are akin to examples from Billingsgate Buildings

(Miller & Rhodes 1980, 119 and fig 66) and Valkenburg (Hoevenberg 1993, 234 and fig 6), while Goodfellow and Thornton noted stamped concentric circles on 16 sandals from the Bank of England and other London sites (1966, 20, 30). There are two spread eagle stamps on <418>, the one positioned at the seat being extremely worn. This stamp has previously been found on a sandal insole from the Bank of England site in London, MoL acc no. 28.140/9a. There is also an example from Vindolanda (Carol van Driel-Murray, pers comm). It remains to be seen whether this was the trademark of a particular sandalmaker.

No. <329> (see Fig 26: <L6>) has two rosette stamps similar to Billingsgate Buildings examples (Miller & Rhodes 1980, 119 and fig 66). This same sandal also has a band of reversed S shapes stamped across the tread, a design previously known from London (Goodfellow & Thornton 1966, 21).

Stitched shoes

The five stitched shoes which form 10% of the total consist of two insoles, two soles and a repair piece from a sole. At Billingsgate Buildings 14% were stitched shoes (Miller & Rhodes 1980, 115). Hoevenberg (1993, 238) has commented that the upper of the stitched shoe or *soccus* may have been a sock-like lightweight one without fastenings. As Rhodes has already pointed out (Miller & Rhodes 1980, 117), stitched shoes would most likely have been worn indoors as slippers or house shoes. The Suffolk House examples are well worn; the grain surfaces of both soles and repair piece are completely worn away.

Sizes

The sizes all fall within the smallest adult range suggesting the wearers were women/young people. This tallies with the findings from other sites such as Billingsgate Buildings (Miller & Rhodes 1980, 116), Carlisle (Padley 1991, 233) and Valkenburg (Hoevenberg 1993, 239) where the stitched shoes were consistently of child and small adult sizes.

Nailing

Shoe <420> (see Fig 19: <L9>) is unusual in that it has five nails set along the edge of the inside forepart. The nails may have been intended to reinforce this part of the shoe which appears to have been subject to extra pressure by the wearer, the leather here having worn very thin. Stitched shoes with subsequent additions of nails are known from other footwear assemblages at Billingsgate Buildings (Miller & Rhodes 1980, 116), Valkenburg (Hoevenberg 1993, 319 and fig 62, no. 031.0693B) and Carlisle (Padley 1991, 241, fig 214, no. 987).

Bottoms

Stitching or thonging alone was used to unite the sole, insole and upper; all of the Suffolk House bottom unit layers have marginal tunnel stitch holes on the flesh surface running parallel to the edge of the sole/insole. Impressions of cross-bracing threads are visible on the flesh surface of three of the shoes <309> <400> (see Fig 19: <L7>) and <420> (see Fig 19: <L9>). The tunnel-stitched insoles and soles from Suffolk House are similar in appearance to those from Billingsgate Buildings (Miller & Rhodes 1980, 108 and fig 61, nos 601, 611) and Carlisle (Padley 1991, 241 and fig 214, nos 981, 983, 984).

One-piece shoes

There are fragments of 10 one-piece shoes or *carbatinae* forming 20% of the footwear total. A similar proportion of this shoe type was found at the Billingsgate Buildings site (Miller & Rhodes 1980, 121). The *carbatina* was cut from a single piece of leather which was seamed across the base of the heel and up its back. An arrangement of fastening loops closed the shoe over the instep. The simplicity of manufacture and probable cheapness of production of this type of shoe have been remarked on by researchers such as Hoevenberg (1993, 236) and Miller and Rhodes (1980, 127).

Sizes

At Suffolk House, the sizes are predominantly child and small adult but there are also two larger adult examples <391> (see Fig 19: <L10>) and <308> (see Fig 26: <L13>), the latter being of similar design to the child size <318>.

Bottoms

In nearly all cases, the shoes are represented by one side of the quarters alone with part of the heel seam and one or two of the fastening loops surviving. Most have plain solid quarters with no ornament, for example <423> (see Fig 26: <L12>), but a few have knife-cut designs such as <391> (see Fig 19: <L10>) with squares and triangles, and <428> which has large square and D-shaped cut-outs. Shoe <394> (see Fig 19: <L11>) has crude knife-cut rounded tabs at the base of the fastening loops.

Shoe <423> has additional stitch holes at the heel end which suggest that a repair piece was once attached. Repairs to *carbatinae* are fairly common, with some examples coming from Billingsgate Buildings (Miller & Rhodes 1980, 126) and Valkenburg (Hoevenberg 1993, 236).

Summary

The Suffolk House shoes represent a collection of well-worn cast-offs that emanated from a mixed civilian source of men, women and children living in Roman London in the first two or three decades of the 2nd century. The full range of footwear styles of the period is well represented. The civilian nature of the material is underlined by the absence of the military boot or *caliga* – also absent from the larger footwear collection at Billingsgate Buildings.

Catalogue

Nailed shoes

<413> [528] (3.3) W4
Probable repair or wedge from an outer sole. There is marginal tunnel stitching on the flesh surface indicating that it was first stitched to the underside of the sole. The single marginal row of nails is discontinued at the waist. Dimensions (112mm) x 29mm x 18mm.

<411> [527] (3.4) W4
Repair piece from toes end of outer sole. The inner facing edge of this is not skived or chamfered but is thinner than the outside edge. Tunnel stitch holes run around the edge on the flesh surface indicating that the patch was first sewn on to the sole. There is sparse marginal nailing. Dimensions 50mm x 84mm.

<334> [689] (4.4) W4
Reinforcement wedge from seat/waist/lower forepart. This would have fitted between an insole and sole and is chamfered along its inner edge for a smooth fit. There are two pairs of marginal thong slots. Nailing is sparse. Dimensions (160mm) x 32mm.

<335> [689] (4.4) W4
Waist/lower forepart fragment of insole. Double row of closely spaced nail holes along outer edge; single row along inside edge. Dimensions (100mm) x 60mm.

<336> [689] (4.4) W4
Seat fragment of outer sole. Single marginal row of widely spaced nails with pairs of stitch holes on same alignment. Dimensions (75mm) x (44mm).

<393> [689] (4.4) W4
Incomplete right insole; toes and seat ends missing. There are three centrally placed pairs of thong slots in seat, above waist and towards toes end. There is a single marginal row of closely spaced nail holes with three parallel rows down tread. Dimensions (185mm) x (70mm) x (52mm).

<396> [689] (4.4) W4
Complete bottom unit; insole and outer sole still joined by nails

with a probable middle layer partly visible between. Gently pointed toe. There are pairs of thong slots centrally placed in the waist and both centrally placed and towards the edges of the forepart of the insole. Single row of sparsely placed nails around the edge of the outer sole with a further two nails in tread and two in heel. Child size. Dimensions 190mm x 65mm x 55mm.

<398> [689] (4.4) W4
Right insole, almost complete. Slender shape with gently pointed toe. There are marginal tunnel stitch holes on the flesh surface indicating where the lasting margin of the upper was attached. There is a single marginal row of fairly closely spaced nails. Small adult size. Dimensions 222mm x 70mm x 45mm.

<404> [689] (4.4) W4
Heel seat wedge; chamfered at inside edge. Single row of sparsely placed marginal nails. Dimensions 80mm x 30mm.

<408> [689] (4.4) W4
Complete right insole. Slender shape. Pointed toe. Single row of closely spaced nails around edge with a row of tunnel stitch holes on the flesh surface set within the line of the nails. There is no central nailing. Child size. Dimensions 209mm x 65mm x 40mm.

<415> [689] (4.4) W4
Fragment of tread/toes end of outer sole. There is a single marginal row of fairly closely spaced nails. Dimensions (78mm) x 70mm.

**<419> [689] (4.4) W4 <L1>
(Fig 19)**
Right insole. Slender shape. Gently pointed toe. This shoe is similar to <398>. There is a single marginal row of fairly closely spaced nail holes with a double row at the outside edge. On the flesh surface there is a row of tunnel stitch holes set within the line of the nails. Small adult size. Dimensions (218mm) x 70mm x 45mm.

<421> [623] (5.1) W4
Nearly complete right insole, middle and sole. Portion missing at heel and toes end of insole; tread of sole and middle is worn

away. Gently pointed toe. Slender middle layer is set within space delimited by the now missing lasting margin edges of the upper. Both insole and middle have corresponding pairs of thong slots at the seat and lower forepart. There is a double row of marginal nailing all along outside edge from toes end to heel. Adult size. Dimensions 266mm x 93mm x 63mm.

<422> [623] (5.1) W4
Nearly complete insole and outer sole. Slender shape. Gently pointed toe. Outer sole has a repair piece at the inside/back of the heel held in place by nails. The insole has centrally placed pairs of thong slots at the seat, above and below the waist and at the toes end. There is a single marginal row of closely spaced nails with two straight rows in the forepart and the heel and a single nail centrally placed in the waist. Small adult size. Dimensions 230mm x 75mm x 52mm.

<424> [623] (5.1) W4
Insole fragment; waist/lower forepart area. Pair of thong slots centrally placed below waist. Single row of closely spaced marginal nail holes with four tiny nail holes in centre waist – set in a lozenge shape. Adult size. Dimensions (150mm) x (75mm) x 63mm.

<427> [623] (5.1) W4
Fragment of insole. Closely spaced marginal nailing. Dimensions (120mm) x (43mm).

<430> [623] (5.1) W4
Insole fragment; waist/lower forepart area. Pair of thong slots centrally placed in lower forepart. Single row of marginal nail holes. Dimensions (107mm) x (60mm).

<304> [698] (5.1) W4
Fragment of right outer sole; waist/lower forepart. Some marginal tunnel stitching on the flesh surface. Single marginal row of closely spaced nail holes with single central row down waist and seat. Small adult size. Dimensions (188mm) x (85mm) x 61mm.

**<305> [698] (5.1) W4 <L2>
(Fig 26)**
Fragment of forepart of right outer sole. Single row of fairly closely spaced marginal nails each

c 6mm in diameter. There are six smaller and more closely spaced nails at the toes end, presumably intended to make this area more durable. There is a single nail in the centre of the tread. Adult size. Dimensions (190mm) x (85mm) x (60mm).

**<306> [698] (5.1) W4 <L3>
(Fig 26)**
Nearly complete left insole, middle and outer sole. Toe shape is blunt. A portion of the upper (maximum height 25mm) survives in situ at the outside forepart and at the inside and outside waist. The upper is attached to the bottom unit by means of a lasting margin sandwiched between the insole and sole. The upper is solid with no signs of openwork. A slender middle layer lies, grain surface up, between the edges of the upper lasting margin. There are six pairs of thong slots on the insole with corresponding pairs on the middle layer. There is a single marginal row of fairly widely spaced nails with a double row at the outer forepart and a single central row in the seat. The surviving nails are worn flat (diameter is 6mm) except for three conical ones at the inside waist/lower tread. Adult size. Dimensions (245mm) x 82mm x 54mm.

<307> [698] (5.1) W4
Forepart and waist of right insole. Gently pointed toe. Scrap of lasting margin of upper in situ against the flesh surface at outside seat. Single marginal row of closely spaced small nails. Damage to tread renders nail pattern here uncertain. Small adult. Dimensions (185mm) x 82mm x 52mm.

<319> [698] (5.1) W4
Seat fragments of outer sole and middle, the latter cut straight across at the waist. Some thong slots around edge. Widely spaced marginal nailing. Dimensions (55mm) x 46mm.

<320> [698] (5.1) W4
Fragment of insole waist. Widely spaced marginal nailing. Dimensions (70mm) x (50mm).

<322> [698] (5.1) W4
Fragment of left insole; waist lower forepart. Some pairs of marginal thong slots. Single marginal row

of fairly closely spaced nails. Dimensions (98mm) x 72mm x 50mm.

<323> [698] (5.1) W4
Fragment of insole; waist/lower forepart. Tunnel stitching around flesh edge. Sparse marginal nailing. Small size. Dimensions (105mm) x (55mm) x 44mm.

Sandals

<333> [689] (4.4) W4
Portion of a cut-and-expanded middle shaped for the outer edge of a bottom unit. Has a row of nail holes and pairs of stitch holes on the same alignment. Dimensions (115mm) x 22mm.

<403> [689] (4.4) W4
Possible reinforcement or repair piece from the toes end of a right-foot sandal. Slender style with toe scallops. There is one large slot which would have held the end of a between-toes strap. The inner facing edge of the piece is cut straight across but also partly torn. There is a single marginal row of tiny widely spaced nail holes. There are some small marginal thong holes on the flesh side. Small size. Dimensions 55mm x 70mm.

<407> [689] (4.4) W4
Fragment of insole and middle sole still joined by nails; heel seat only. The grain of the insole is very worn. The insole has split into two laminae. There are pairs of stitch slots around the edges of both layers and a single marginal row of closely spaced small nails. Small size. Dimensions (100mm) x 52mm.

<414> [689] (4.4) W4 <L4> (Fig 19)
Right forepart only; insole, two middle layers and outer sole (lamina only of outer sole survives). Slender shape. Toes end very worn and marked out by scallops. The tread of the insole is also very worn. Both middles are of the cut-and-expanded type. On the lowermost middle layer, the slash extends to the widest part of the tread and the cavity is filled by a loose piece of leather roughly corresponding to the shape of the cavity. On the uppermost middle layer, the slash extends from the

lower forepart to below the waist. The grain surfaces of both middles face upwards. There is a pair of thong slots at the toe end to hold the between-toes upper strap. There are some pairs of stitch holes around the edges of the layers. There is a single marginal row of fairly sparsely placed nails with a row of three centrally placed down the forepart. Small adult size. Dimensions (174mm) x 76mm.

<418> [689] (4.4) W4 <L5> (Fig 20)
Incomplete right insole, middle and outer sole; seat/waist/lower forepart. The grain surface of the insole has a number of stamped motifs. Centrally placed above the waist is an eagle design set within a circle. The same stamp occurs again in the centre of the seat but this is extremely worn. Around the edges of the insole are a further 14 stamps of ring-and-dot motifs. Traces of an impressed line, running parallel with the edge of the insole, survive to the inside of the row of stamps. The middle layer is a cut-and-expanded one. The three expanded spaces are each filled by a piece of leather roughly equating to the shape of the cavity. The three layers were joined by marginal thonging or stitching; pairs of stitch slots run around the edges of all three layers. The sandal is nailed at the heel only, where a single row of nails runs around the outer edges. See Billingsgate Buildings for parallel (Miller & Rhodes 1980). Small adult/child size. Dimensions (138mm) x 43mm.

<338> [623] (5.1) W4
Insole fragment; waist. There are five stamped motifs of concentric circles, two at both inside and outside waist and one at the waist centre. Single row of fairly widely spaced nails around the edge with pairs of marginal thong slots on the same alignment. Small size. Dimensions (76mm) x 46mm.

<339> [623] (5.1) W4
Small fragment of outer sole with remnants of three cut-and-expanded layers still attached. The surviving edges are nailed and have pairs of thong slots. Two detached cut-and-expanded fragments may also belong. Nails are flattened and measure 11mm in diameter.

<321> [698] (5.1) W4
Fragment of left insole; forepart with toes end missing. Pair of thong slots at toes end to hold a between-toes strap. Sparse marginal nailing with some thong slots on the same alignment. Child's size. Dimensions (92mm) x 55mm x 35mm.

<329> [698] (5.1) W4 <L6> (Fig 26)
Right incomplete insole and outer sole; forepart/waist. Slender form. Scalloped for big toe. This is a thonged sandal; there are no nails. The layers still joined by marginal thonging which survives in part along the outer forepart and waist and is visible on both the grain surface of the insole and the underside of the sole where the grain has worn away. This thonging is very thin, 3mm wide, and probably of goat leather. There is a single thong slot at the toes end of the insole and outer sole to hold the end of a between-toes strap. The insole has a stamp at the waist and the lower forepart of an eight-petalled rosette motif. Across the tread is a faint stamped band of reversed S motifs. Rather surprisingly, a piece of the sandal's upper strapwork has survived, now detached from the rest of the sandal. This is of very thin – probably goat – leather. The strap measures 144mm in length and 28mm across its maximum width. The end which is now creased and bunched up has stitch/thong holes and was sandwiched between the insole and outer sole at the inside waist/lower forepart junction. The other end of the strap has a single thong slot and would have been affixed to a between-toes strap. The irregular shape – and flimsiness – of the strap suggest that it is a repair. Small adult/child size. Dimensions (170mm) x 61mm x 38mm.

Stitched shoes

<400> [689] (4.4) W4 <L7> (Fig 19)
Right outer sole fragment; tread-waist-seat area. Marginal tunnel stitch holes on flesh surface. Some impressions of cross-bracing threads also on flesh surface. Grain surface worn away. Very small adult size. Dimensions (200mm) x (70mm) x 52mm.

<401> [689] (4.4) W4
Nearly complete left insole. Slender shape. Pointed toe. Tunnel stitch holes around marginal edge on flesh surface indicate where lasting margin of upper was attached. Very small adult size. Dimensions 210mm x 60mm x 39mm.

<406> [689] (4.4) W4 <L8> (Fig 19)
Repair piece from seat-waist area of outer sole. There are marginal tunnel stitch holes on the flesh surface as well as some pairs of stitch holes. The grain surface is worn away. Dimensions 120mm x 60mm x 50mm.

<420> [689] (4.4) W4 <L9> (Fig 19)
Left outer sole; back of seat missing. Gently pointed toe. Marginal tunnel stitch holes occur on flesh surface as well as some impressions from cross-bracing threads. Although primarily a stitched shoe, there are five nails set along the edge of the inside forepart. The leather is worn very thin in this area and the nails may have attached a now missing wedge or served to reinforce this part of the shoe. The grain is worn away on the underside of the sole. Small adult size. Dimensions (224mm) x (70mm) x 55mm.

<309> [698] (5.1) W4
Part of right insole; tread and toes end missing. There are marginal tunnel stitch holes on the flesh surface as well as some criss-cross impressions of bracing thread. Small adult. Dimensions (185mm) x 45mm.

One-piece shoes

<391> [689] (4.4) W4 <L10> (Fig 19)
Fragment of right side of quarters with upright heel seam. The leather has delaminated into two layers. Upper part of quarters has decorative cut-outs consisting of a row of squares above a row of triangles. The design has been fairly crudely executed with a knife. ?Adult size. Dimensions (183mm) x (84mm).

<392> [689] (4.4) W4
Fragment of left side of quarters with heel seam and five

semicircular scoops marking the base of the fastening loops. Plain solid design. Child size. Dimensions (140mm) x (61mm).

<394> [689] (4.4) W4 <L11> (Fig 19)
Part of left side of quarters/forepart. The conjoined fastening loops decrease in size towards the front of the shoe. There are rough knife-cut rounded tabs at the base of the loops. Dimensions (180mm) x (105mm).

<405> [689] (4.4) W4
Fragment of left side of quarters with heel seam and a portion of the main instep fastening loop. Plain solid design. Child size. Dimensions (100mm) x (53mm).

<428> [623] (5.1) W4
Fragment of left side of quarters with upright heel seam and principal fastening loop. Knife-cut openwork cut-outs. Child size. Dimensions (80mm) x (44mm).

<429> [623] (5.1) W4
Small fragment of sole. No features. Dimensions (90mm) x (50mm).

<423> [623] (5.1) W4 <L12> (Fig 26)
Part of right side of quarters. Plain solid style with basic type of fastening loops. Stitch holes at heel end suggest attachment of repair piece. Small adult size. Dimensions (190mm) x (50mm).

<308> [698] (5.1) W4 <L13> (Fig 26)
Fragment of left side of quarters with heel seam and three fastening loops only one of which is intact. The plain solid design is similar to the smaller <318>. Adult size. Dimensions (195mm) x (110mm).

<318> [698] (5.1) W4
Fragment of left side of quarters with heel seam and principal fastening loop. Solid plain design (no cut-outs). Style is similar to the larger <308>. Child size. Dimensions (121mm) x (47mm).

<324> [698] (5.1) W4
Small fragment of back part of quarters with upright heel seam. Decorative openwork of trellis design. Dimensions (78mm) x (40mm).

Waste

<71> [698] (5.1) W4
Tiny roughly cut-out sole shape. No stitching or other markings. Its crudeness suggests that it is neither a miniature shoe nor a pattern sample, simply a waste 'doodle'. Dimensions 91mm x 31mm x 20mm.

6.8 The Roman non-shoe leather

Jackie Keily

Introduction

A quantity of Roman non-shoe leather was recovered from the site. All the material came from the waterfront dumps, mainly associated with Waterfront 4, and was in a very good state of preservation when excavated. The leather was washed and simple 1:1 outline drawings were made, prior to conservation. The pieces were conserved by the freeze-drying method in the conservation laboratory at the Museum of London. A shrinkage of approximately 10% has been noted with the shoe leather (see 6.7 above) and this is reflected in the present assemblage.

The assemblage

Sixteen non-shoe leather accessions were recovered from the site. Most of the fragments have stitch holes and were parts of incomplete objects. The material has been split up into the following categories: shoe sole offcut waste (2 fragments); binding (1); reused fragments, that is objects that have been cut up for reuse (5); panels, possibly from tents or covers (2); and unidentified pieces (6). It should be noted that two of the reused pieces, <317> and <326> (see Fig 27: <L18> <L19>), are thought to have come from panels, possibly tents, as well. It is of interest to note that no fragments of the unusable parts of a hide were found and that very little offcut waste was recovered. The majority of the material showed signs of reuse. The excavations of similarly dated waterfront deposits at Billingsgate Buildings in the City of London produced a larger assemblage of leather with a much higher quantity of leather shoemaking waste (Miller & Rhodes 1980, 95). Of the leather artefacts recovered from Billingsgate Buildings, most (13 out of 17) had been cut up for reuse.

Identifications have been made by comparison with other published groups of leather from London (Miller & Rhodes 1980, 95–102), Carlisle (Winterbottom 1991, 244–328) and Castleford (van Driel-Murray 1998, 285–334). The hem and seam classification is based on that devised by Groenman-van Waateringe (1967) with further revisions (see Padley & Winterbottom 1991; van Driel-Murray 1998). Incomplete measurements (those with torn edges) are put within brackets.

Date and context

All of the leather recovered from this site came from the waterfront dumps dating to the first half of the 2nd century AD. Two leather artefacts came from deposits associated with the construction of Waterfront 2, the remainder were associated with Waterfront 4, including three fragments from dumps (3.3–4) over Waterfront 2 in the south-west (EN11), and 11 fragments from dumps in front of and over Waterfront 3 (4.4, 5.1) in the south-east (EN20). These figures are summarised in Table 14.

Table 14 Provenance of leather objects by type and land use

Land use/ subgroup	Unidentified	Binding	Shoemaking waste	Reused pieces	Panels
W2 (2.3)	l		l		
W4 (3.3–4)			l	2	
W4 (4.4)	2	l		l	l
W4 (5.1)	3			2	l

As can be seen from above, the non-shoe leather was mainly recovered from Waterfront 4, from the same deposits as the shoe leather (see 6.7 above). It is of interest to note that the only fragments thought to have come from shoe manufacturing came from the south-west (EN11), and the fragments of leather panels came from the south-east (EN20). The assemblage is typical of a waterfront group from this period in London, being a mix of offcuts, reused pieces and parts of panels and other unidentifiable objects. As a whole the assemblage is too small, however, to be able to infer much about the types of leatherworking and associated processes that were occurring in London at that time.

Catalogue

Unidentified

<328> [529] (2.3) W2
Incomplete: maximum length (67mm), maximum width (46mm). A small fragment of leather with the remains on one side of a shallow folded-over hem with a line of fine tunnel stitching below it. The hem is folded over on to the flesh side and the stitching is not visible from the grain side. The tunnel stitching and the impressions left in the leather indicate that this is the remains of a Narrow Reinforced Seam, type a(i) (NRa(i)). The stitching is very fine and this fragment may have come from a garment.

<399> [689] (4.4) W4 <L14>
(Fig 21)
Incomplete: maximum length (193mm), maximum width 54mm. Two fragments of leather, both decorated with parallel lines of finely stabbed holes. At first these holes were thought to be stitch holes but they are quite finely made and very close together and there are no thread impressions, which given the number of holes would be very unusual if they had been used as stitching holes. Both fragments have two long cut edges and one cut end and one torn, incomplete end. It is of interest to note that the grain surface between the lines is highly polished. The function of these fragments is unknown but they may have come from upholstery or a garment.

<402> [689] (4.4) W4
Incomplete: maximum length 78mm, maximum width (95mm). A decoratively cut piece. The upper edge has a line of stitch holes running along it. The lower edge is cut into what appears to be a decorative fringe of alternating long rectangular strips and short semicircles. One end is cut and the other is torn and missing. This piece

may have come from a garment or may have been used as a decorative trim, for example on upholstery.

<330> [623] (5.1) W4 <L15>
(Fig 27)
Incomplete: maximum length 130mm, maximum width 26mm. A slightly curving, rectangular fragment of leather with roughly cut edges. The grain surface is decorated with horizontal and vertical impressed parallel lines. There is a fragment of leather from the Billingsgate Buildings excavations at Lower Thames Street in the City of London, which has a similar type of decoration forming a lattice (Miller & Rhodes 1980, 99, fig 58, no. 505) which is thought to have possibly come from a garment or upholstery.

<337> [623] (5.1) W4 <L16>
(Fig 27)
Complete(?): length 88mm, maximum width 39mm. A small fragment of leather with a rounded top and tapering to a flat base. There are no signs of any stitching and the edges are quite roughly cut. A round hole has been cut through the upper, wider part of the piece with a narrow rectangular perforation cut below it. The function of this fragment is unknown. The leather is quite thick and similar to leather used for soles. It may, therefore, be a sole offcut, but this would not explain its shape or the presence of the two perforations. It is more likely to be a unique piece made for a particular function, such as reinforcement.

<425> [623] (5.1) W4
Incomplete: maximum length (70mm), width 57mm. A small and very fragmentary piece of leather with one stitched edge and a cut edge parallel to it. The remaining edges are torn. There is a single line of small round stitch holes near one edge, which has a slight curve to it. The impressions

in the flesh side would indicate that there was a binding or hem on this edge. The leather is too worn to be able to identify the form it may have taken.

Binding

<332> [689] (4.4) W4
Incomplete: maximum length (145mm), maximum opened-out width 26mm. One end is cut and one end is torn and missing. The edges are quite crudely and unevenly cut, presumably after use. The stitch holes are quite large and widely spaced (c 18mm apart).

Shoemaking waste

<327> [529] (2.3) W2
Incomplete: (58mm) x 53mm x (30mm). A small triangular fragment; one corner is torn and missing. There is an oval hole cut through the centre of the triangle. The long side is slightly curved. Possibly a fragment of waste offcut from the production of shoe soles. This fragment is not as thick as <410>.

<410> [527] (3.4) W4 <L17>
(Fig 21)
Incomplete: 53mm x (42mm) x (47mm). A small triangular fragment; one corner is torn and missing and one corner is cut off. One of the sides of the fragment is slightly curved. There is a small oval hole cut through the centre of the triangle. The leather is thick and similar to sole leather. Similar triangles have been found at Carlisle (Winterbottom 1991, 318 and figs 281, 282) and they have been identified as parts of the offcuts created when shoe soles are cut from a sheet of leather. Since two of the sides of the present example are straight, it is likely that the piece came from the edge or corner of the sheet. None of the Carlisle fragments have holes in them. It is possible that this slit was made to peg down the sheet while it was being worked on.

Reused pieces

<412> [528] (3.3) W4
Incomplete: four very fragmentary pieces of leather, all with stitch holes. Three probably come from the same piece of leather, having a

hemmed edge with a double row of fine stitching running parallel to it and c 30mm apart from it. On the other side of this finer stitching the leather has been cut, at a slight diagonal to the stitching. Running parallel and close to the hemmed edge is a line of tacking, which appears to have been done with a thong or thick thread, the impression of which can be seen between the stitch holes. The other edges of the piece are torn and missing. The fourth fragment of leather is of a similar type and texture but has different seams. This fragment is roughly triangular, having two corners and then being cut diagonally across one of its long sides. It therefore now forms a triangle with one blunt corner and altogether has four sides. The three original edges all have a simple line of stitching running parallel and close to the edge. The slightly odd shape of this piece (even before it was cut) would indicate that it may have been used as an appliquéd patch or may possibly have been part of a garment.

<409> [527] (3.4) W4
Incomplete: maximum length 132mm, maximum width 19mm. A long thin fragment of leather with a binding strip attached to its outer edge by a single line of stitching, a IVa hem. The inner edge and both ends of the fragment have been cut indicating that this hemmed edge was removed from a piece of leather which was, presumably, required for reuse. The binding has been folded grain side out over the edge of the panel.

<395> [689] (4.4) W4
Incomplete: two fragments: (1) maximum length (160mm), maximum width 65mm; (2) maximum length (190mm), maximum width 108mm.

1) A fragmentary piece of leather with one long side cut and the other stitched, both ends are torn and missing. The stitched edge has fine oval stitch holes close to the edge, with the remains of a line of tunnel-stitch holes running parallel to and c 15mm from the other stitching on the flesh side. Too little remains and in too fragmentary a condition to be able to identify the type of seam used.

2) One long edge is sewn and the other is cut, both of the ends are torn, although one is also partly cut. The stitched edge has a row of stitch holes running parallel to the edge and another row above the first one, very close to the edge. Since there is no impression of a binding strip it is possible that this edge formed part of a seam, probably a type II seam.

<317> [698] (5.1) W4 <L18> (Fig 27)

Incomplete: two fragments: (1) length 59mm, maximum width (292mm); (2) maximum length 267mm, maximum width 190mm. Two fragments from leather panels.

1) A corner fragment of a leather panel. The long edge has two lines of stitching and a portion of binding, now in three pieces, which would have been attached to it, forming a hem IVb. This type of hem is found mainly on tent leather (Winterbottom 1991, 251). The other edge has the remains of what appears to be a shallow curving row of stitch holes, suggesting that a circular appliquéd patch may originally have been attached here. The inner edge of this fragment is cut and the rest of it is missing, indicating that this may have been a tent panel, which, once no longer required, had its centre portion cut out for reuse. The other end of this fragment is torn.

2) A largely torn fragment from a leather panel, with part of an edge with a double row of stitching remaining. This edge would have had binding attached to it. Two edges are partly torn and partly cut. One of the cut edges is straight and the other is curved. This would indicate that the panel was also cut up for reuse. The leather of this fragment would appear to be slightly thinner than that used in fragment (1).

These fragments may be associated with <326>.

<326> [698] (5.1) W4 <L19> (Fig 27)

Incomplete and very fragmentary: three small fragments with torn and cut edges. Two of these fragments have the remains of two circular or semicircular lines of stitch holes. Similar features are found on tent panels where circular appliquéd patches were attached to

reinforce certain points of the tent (eg Winterbottom 1991, figs 254, 255; van Driel-Murray 1998, fig 143). Possibly associated with <317>.

Leather panels

<397> [689] (4.4) W4 <L20> (Fig 21)

Incomplete: length (170mm), maximum width (80mm). Part of a panel with a double row of stitch holes along one edge, which was presumably edged with a binding strip and hem IVb. The binding is now missing but there is a distinct sheen to the area where it would have been. One end of this edge is torn and missing. The other end is complete to the corner. The other edge of the corner has a single line of stitch holes but little remains of this as it is torn and missing. A single line of stitch holes extends down from, and at a slight angle to, the first edge near to the corner. Another line of stitch holes extends out from the corner point. This presumably would have held a reinforcement patch, similar to an example from Carlisle (Winterbottom 1991, 292, fig 254, no. 1171). As with the bound edge, this area has a slight shine to it, a feature also noticed on the leather from Carlisle with areas of appliqué (Winterbottom 1991, 293).

<431> [623] (5.1) W4 <L21> (Fig 27)

Incomplete: maximum length (395mm), maximum width (148mm). A fragment from a leather panel or sheet with two pieces of binding. The binding fragments have two rows of stitch holes in line with hem type IVb, whereas the only remaining edge of the panel has a single row of stitching. This edge, however, does have the impressions of a binding strip and the fragments of binding would fit. It may, therefore, be the case that the binding was only actually attached by the lower row of stitching. This type of hem, as noted with <317>, is mainly associated with tent panels (Winterbottom 1991, 251). In the present context, however, it is difficult to see why it may not equally have come from something such as an awning or a wagon cover or some other type of object associated with the daily life and trade of a large town.

6.9 The Roman building material

Terence Paul Smith

Introduction

The site produced both medieval and post-medieval brick and tile, although most of the material is of Roman date. Some non-ceramic material is also represented. The ceramic materials were examined using binocular microscopy (x10) in order to ascertain fabric types.

A multi-period list of fabric types referred to in the text is included in section 6.16 below (see Table 24).

Ceramic building materials

The Roman fabrics represented include those typical of the pre-Boudican and 1st-century period, predominantly the 2815 group (made probably at several locations in the region of London, notably between St Albans and London itself but perhaps also to the south-west of London), together with the yellow/cream type 2454, 2455 and 3022 (from Eccles in Kent, where they were probably made on the estate associated with the Roman villa there), and fabrics 3023 and 3060 from the Radlett kilns in Hertfordshire. Other 1st-century fabrics noted are 3028 and 3054 (which has been found on many Sussex sites and may have been manufactured there) and 3069 (the provenance of which is not known). Early 2nd-century types 3009 and possibly 3019 (both from kiln sites at Braxells Farm and Little London in Hampshire) were noted.

Clearly, the Suffolk House area, as indeed the Roman city of London generally, was able to draw on a number of different sources for its ceramic building materials in these early centuries, although the overwhelming quantity came from those kilns between London and St Albans.

The late Roman period is represented mainly by fabrics of the later 2815 group, including 2459B and small amounts of fabrics from more distant sources: calcareous fabric 2453 (probably made on or near the south coast, possibly in Hampshire); shelly fabric 2456 (similar to that from the kilns at Harrold in Bedfordshire); and fabric 3050 (probably from the Reigate area of Surrey) and the related fabric 3061, none of which has been recorded from London before the mid to late 2nd century. Also present is fabric 3236, the date range of which is not at present known. In these later centuries, London was reliant on some sources more distant than in earlier times, perhaps because of a decrease in production in the yards which had formerly met most of London's demands. In these later centuries too, earlier materials were not infrequently reused.

Some of the Roman materials were from primary contexts, including Buildings 1–5. Building 1 included materials indicating some status: tesserae in both ceramic and stone, *opus signinum* (in a very crushed, powdery state) and a fragment of flue tile. Building 2 also included flue tile as well as a fragment of Purbeck marble, probably used for paving. Building materials recovered from Building 3, which is known from the archaeological record to have had some mosaic and plain tessellated floors as well as underfloor heating and plastered and painted walls, included several flue-tile fragments and a single tessera, though it also included mudbrick. The percentages of ceramic building materials from Building 3 are: bricks 34·8%, tegulae 52·4%, imbrices 12·0% and flue tiles 0·7% (total = 99·9%). It was from an early medieval pit near the south-east corner of this building that the Tuscan column was retrieved. Buildings 4 and 5 also included flue tiles, which were, of course, used for the construction of hypocaust heating systems. Like Building 3, the evidence suggests that Building 1 combined these with tessellated floors, although the range of rooms excavated in 1969 and 1994–7 were of relatively low quality.

Bricks

The site produced a good sample of bonding bricks, many of which appear to be from in situ buildings. Those from Building 3 (8.1: [895]) have a mortar joint of 30mm. Most were of fabrics in the local 2815 group. The complete or near complete bricks are of various known types (for which see Brodribb 1987, 34–47), including a very thick brick (probably a bipedalis or sesquipedalis from a hypocaust) in a grog variant of 2815. Complete bricks include a bessalis brick from an early medieval pit in Open Area 4 (11.1: [473]), and two lydion bricks, used as bonding bricks, from Building 4 (9.4: [577]). A possible lydion from Building 2 (7.5: [632]) has a hobnailed boot impression in it. A complete section of Roman rubble and mortar walling from Building 5, with flint foundations and brick coursing, was retained for possible display.

Small paving bricks were found in fabrics 3006 and 2454 in dumps behind Waterfront 4 (5.1: [623] and 3.4: [527] respectively); the latter context also yielded an overfired brick, probably in fabric 2815. The dimensions of the example from Waterfront 4 are 138mm x 77mm x 30mm, and one side is abraded, showing that it had been subjected to heavy wear in a floor, in which it would have been set on edge, perhaps in the usual herringbone arrangement (opus spicatum); the overfired example from [527] measures 127–128mm x 66–70mm x 33–36mm; the other example from the quay infill is not complete, but is 65mm wide by 24–25mm thick (for a treatment of opus spicatum bricks see Brodribb 1987, 50–4).

Roofing tiles (tegulae and imbrices)

Most of the roof tiles are in fabrics of the 2815 group. Items of interest include some fragments of tegulae, three with nail holes made before firing, and a further tile in which an attempt had been made, probably unsuccessfully, to bore a nail hole after firing. Tegulae were heavy enough to remain in place without nailing, and nail holes are therefore infrequent; the nailed examples were probably in fairly insecure positions – at the eaves or verges of a roof. The evidence therefore indicates that nailed tiles were sometimes prepared at the tilery but that in other cases nail holes were made (or attempted) on fired products,

presumably as and when needed at the building site. Tegulae with their flanges apparently deliberately removed were recovered from Building 1 (6.10: [34], fabric 3028) and Building 2 (7.3: [676], fabric 2454); the latter also has a worn surface suggesting that it had been used flat for paving. It is by no means unknown for modified tegulae to be used in this way. Removal of the flanges could also enable the tiles to be used as bonding bricks, although tegulae were used as proxy bricks with their flanges still intact – their outer edges resembling the edges of bricks in a completed wall as was the case in a structure with a flint foundation from the earliest phase of Building 1. Four complete but broken imbrices were recovered (Table 15): three from Building 5 (10.3: [514]) and a further example from Building 3 (8.15: [901]).

Table 15 Dimensions of four complete imbrices

Subgroup	Length	Breadth			Thickness
		Top	Middle	Bottom	
8.15	435	146		204	22–5
10.3	444		187		17
10.3	448	148		158	18–20
10.3	448	165		179	15

Dimensions (mm)

Flue tiles

Although not present in large quantities, two types of box-flue tile were noted.

COMBED

This is the more common type from the site and several examples came from early medieval pit fills in Open Area 4 (12.1), as well as late Roman 'dark earth' (11.1–2) and Roman buildings, including Buildings 2 (7.4), 3 (8.12, 8.15), 4 (9.3) and Structure 1 (10.1), mostly in fabric group 2815 (especially 2452). That from Building 4 (9.3: [576]) is in shelly fabric 2456 and may have been a small fragment of voussoir tile rather than a square flue tile. Voussoir tiles were used in the construction of arches and vaults; they could form part of a hypocaust heating system (particularly in bath-houses), but they were also used independently of such heating systems because of their light weight. The example from Structure 1 (10.1: [510]) has a fingerprint from where the tile had been handled while still soft. The plain sides of flue tiles were recovered from Open Area 3 (6.2: [100]) below Building 1, and early pits in Open Area 4 (12.1: [212], [245]).

ROLLER-STAMPED

These, their patterning formed by rolling so as to impress a pattern in the still soft clay, were less common than the combed variety. The rollers (or 'dies') used are well recognised; where possible the pieces from this site have been given their die type numbers (Betts et al 1994), although in some cases the fragmentary nature of the presence of mortar covering did not allow this. The roller-stamped examples were recovered as before from a variety of provenances (Table 16) including Building 3 (8.12: [893], 8.15: [903]), Waterfront 4 (3.3: [528], 4.4: [689]), an early medieval pit in Open Area 4 (12.13: [358]) and the sunken-floored early medieval Building 8 (15.4: [149]).

Table 16 Roller-stamped box-flue tiles

Subgroup	Fabric	Die	Comments
3.3	3006	85?	
4.4	3006?	?	die of group 5
8.12	3006	?	die of group 5
8.15	3006	3	
12.13	2452	?	lattice pattern obscured by *opus signinum*
12.13	3006	12	
12.13	3059	21	
15.4	3054	23	

OTHER ASPECTS OF THE FLUE TILES

A fragment of a box flue in fabric 3006 with the complete width of the plain face (128mm) was recovered from Building 1 (6.10: [34]). Two unusual types were noted within a modern context (31.1: [570]): a plain fragment in late Roman fabric 3061, and a plain fragment in fabric 3006 with a very small (c 25mm in diameter), knife-cut, circular vent. A group 5 roller-stamped box-flue tile from Building 3 (8.12: [893]) also has part of a knife-cut circular vent in its plain side; this same tile has thickish *opus signinum* adhering to it. A residual example from the early medieval Building 9 (16.2: [179]) in fabric 2815 may have been part of a half-box tile, used against an inner wall face as yet another way of creating a cavity in connection with a hypocaust system (Brodribb 1987, 65–7).

Tegula mammata

A tegula mammata with a single central boss was noted in fabric 2452 from Building 9 (16.2: [179]), with a second possible example, in fabric 3006, with a very small central boss, in Waterfront 4 (3.5: [526]). These are likely to have been of 1st-century AD date. Tegula mammata bricks were used vertically against a wall, their bosses (*mammatae*) placed against it, and held in place with metal clamps in order to form a cavity wall for hypocaust heating as an alternative to the use of flue tiles built into the walls (Brodribb 1987, 63–5).

Ceramic tesserae

Some tesserae were recovered, most of them of ceramic material (but see below for stone tesserae). The ceramic pieces were not specially made but were cut from other ceramic building materials such as tegulae and imbrices. From this site they are either in fabric 2815 or 2454, both very common. Those in fabric 2815

would have provided colour in various shades of orange, red or ruddy brown. They were recovered from structures of all periods, including Waterfront 4 (5.4), Buildings 1 (6.7, 6.9) and 3 (8.16), Structure 1 (10.1, 10.7), late Roman 'dark earth' (11.5), the early medieval Building 9 (15.4), and pit fills in Open Areas 4 (12.1) and 6 (22.1). Those in fabric 2454 would have provided colour in buff-yellow, off-white or pinkish. They were recovered from Buildings 1 (6.9) and 5 (10.7).

Non-ceramic building materials

Tuscan order dwarf column

Trevor Brigham

A 0.95m fragment of column capital in oolitic limestone (see Fig 43) was recovered from an early medieval context at the south-east corner of the Roman townhouse, Building 3 (12.13: [367]). The section consisted of a shaft 260mm in diameter, tapering slightly towards the capital, with 0.29m taken up with the moulded capital itself, under a 440mm square cap with a small 50mm deep rectangular socket in the centre of the upper face for attachment to the architrave. Below the cap was a circular corona or large flat fillet acting as a main element. This was succeeded by a quirked cavetto (concave section with the upper edge undercut to emphasise it), separated from a second quirked cavetto by a beaded or rounded fillet. A pair of contiguous beaded fillets below the cavettos preceded a broad plain band, and below this, a narrow torus preceded by a beaded fillet, and succeeded by an ogival fillet or cyma recta angled acutely back to the shaft.

This type of dwarf column is known from other excavation sites in the City of London: the base of a similar example was found at Regis House in 1929–31 (Brigham & Watson in prep). The source of the stone was probably in the Cotswolds where stylistically similar columns exist, including a complete example at Cirencester, for example (Blagg 1984, pl II), although the Suffolk House column was not as aesthetically balanced, partly because of the presence of a second cavetto, which attenuates the capital. Variations in the details of such columns, even where several more or less identical examples occur – as in the villa at Great Witcombe, Gloucestershire (Blagg 1977, 56–9) – make any attempt to reconstruct the height of the Suffolk House example difficult, although it is likely to have been over 1.5m, and perhaps a little over 2.0m.

Stone rubble

Non-ferruginous sandstone rubble was recovered from dumps behind the early 2nd-century Waterfront 4 (4.3). Kentish rag rubble was widely used, for example in the foundation of the west wall of the rebuilt Building 4 (9.4), while flint nodules were also used, in both early and late contexts, such as in the west wall of Building 5 (10.7). All these would have been fairly easily available within south-east England, the sandstone from various outcrops, the Kentish ragstone from the quarries in the

Maidstone area, and the flint from the chalk hills. From a more distant source was oolitic limestone rubble in the post-Roman dumping over Building 3 (12.13: [353]), possibly from the quarries at Barnack in Northamptonshire. This was almost certainly from the building itself, since it was located with other Roman rubble including the Tuscan column.

Paving and inlay

Carrara-type marble inlays (veneers or paving) were recovered from dumps associated with Waterfront 4 (4.4: <274> [689], 5.1: <367> [698]), both recut and reused. They indicate high status, although unfortunately neither piece was necessarily associated with a particular building from the site. Purbeck marble came from an early level within Building 2 (7.3: <434> [676]) and make-ups over the box-drain associated with Waterfront 4 (5.4: <636> [549]), also reused. A piece of white imported marble from Building 1 (6.11 or 6.13) could not be found for this report, while a small fragment of sandstone also noted in dumps behind Waterfront 4 (4.3: [161]) may have been part of a paving slab.

Daub

Daub was found within Building 1, where it perhaps represents interior (party) walls of wattle and daub, presumably plastered over, since there is evidence for quite high status in this building. Residual Roman daub was also recorded from many of the early medieval contexts examined, much of it in an abraded condition. However, a quantity of daub in good condition with wattle impressions was noted from early medieval dumps in Open Area 6 (22.3), within Building 8 (15.4) and pit fills in Open Area 4 (12.1); other more fragmentary pieces with no impressions were also recovered.

Mudbricks

Mudbricks of Roman date were recovered from the late Roman 'dark earth' (11.2), as well as in medieval contexts, including Open Area 4 (12.1) and Building 8 (15.2). Unfortunately, none was complete and it is not possible to determine dimensions. A fragment from Open Area 3 under Building 1 (6.3: [82]) may have been a large piece of daub, but has no wattle impressions and was probably a fragment of mudbrick; it is partly burned. The contexts in which the mudbricks (and the possible mudbrick) were found all contained exclusively Roman building materials.

Painted wall plaster

Roman painted wall plaster was noted in Buildings 1 (6.13) and 3 (8.12, 8.15), and Open Area 3 (6.2–5), but residual fragments were also recorded in post-Roman contexts, including Open Area 6 (22.1–2), and Buildings 8 (15.4), 9 (16.5) and 12 (19.1). The quality varies from a rough white skim to good-quality red paint; quantities, however, were small. A piece from Building 3

(8.24: [320]) has a flattish impression, as of a timber post against which the plaster would have been laid. This and other painted wall plaster associated with Building 3 indicates a high status, apparent too in the ceramic building material from this building.

Stone tesserae

A few stone tesserae of Roman date were recovered, all of the hard form of chalk known as 'clunch'; they would have provided a white or off-white colour, contrasting with the darker colours of the red or even blackish (if overfired) ceramic tesserae. An example was found in dumps behind Waterfront 4 (5.1: [698]), and three were recovered from Building 1 (6.7: [53], 6.9: [41], [47]), one being a possible example of roughly rectangular shape.

6.10 The Roman plant remains

Lisa Gray

Introduction

This section describes the general methodology used for the processing and analysis of botanical samples of all periods, but deals mainly with the Roman plant remains: the prehistoric and post-Roman samples are dealt with elsewhere (6.1 above, 6.17 below). The results are analysed and discussed with reference to research questions defined prior to the main investigation taking place (Brigham et al 1998).

Sampling and processing methods

Seventy environmental samples were taken during the evaluation in 1994 and excavations in 1996. Of these, 33 samples of all periods were selected for assessment on the basis that dates for the associated contexts were present (Giorgi in Ainsley et al 1996, 14–19).

Eighteen samples with dates, archaeological information and plant remains which could give information about diet, economy or environment were recommended for further analysis, of which four were Roman. Details of the Roman samples are given in Table 17.

Table 17 Provenance of the Roman environmental samples

Period	Land use	Subgroup	Context no.	Sample no.	Feature type
Roman	W4	3.4	527	48	peat
Roman	W4	3.3	528	49	peat
Roman	W4	5.3	610	53	drain fill
late Roman	OA4	11.1	473	47	dark earth

The plant remains were identified as closely as their quality of preservation allowed, using modern reference collections and manuals for the identification of the seeds. A small number of charred cereal grains and chaff were also identified according to criteria designed by Hillman (G C Hillman, pers comm; Hillman 1972). Charred remains were counted, and waterlogged remains were given estimated levels of abundance as shown in the Key to Table 18. Identifications were made to species where possible, and genus and family where diagnostic features were less clear.

Results

The plant remains at Suffolk House were preserved by charring, mineralisation and waterlogging. The greatest number of charred remains were present in the sample from the Roman ditch/drain.

Charring occurs when plant remains are exposed to high temperatures in fires with limited oxygen supply. This converts the organic material in the plant remain to carbon that is then immune to the decaying effects of bacteria or fungi (Zohary & Hopf 1993, 3–4).

Waterlogged remains are preserved by anaerobic conditions in contexts such as waterlogged ditches, ponds, wells and marshland that prevent the decomposition of plant remains.

Mineralisation occurs when organic remains are exposed to urine or lime that replaces the organic compounds in the remains with calcium phosphate (Greig 1982, 49), calcium carbonate or silica (Zohary & Hopf 1993, 6).

Full details about the species present in the samples will be found in Table 18. This section describes the modes of preservation and taxa present. Interpretations are made in the discussion.

Revetment infill

{49} [528] (3.3); {48} [527] (3.4) W4
Most of these remains were preserved by waterlogging.

HABITAT
Like the prehistoric marsh deposits, the Roman revetment infill contained plant macro-remains from a range of disturbed, woodland/scrub and wetland habitats. Also significant in this phase were plant seeds from grassland habitats. In sample [527] {48} woodland/scrub/hedgerow plants appeared to dominate followed by waste/disturbed ground and grassland plants. Sample [528] {49} was dominated by weeds of cultivation and waste/disturbed ground plants. The only purely semi-aquatic/aquatic plant remains for this phase were seeds of spike-rush and marshwort (Apium sp), rush and sedge.

The plant macro-remains in this phase contained a greater range of seeds from plants of cultivated, waste/disturbed ground and grassland than the prehistoric phase. Wild radish/charlock was present along with corncockle (Agrostemma githago L) – a plant found in nutrient-rich soil (Hanf 1983, 293), sheep's sorrel (Rumex acetosella L) – an indicator of poor arable and

woodland soils (Hanf 1983, 403), common sorrel (Rumex acetosa type) – present in nutrient-rich meadows and pastures (Hanf 1983, 403), henbane (Hyoscyamous niger L) – found in open, frequently disturbed soils, and a large number of weld/dyer's rocket (Reseda luteola L) – seeds present in dry areas and in perennial crops (Hanf 1983, 419).

ECONOMIC USES
Remains of edible plants were present. These included fragments of coriander (Coriandrum sativum L), fig seeds, an olive (Olea europaea L) stone, a stone pine scale (Pinus pinea L) and a fragment of walnut (Juglans regia L) shell. Also present were hazelnut shell fragments (Corylus avellana L) and a flax (Linum sp) seed. A sample taken from other waterfront dumps in 1994 ({13} [122]) included grape pips (Vitis vinifera L).

Box-drain fill

{53} [610] (5.3) W4

HABITAT
Like the previous samples, plant remains from waste/disturbed ground, grassland and cultivation dominated. These were associated with sedge seeds.

ECONOMIC USES
Wild edible plants were represented by stinging nettle seeds, blackberry/raspberry seeds and elder (Sambucus nigra L). Of greater significance here was the recovery of charred spelt (Triticum spelta L) wheat grains and chaff. One spelt wheat grain, 10 spelt glume bases and eight spelt wheat rachises were present.

'Dark earth'

{47} [473] (11.1) OA4

HABITAT
Plants of waste and disturbed ground and woodland/scrub/hedgerow dominated this sample. These included fat hen (Chenopodium album L), elder and campion/catchfly (Silene sp) seeds, and to a lesser extent seeds from plants of grassland and semi-aquatic habitats, for example spike-rush (semi-aquatic) and hemlock (Conium maculatum L) (waste ground). This sample is similar to the Roman samples, with spike-rush being the only aquatic/semi-aquatic plant species present. Hemlock and mallow (Malva sylvestris L) were recorded at the site for the first time in this sample. Mallow grows in disturbed ground, woodland/scrub/hedgerow and grassland.

ECONOMIC USES
Like the Roman samples, stinging nettle, elder and blackberry/raspberry were among the edible wild plants. Hop (Humulus lupulus L) was present in very small quantities. Two charred spelt grains and one charred barley grain were also

present. A sample taken during the 1994 evaluation ({43} [310] 11.2) consisted almost entirely of large numbers of elder seeds.

Discussion

Revetment infill: Waterfront 4

The dominance of plants from disturbed/waste ground, grassland and wood/scrub/hedgerow habitats and the relative lack of aquatic plants could indicate that drier conditions were becoming prevalent whether through natural causes or by human activity.

The edible plant remains of coriander, fig, olive, stone pine and walnut are exotic species and Roman introductions. Also present were hazelnut shell fragments which could have been gathered from the surrounding environment. A flax (Linum sp) seed was recovered but it is more likely that it was present as a weed of cultivated ground or grassland rather than representing a crop.

A large number of weld/dyer's rocket (Reseda luteola L) seeds were present in both samples. This is a dye plant and its seeds have been noted as occurring where dyeing has actually taken place (Wilcox 1977, 280). As it was only present in these two samples they may have economic importance.

Box-drain: Waterfront 4

The taxa recovered from this sample give the same picture of the natural environment to that given by the Roman peat deposits: one of marginal agricultural land, damp meadows and scrub.

The waterlogged edible plant remains are not present in numbers high enough to suggest they have been gathered for food but would have been available as a wild resource. Of more interest is the charred cereal assemblage. As more chaff was present than grain it is probable that this represents a by-product of crop processing.

'Dark earth': Open Area 4

The plant taxa identified in this sample seem to confirm the change from wetland in the prehistoric period to gradually drier conditions during Roman activity, a process which appears to continue into this phase. The presence of a very small quantity of hop seeds need not suggest that activity was taking place using hops, because a larger assemblage of hop seeds were recovered from a late medieval or post-medieval well further west; this example could be intrusive, although the well (in EN11) was some distance from the location of the sampled dark earth (EN20). Similarly two charred spelt grains and one barley grain were present in this sample. These may also be residual, possibly associated with the Roman activity at the site rather than meaning that cereals were being processed at the time of the creation of this deposit. The large number of elder seeds present in a 1994 sample do, however, imply an economic use.

Table 18 Details of pre-Roman and Roman botanical remains

Land use			Pre-Roman marsh OA2 (1.5) [18] {2}
Bulk sample volume (litres)			6
Flot volume (millilitres)			250g subsample
Scientific name	English name	Habitat and use codes	
Charred remains			
Indeterminate stem fragment	–	–	–
Indeterminate seeds	–	–	–
Indeterminate wood fragments	–	–	–
Eleocharis sp	Spike-rush	E	–
Triticum spelta L	Spelt wheat grains	FI	–
Triticum spelta L	Spelt wheat glume bases	FI	–
Triticum spelta L	Spelt wheat rachises	FI	–
Hordeum sativum L	Barley grain	FI	–
Vitis vinifera L	Grape	FI	–
Waterlogged remains			
Raphanus raphanistrum L	Wild radish/charlock	A	–
Sonchus asper (L) Hill	Spiny milk-/sow-thistle	AB	–
Agrostemma githago L	Corncockle	AB	–
Chenopodium murale L	Nettle-leaved goosefoot	AB	+
Onopordium acanthium L	Scotch thistle	ABC	+
cf Lamium sp	Dead-nettle	ABC	–
Lamium sp	Dead-nettle	ABC	+
Rumex acetosa/ crispus/obtusifolius	Dock	ABCD	–
Galium sp	Bedstraw	ABCDE	–
Polygonum sp	Knotgrass	ABCDEFG	–
Rumex sp	Dock	ABCDEFG	+
Ranunculus acris/repens/bulbosus	Buttercups	ABCDEG	–
Silene sp	Campion/catchfly	ABCDF	+
Chenopodium sp	Goosefoot	ABCDFH	–
Viola sp	Violet	ABCDG	+
Mentha sp	Mint	ABCEFGI	–
Carduus/Cirsium sp	Thistles	ABDEG	+
Polygonum persicaria L	Persicaria	ABEH	+
Atriplex sp	Orache	ABFGH	+
Brassica/Sinapis sp	Cabbage/mustard	ABFGHI	–
Chenopodium album L	Fat hen	ABFH	+
Polygonum aviculare L	Knotgrass	ABG	–
Reseda luteola L	Weld/dyer's rocket	ABGHI	–
Mentha cf arvensis	Corn mint	ACE	–
Stachys sp	Woundwort	ACEG	–
Rumex acetosella L	Sheep's sorrel	AD	–
Juncus sp	Rush	ADEH	+
Linum sp	Flax	ADHI	–
Rumex crispus L	Curled dock	BC	–
Potentilla sp	Cinquefoil/tormentil	BCDEFGH	+
Urtica dioica L	Stinging nettle	BCDEFGH	++
Malva cf sylvestris	Mallow	BCDF	–
Prunella vulgaris L	Self-heal	BCDG	–

Pre-Roman marsh OA2 (1.5) [19] {1}	Pre-Roman marsh OA2 (1.5) [569] {57}	Pre-Roman marsh OA2 (1.5) [569] {60}	Pre-Roman marsh OA2 (1.5) [693] {73} 0–100mm	Pre-Roman marsh OA2 (1.5) [693] {75} 2–300mm	Pre-Roman marsh OA2 (1.5) [693] {77} 4–500mm	Pre-Roman marsh OA2 (1.5) [693] {79} 6–700mm	Pre-Roman marsh OA2 (1.5) [693] {81} 8–900mm	Roman quay fill W4 (3.4) [527] {48}	Roman quay fill W4 (3.3) [528] {49}	Roman drain fill W4 (5.3) [610] {53}	Dark earth OA4 (11.1) [473] {47}
6	10	10	10	10	10	10	10	10	18	16	20
250g subsample	250g subsample	250g subsample	250g subsample	250g subsample	250g subsample	250g subsample	250g subsample	300ml +250g subsample	255ml	255ml	90ml
–	–	–	–	–	–	–	–	–	–			–
–	–			–	–	–	–	–	–	–	–	–
–	++	++++	–	–	–	++++	–	++++	++++	++++	–
–			–	–	–	–	–	–	–	–	–	–
–	–	–	–	–	–	–	–	–	–			2
–	–	–	–	–	–	–	–	–	–	10	–
–	–	–	–	–	–	–	–	–	–	8	–
–					–	–	–	–	–	–	–	–		
–			–	–	–	–	–	–	–	–	–	–
–	–	+	–	–	–	–	–	–	+	–	–
–	+	–	–	–	–	–	–	+	+	–	–
–	–	–	–	–	–	–	–	+	–	–	–
–	–	–	–	–	–	–	–	–	+	++	–
–	–	–	–	–	–	–	–	–	–	–	–
–	–	+	–	–	–	–	–	–	–	–	–
–	–	–	–	–	–	–	–	–	–	–	+
–	++	++	–	–	–	–	–	–	–	–	–
–	–	–	–	–	–	+	–	–	–	–	–
–	+	–	–	–	–	–	–	+	–	–	–
–	+	+	–	–	–	–	–	–	–	–	–
+	+	+	+	+	–	–	–	+++	++	++	–
–	+	+	–	–	–	–	–	+	+	+	+
+	+	+	–	–	–	–	–	+	–	–	–
–	+	+	–	–	–	–	–	+	–	++	–
–	–	–	–	–	–	–	–	–	+	–	–
–	+	+	–	–	–	–	–	–	–	–	–
–	++	+	–	–	–	–	–	–	–	–	–
–	–	–	–	–	–	–	–	+	–	–	–
–	–	–	–	–	–	–	–	+	–	+	+
–	+	+	–	–	–	–	–	–	+	–	–
–	–	–	–	–	–	–	–	+++	+++	–	–
–	–	+	–	–	–	–	–	–	–	–	–
–	–	–	–	–	–	+	–	–	–	–	–
–	+	–	–	–	–	–	–	–	+	–	–
–	–	–	–	–	–	–	–	++	–	–	–
–	–	–	–	–	–	–	–	–	+	–	–
–	+	–	–	–	–	–	–	–	–	–	–
–	–	+	–	–	–	–	–	+	–	+	–
+	+	–	+	+	–	+	+	–	–	+	+
–	–	–	–	–	–	–	–	–	–	–	+
+	–	–	–	–	–	–	–	++	–	–	–

(*Table 18 cont*)

Land use			Pre-Roman marsh OA2 (1.5) [18] {2}	Pre-Roman marsh OA2 (1.5) [19] {1}	Pre-Roman marsh OA2 (1.5) [569] {57}	Pre-Roman marsh OA2 (1.5) [569] {60}	Pre-Roman marsh OA2 (1.5) [693] {73} 0–100mm	Pre-Roman marsh OA2 (1.5) [693] {75} 2–300mm	Pre-Roman marsh OA2 (1.5) [693] {77} 4–500mm
Bulk sample volume (litres)			6	6	10	10	10	10	10
Flot volume (millilitres)			250g subsample	250g subsample	250g subsample	250g subsample	250g subsample	250g subsample	250g subsample
Scientific name	**English name**	**Habitat and use codes**							
Sambucus nigra L	Elder	BCFGH	+	+	+	+	+	+	–
Leontondon sp	Hawkbit	BDF	–	–	–	–	–	–	–
Hyoscyamous niger L	Henbane	BDG	–	–	–	–	–	–	–
Solanum nigrum L	Black nightshade	BF	++	–	+	+	–	–	–
Stellaria graminea L	Lesser stitchwort	CD	–	–	–	–	–	–	–
Ajuga reptans L	Bugle	CDE	+	–	+	+	–	–	–
Potentilla erecta L	Tormentil	CDEGH	–	–	–	+	–	–	–
Cyperaceae	Sedges	CDEH	–	++	–	–	–	–	–
Carex sp	Sedge	CDEH	++	–	+	+	+	–	–
Carex spp	Sedge	CDEH	–	–	–	–	–	–	–
Rumex acetosa type	Common sorrel	CDF	–	–	–	–	–	–	–
Alnus glutinosa L	Alder seeds	CE	–	+	+	+	–	–	–
Alnus glutinosa L	Alder catkins	CE	–	+	–	–	+	–	–
Conium maculatum L	Hemlock	CEG	–	–	–	–	–	–	–
Corylus avellana L	Hazelnut shell fragment	CF	–	–	–	–	–	–	+
Rubus fruticosus/idaeus	Blackberry/raspberry	CFGH	++	+	++	++	+	–	–
Prunus avium/cerasus	Sloe/cherry	CFGI	–	–	+	+	–	–	–
Humulus lupulus L	Hop	CGHI	–	–	–	–	–	–	–
cf Oenanthe aquatica L	Fine-leaved water dropwort	E	–	–	–	+	–	–	–
Eleocharis sp	Spike-rush	E	–	–	–	+	–	–	–
Iris pseudacorus L	Yellow iris/yellow flag	E	–	–	–	+	–	+	–
Potamogeton sp	Pondweed	E	+	–	+	–	–	–	–
Ranunculus sceleratus L	Celery-leaved crowfoot	E	+	–	+	–	–	–	–
Ranunculus subgen Batrachium	Crowfoots	E	–	–	–	+	+	–	–
Sparganium erectum L	Bur-reed	E	–	+	+	–	–	–	–
Apium sp	Marshwort	EFI	+	–	+	+	–	–	–
Ranunculus flammula L	Lesser spearwort	EG	–	–	–	+	–	–	–
Lycopus europaeus L	Gipsy-wort	EH	+	–	+	+	–	–	–
Coriandrum sativum L	Coriander	FGI	–	–	–	–	–	–	–
Ficus carica L	Fig	FGI	–	–	+	–	–	–	–
Juglans regia L	Walnut shell fragment	FHI	–	–	–	–	–	–	–
Olea europaea	Olive	FGHI	–	–	–	–	–	–	–
Pinus pinea L	Stone pine shell fragment	FHI	–	–	–	–	–	–	–
Indeterminate Bryophyta sp	–	–	–	–	++	+	++	+	–
Indeterminate leaf fragments	–	–	–	–	–	–	–	–	++
Indeterminate bud fragment	–	–	–	–	–	+	–	–	–
Indeterminate stem fragments	–	–	++++	–	++++	++++	–	++	++
Indeterminate wood fragments	–	–	++++	++++	++	+++	++++	–	++
Indeterminate seeds	–	–	–	–	–	–	–	–	–

Key

Habitat/use codes: A – weeds of cultivated land; B – ruderals, weeds of waste places and disturbed ground; C – plants of woods, scrub and hedgerow; D – open grassland/heath; E – plants of damp/wet environment and aquatics; F – edible plants; G – medicinal and poisonous plants; H – commercial/industrial use; I – cultivated plants

Estimated levels of abundance: + = 1–10; ++ = 11–50; +++ = 51–150; ++++ = many 100s

Pre-Roman marsh	Pre-Roman marsh	Roman quay fill	Roman quay fill	Roman drain fill	Dark earth
OA2 (1.5)	OA2 (1.5)	W4 (3.4)	W4 (3.3)	W4 (5.3)	OA4 (11.1)
[693] {79}	[693] {81}	[527] {48}	[528] {49}	[610] {53}	[473] {47}
6–700mm	8–900mm				
10	10	10	18	16	20
250g subsample	250g subsample	300ml +250g subsample	255ml	255ml	90ml
–	+	–	–	+	+
–	–	–	+	–	–
–	–	+	–	+	–
–	–	–	–	+	–
–	–	+	–	+	–
–	–	–	–	–	–
–	–	+	+	–	–
–	–	–	–	–	–
–	+	–	–	++	+
–	–	++	+	–	–
–	–	++	–	–	–
–	–	–	–	–	–
–	–	–	–	–	++
–	–	++	++	–	–
+	+	+	–	+	+
–	–	+	–	–	–
–	–	–	–	–	+
–	–	–	–	–	–
–	–	++	+	++	+
–	–	–	–	–	–
–	–	–	–	+	–
–	–	–	+	–	–
–	–	–	–	–	–
–	–	–	–	+	–
–	–	+	–	–	–
–	–	+	–	–	–
–	–	+	–	–	–
–	–	+	–	–	–
–	–	+++	+++	+	–
++++	++++	–	–	–	–
–	–	–	–	–	–
++++	++++	++++	–	–	–
–	–	++++	–	++++	++++
–	–	+	+	+	–

6.11 The Roman animal bone

Introduction

This section is concerned with the animal bones recovered from Roman contexts at Suffolk House during both phases of excavation work in 1996, and is based on the results of the original post-excavation assessment by Charlotte Ainsley, which described and quantified the hand-collected bones and assessed the potential for further study. It has not been possible within the scope of this publication to carry out more specific analysis on this material, although it is retained within the archive for future research.

Sampling and processing methods

The animal bones were mainly collected together with other categories of material, such as pottery, and were not the result of specific sampling, although smaller bones are often recovered from environmental samples. In this instance, 38.68kg of animal bone (about 1000 fragments) were recovered from 43 contexts of all periods during the 1996 excavation, and a further 30.60kg of bone from 69 contexts in 1994, although these were mainly of medieval date and added little to the Roman assemblage; records of these are retained in the Museum of London archive.

Results

Most of the animal bone was sufficiently well preserved to allow the identification of butchery marks and measurement points, although the degree of fragmentation and the quality of preservation of the bone fluctuated from context to context. The majority of the bone within the Roman building deposits, despite being burnt, was well preserved and in fragments between 20mm and 70mm long. The results are discussed below in terms of phase and context.

Early foreshore and dumps

[691] (4.1) OA2
The early foreshore below Waterfront 3 contained remains of cattle and pig. One cattle tibia showed distinctive marks which suggested that it was the waste product of boneworking.

Revetment infill

[596] (4.2) W3
The uppermost dumps behind Waterfront 3 produced remains of cattle, cattle-size mammals, sheep/goat, chicken (humerus and tibia) and horse. The last species was represented by a single chopped humerus. Butchery was also common on the cattle upper limbs present.

Revetment infill

[527] [528] (3.3–4); [122] (4.3); [689] (4.4); [623] [698] (5.1) W4
The lower deposits in front of Waterfront 3 (3.3–4), associated with the construction of Waterfront 4, produced a mix of cattle,

pig, sheep, cattle-size and sheep-size bones. A single dog tibia [527] and a roe deer metatarsal [528] were recovered. As there was no consistency in the skeletal representation or the positioning of butchery marks it appeared probable that they represented domestic rubbish, rather than industrial waste. This was borne out by the range of other artefacts which suggested that they had been rubbish dumps. Both [527] and [528] contained a number of oyster and winkle shells (0.227kg in total) and a section of cuttlefish shell was present in the latter. A large amount of material was recovered from [689] (4.4), a deposit containing approximately 50 bones, predominately cattle and cattle-size fragments. A notable find was a foetal or newborn cattle humerus. Pigs, sheep/goat, sheep-size mammals, chicken and unidentified fish vertebrae were also present. In addition a single mandible showed the presence of horse. Butchery was evident on the upper limbs of both pigs and cattle. From the upper deposits (5.1) an interesting find was a sawn antler tine [698] which suggests that they included industrial-processing waste. A fragment of sea urchin was also present [623]. A single eel vertebrae (*Anguilla anguilla*) was found in dumps some distance behind the main waterfront area (4.3: [122]), although it is interpreted as part of the same phase of activity.

Occupation deposits

[678] (7.2); [676] [677] (7.3); [671] [672] [673] [675] (7.4) B2

Animal remains were recovered from two separate building deposits and a pit fill. These represented either an *in situ* hearth deposit [676] or the rake-out from domestic fires that had been trampled into the ground by the occupants [671], [672], [673], [675] and [677]. A mixed distribution of skeletal remains was recovered of cattle, pig sheep/goat and limb bones of chicken. Roe deer presence is indicated by a scapula [672]. The majority of these bones were burned and fragmentary, supporting the idea of trampled domestic refuse, perhaps cooked on the nearby hearth, although the discovery of a gold-refiner's crucible may imply an industrial usage. Butchered cattle bones (rib, tibia and radius) were in a rare pit deposit [678] within Building 2.

Box-drain fill

[610] (5.3) W4

Fragmentation of the bones from the drain behind Waterfront 4 was high, the majority being less than 25mm in length, consistent with silt deposition. Identifiable remains were all cattle (vertebrae, rib and a section of metapodial).

'Dark earth'

[473] (11.1); [309] [310] (11.2) OA4

A range of animals was represented within this layer, which included sheep-size vertebrae and ribs, a single foetal or neonatal pig tibia, rat, mouse and vole, including vole teeth [310] and chicken limb bones. All the bones were highly fragmentary. The same contexts also produced shellfish, the majority of which was oyster with a few terrestrial species.

Discussion

The majority of the bones recovered were representative of general household processing and food waste, provided mainly by the three main domesticates. It is possible that [527] and [528] (Waterfront 4) were industrial-processing waste rather than domestic rubbish, although this is unlikely given the nature of the rest of the finds assemblage; a cattle tibia from [691] did, however, show evidence of boneworking. Evidence of butchery, particularly in [678] and [689], probably represents the dressing, halving and jointing processes.

A small quantity of wild animal bone was present, including roe deer, possibly red deer (found in 1994), and duck, indicating the importance of hunting to vary the diet. They may also be an indicator of status, either through the ability to purchase such relatively expensive items, or through time available for hunting. This may be related to the presence of high-quality buildings at Suffolk House. Normally non-edible species – such as dog, cat and horse – were rare, although a chopped horse humerus was recovered, perhaps indicating food use. Small mammals – such as voles, rats and mice – would have been local pests, the presence of vole presumably reflecting the proximity of the river or wet areas.

A low proportion of fish bone, including eel and oyster and other marine shells, were recovered through all phases of the site, but not in sufficient quantities to suggest that they were part of the diet to any notable degree. A sea urchin shell suggests some dietary variety. This general absence is surprising considering the proximity of the river, and contrasts sharply with the very large industrial-scale dumps of oyster found around the bridge at Regis House and Pudding Lane (Brigham & Watson in prep), and the variety of fish found in the pit assemblages at Fennings Wharf which imply both river and saltwater fishing (Rielly in Watson *et al* 2001).

In summary, it can be seen that the bones were the remains of general waste, provided mainly by the major mammalian domesticates, which reflect economic and domestic practices from the Roman period. The proximity of high-status buildings was not reflected in the range of species represented: more examples of rare or exotic game species might have been expected, for example.

6.12 The Roman goldworking evidence

Megan Dennis and Malcolm Ward
Ancient Monuments Laboratory

Introduction

Goldworking debris excavated from Area 4 of Bush Lane House in 1972 (Marsden 1975, 9–13) and Suffolk House in 1996 has been assessed together. The debris includes crucibles for melting gold, crucibles for cupellation, parting vessels and lids and luting fragments. Gold dust was also recovered from Bush Lane House.

Through X-ray fluorescence analysis and scanning electron microscopy techniques, it was possible to distinguish between gold-melting and cupellation vessels. The objects produced on site are unknown.

The material from Bush Lane House was concentrated in the fill of a well and pit dated AD 80–100 by the pottery contained within it (Marsden 1975, 12). The assemblage included gold dust, parting vessels, lids, a crucible, and clay fragments used to seal lids on to the parting vessels (luting), which were examined by Mavis Bimson of the British Museum Research Laboratory at the time of original publication (Marsden 1975, 100). Since then there have been significant advances in the recognition of evidence of different precious metalworking processes. During assessment of the new material from the site the evidence from the original investigations has been reassessed.

The Suffolk House assemblage from Buildings 2 and 4 and the waterfronts further south comprises one complete crucible and several fragments of two other crucibles (see Fig 73); fragments of a fourth crucible were not examined.

Background

Gold and copper objects have been made and used in the British Isles since 2000 BC (Bayley 1992a, 314). During the Roman period they were primarily used for the production of coinage and jewellery (Adkins & Adkins 1982, 113). The processing of gold is made up of several different procedures: mining, assaying and refining, melting and casting. The collection of native gold during the Roman period was probably limited to a small number of areas; the only known British mine during this period was at Dolaucothi, Carmarthenshire, Wales, where metal was extracted from a series of deep shafts and open-cast mines. Aqueducts brought water 11km from the nearby river to create settling tanks in which gold separated out from rock and soil. The mines remained in production up to the late 1860s (Sutherland 1959, 92).

Assaying and refining were performed from the Late Iron Age to the late medieval period in three different ways: using touchstones to assess colour; by careful calculations of density; and by cupellation and parting. The first two methods produce little diagnostic archaeological evidence. Touchstones utilise the streaks of colour that can be made on a black stone with soft metal such as gold. Comparisons of the colours of various alloys can reveal compositions, but leave no archaeological evidence other than the touchstones themselves (Moore & Oddy 1985). Sets of scales, such as those needed to calculate density, are often found, but have many varied uses.

Cupellation is a chemical process. During the Roman period it was carried out in reduced-fired ceramic dishes, crucibles or on pot sherds. The process involved weighing a sample of the gold which was then melted with an excess of lead ('fused with lead': Bailey 1929, 91) and a blast of air blown across it. This oxidised the lead to form litharge (PbO). Any base metals in the gold would also be oxidised and then dissolve into the lead oxide, and the pure gold or silver would then coalesce and could be reweighed once cooled. Any loss in weight would be calculated to reveal the original composition of the gold. Cupellation is carried out on a larger scale to refine larger quantities of precious metals, and cannot separate silver from gold, a process known as parting.

Theophilus, writing in the medieval period, mentions two such processes – salt and sulphur methods (Hawthorne & Smith 1979, 147). Archaeological evidence only survives for the salt process, which involved the layering of the metal in fine sheets between a mixture of salt and finely powdered brick, tile or clay. To this a weak acid was added (for example fresh urine) and the whole container was carefully sealed with luting clay and heated (Bayley 1991, 20). This would result in the creation of silver chlorides which were absorbed into the 'cement', leaving the pure gold. The silver could afterwards be recovered.

Precious metals were melted in crucibles very similar to those used for the melting of base metals, although these were often smaller because of the increased worth of the precious metals and consequently the smaller quantities used at one time. They would then be cast into intricate finished objects or simple ingots ready to be worked.

Description of the debris

The debris from both excavations was examined visually, but the crucibles were carefully studied and analysed in detail.

A fragment of one crucible was excavated by Marsden (Guildhall Museum acc no. 24505) and has been re-examined. Fragments from two further crucibles and a complete crucible were found and examined during the later excavations (<440> <232> and <243>): a fourth (<443>) showed no visible traces of metal, and was not analysed.

24505 is a quarter of a crucible of reduced fabric, heavily vitrified and beginning to bloat. It is dark grey in colour with some areas of orange colouring on the outer surface that may be due to post-depositional iron staining. It contains small mica and quartz inclusions (less than 1mm in diameter), but no other tempering. Both the inner and outer surfaces show some cracking and crazing from the high temperatures it has been exposed to. The inner surface seems to have been eroded, but there are remains of a green/black glassy layer on the rim, and near the bottom of the fragment a thin coating of orange material which may also be the remains of a vitrified layer. Between these glazes is a very fine scattering of gold droplets. These are concentrated at the base of the fragment, but there are some visible in the black glaze near the rim. Gold droplets can also be seen within the cracks on the surface of the sherd which suggest that it may have been reused.

<440> is a small fragment of fine grey reduced fabric starting to become bloated from the high temperatures involved in goldworking. The inner surface is covered in a thin green/black glassy layer in which gold droplets of up to 1mm in diameter are trapped.

<232> (Fig 73: <S27>) is two fragments of an almost complete spouted crucible. It is made of a heavily quartz-tempered reduced coarse black/grey fabric with temper grains of a uniform size between 0.3–0.5mm. The inner surface is

heavily vitrified, especially on the lower walls and base, where the black vitrified layer is between 0.5–2mm thick. There are several areas of gold droplets, which are mostly concentrated on the upper walls and rim of the crucible, trapped in the thinner layers of vitrification present there.

<243> (Fig 73: <S28>) is a complete vessel of a grey/yellow sandy, quartz-tempered reduced fabric. The temper is finer than in <232>, the grains being only *c* 0.2mm in diameter. There are gold droplets trapped within a yellow/orange vitrified layer

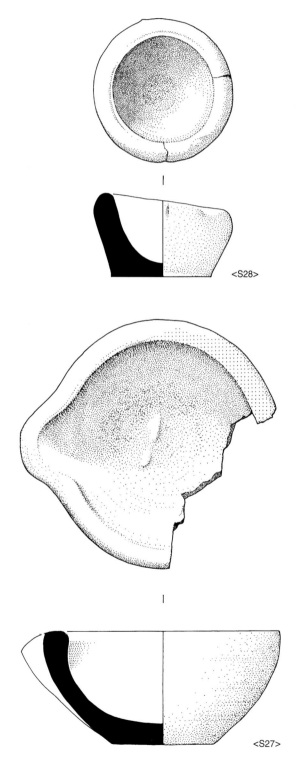

Fig 73 *Goldworking crucibles from Waterfront 4 and Building 4: <S27> <S28> (1:1)*

on the inner surface. This layer is thicker around the area where the gold droplet has cooled and coalesced and then been removed, leaving a pit. In the base of the depression where the gold drop solidified a darker green/black glassy layer can be seen, but it has been quite heavily eroded. The pit rim is parallel to the uneven crucible rim – this suggests that when the crucible was used it stood on an uneven floor. There are some signs of slight vitrification on the upper walls and rim of the outer surface.

The samples were first analysed using X-ray fluorescence which provides a non-destructive method of identifying the elements present in the samples. The results for the samples analysed are presented in Table 19. Further analysis was then carried out using energy dispersive X-ray analysis (EDX) in a scanning electron microscope (SEM).

Table 19 *XRF analysis of goldworking debris from the 'Governor's Palace' area*

Small find no.	Area analysed	Fe	Cu	Au	Pb	Ag
<440>	crucible inner surface	**	*	*	tr	–
<232>	crucible inner surface	**	tr	**	**	–
<232>	crucible rim	*	*	–	***	–
<243>	crucible inner surface	***	tr	**	*	*
24505	crucible inner surface	**	tr	**	tr	–

Key: *** – strong signal; ** – present; * – weak signal; tr – trace element

Interpretation of SEM-EDX analysis results

Sample 990005

<440> [673] (7.4) B2
The XRF results show only a trace of lead which suggests that the crucible was not used for cupellation as this normally produces a highly lead-rich silicate glass on the inner surfaces of the ceramic. This conclusion is reinforced by the SEM-EDX analysis that shows that the gold droplet (A) is relatively pure gold, containing only small amounts of silver and copper and no lead. Darker areas in the gold droplet were shown by analysis to be hydrocarbon stains from cleaning and polishing agents. The glassy layer on the crucible is made up of various silicates and oxides but there is no lead present. The vitrified layers are the result of reaction between the crucible fabric and alkali fluxes or fuel ash at high temperatures.

CONCLUSION
Crucible <440> was used to melt gold.

Sample 990006

<232> [623] (5.1) W4
The XRF results revealed that the two fragments of the crucible contained high levels of gold and also lead. This suggested it

was used for the cupellation of gold, and SEM-EDX analysis was used to identify the different phases present in the sample.

The glassy layer on the crucible has a relatively uniform composition; it is a mixture of lead and alkali silicates. This is the sort of composition to be expected on a ceramic cupel. The gold droplet has an unusual two-phase structure. Both phases contain lead which suggests the conditions became insufficiently oxidising for the lead (which had been added to the gold to cupel it) to be converted to lead oxide. The phase which appears grey is higher in gold and also contains some silver and the copper that had not been extracted by cupellation. This would have solidified first from the molten metal which accounts for its dendritic structure. The remaining metal contains more lead. Some of this phase has corroded during burial, the lead being partly oxidised.

CONCLUSION

This crucible was used to cupel gold, but the process has not gone to completion. The gold still contains some copper and considerable amounts of lead as conditions did not become sufficiently oxidising to complete the reaction.

Sample 990007

<243> [660] (9.1) B4

The XRF results did not show high quantities of lead, suggesting that this complete crucible had been used for melting rather than cupellation. Detailed analysis using the SEM-EDX system, although not quantitatively reliable, did show that the vessel had not been used for cupellation.

The gold droplet examined contained two phases. The grey purified phase contained only gold and silver, the white phase contained some lead (this phase was difficult to identify as it only made up a very small percentage of the whole). Jagged edges and holes in the droplet were formed because it had cooled and solidified after flowing into the surrounding porous ceramic fabric. The black and orange glass phases were revealed not to be of significantly different atomic weight.

CONCLUSION

The crucible has been used for melting of gold. The gold has previously been cupelled, in a different crucible, but still contains a small amount of lead because the process was not completed efficiently.

General discussion

The assemblage from this site has been shown to provide evidence for several stages of gold processing:
1) the cupellation of gold in small crucibles
2) the parting of gold, in larger vessels, using the salt method
3) the melting of gold in crucibles.

During the Roman period most gold objects were wrought (hammered or cold-worked into shape: J Bayley, pers comm) and not cast. Therefore it was unimportant what shape the molten gold was allowed to cool in as it would be reworked

when it was cool. The gold from crucible <243> has only been removed once it has cooled and coalesced into a droplet at the bottom. When it was removed it left a 'pit' in the glassy layer. The glaze on the lower section of 24505 also appears to have become removed. It is possible that it was pulled away from the fabric of the crucible when the solid droplet of gold was removed from the base.

It is unclear whether the cupellation crucible was used for assaying the gold from a large batch to test its purity or to purify a smaller quantity of metal. It may be that both processes were occurring on the site.

Equally it is unclear whether all the evidence came from one workshop. There was no related structure found with the debris during either excavation, although the concentration of the Bush Lane crucibles and parting vessels in a pit and well suggests that the goldsmith may have been working in one small structure. Marsden suggests that this may have been located in or near Rooms 5 and 6 of the later 'Governor's Palace', but it is possible that several goldsmiths were working in the same area in several different workshops and disposing of their debris in the same deposits.

In the Roman period all gold mining was controlled centrally (Wacher 1998, 217), but this does not imply that mining or working gold would necessarily be carried out by Roman officials. It is likely that most jewellers and craftspeople could practise refining processes and only the export and mining of the mineral resources were fully supervised (Wacher 1998, 217).

New gold objects can be made in two different ways: the recycling of old worn-out objects or the utilisation of newly mined native gold. It is impossible to know what type of material the goldsmith in the 'Governor's Palace' area was using as a raw material. The small size of the cupellation dish excavated (<232>) may suggest that he was simply purifying old gold before reusing it. This would be necessary to remove copper and silver which were often used in solders in gold jewellery. Unless these metals are removed before remelting they become mixed with the gold to create an alloy, and this can make it more difficult to work and can change the colour of the metal. It is possible, however, that the small cupellation dish was simply used to test a sample of gold for purity.

The processes of cupellation and parting had been known since the Late Iron Age and had been perfected by the Roman period. However, the sticky residues often formed during these processes, if not properly absorbed, would prevent the gold droplet from completely coalescing. Small gold droplets would become trapped in the slag layers (as can be seen on the walls and rims of the crucibles). This has occurred to a greater degree on the gold-melting crucibles (<440> <243> and 24505). The lead-rich slags produced during cupellation have a lower melting point, and therefore are more liquid allowing the gold droplets to coalesce more easily. The waste caused by this could have been prevented by crushing the crucibles and panning the powder produced to recover the gold. It is strange that the smith has left so much waste within the crucibles, especially as gold is a very valuable metal.

Although crucible 24505 was not analysed using the SEM, by comparing the XRF results it can be seen that it is likely that it was used for gold melting. The low levels of lead within it show that it was not used in cupellation.

Conclusions

The goldworking debris from the 'Governor's Palace' area is diagnostic of gold melting, cupellation and parting. Casting and manufacture of wrought-gold objects may also have been carried out on the site, but there is no physical evidence for these processes. It has been shown that cupels and crucibles used to melt gold can be differentiated through careful elemental analysis of the glassy layers built up through these processes. It is still unclear whether the cupellation process was being used to test the purity of large batches of gold, or to purify small scraps. The output from the site is unknown but may have covered a wide range of objects.

6.13 The dendrochronological dating

Ian Tyers and Gretel Boswijk
ARCUS Dendrochronology

Introduction

A total of 31 samples from Suffolk House were submitted of which 27 samples were suitable for analysis. Dates were obtained from 18 samples. Fig 74 and Table 20 show the date spans obtained from these. All the dated samples were from Waterfronts 2, 3 and a drain associated with Waterfront 4, and

the timbers are of apparently local origin. The undated material has been checked against Roman chronologies from elsewhere in Britain and Europe, as well as earlier and later chronologies from London and elsewhere.

Standard dendrochronological methods were applied to the timbers, which are all oak (*Quercus* spp).

Three types of dating result are usually obtained by dendrochronological analysis. Firstly, where a sample is complete to bark edge a precise year of felling is obtained directly from the date of the last ring of the sample. Secondly, where a sample has some sapwood, but is not complete to bark edge, a felling date range is obtained by applying the maximum and minimum numbers of rings of sapwood normally seen in English oaks to the relevant samples. The range 10–55 is used throughout this report, based on modern and excavated timbers from England (Hillam & Tyers 1987). Finally, where no sapwood survives, a *terminus post quem* (TPQ) date is obtained by adding the minimum number of sapwood rings likely to have been lost to the date of the latest surviving ring. This type of date is very much less useful than the other two types since a very great number of rings could have been lost through either ancient carpentry practice or poor site preservation, and thus the felling date of such material may be considerably later than the tree-ring date.

Results

Waterfront 2: Roman quay tiebacks

Nine samples were dated from this structure. Six of these included some sapwood, and sample [594], which included complete sapwood and bark edge, was felled in spring AD 84. The less complete material appeared to be compatible with this date, since they gave a combined felling date range of AD 83–105.

Table 20 Tree-ring dates for timbers from Suffolk Lane

Context	Land use	Comment	Rings	Sap	Growth rate	Early date	Late date
582	W2		98	0	2.95	35 BC	AD 63
583	W2		63	0	4.27	AD 10	AD 72
584	W2		125	11	2.59	59 BC	AD 66
585	W2		243	23	1.15	170 BC	AD 73
586	W2		85	0	2.39	45 BC	AD 40
587	W2		138	2	1.4	81 BC	AD 57
588	W2		214	10	0.89	144 BC	AD 70
589	W2		75	0	3.96	40 BC	AD 35
594	W2		243	36	1.53	159 BC	AD 84
609 (1)	drain (W4)		90	0	1.92	22 BC	AD 68
609 (2)	drain (W4)		80	0	1.89	19 BC	AD 61
612	drain (W4)		67	1	1.5	AD 36	AD 102
614	drain (W4)		73	25	1.39	AD 56	AD 128
650	W3		90	0	1.63	76 BC	AD 14
682	W3	reused	98	22	1.6	10 BC	AD 88
683	W3	reused	132	12	1.54	54 BC	AD 78
684	W3	reused	96	0	1.58	129 BC	34 BC
685	W3	reused	174	17	1.07	120 BC	AD 54

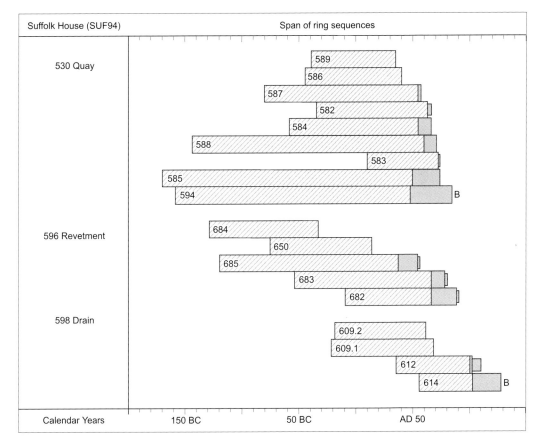

Fig 74 Bar diagram showing dated oak timbers from Suffolk Lane

Waterfront 3: post-and-plank revetment

Five samples were dated from this structure. Three of these included some sapwood, but most ([682]–[685], felled between AD 56 and AD 121) are thought to have been reused from an earlier structure or structures. The possible non-reused timber [650] provided only a *terminus post quem* of AD 14. A felling date range of AD 90–121 is suggested for [682], and bearing in mind the evidence of reuse and the date of AD 128 for a timber from a subsequent drain (see below), the first quarter of the 2nd century might be suggested for the construction of the revetment.

Box-drain

Four timbers were dated from this structure, which is thought to have functioned with Waterfront 4 (beyond the southern site boundary). Two of these included sapwood, and [614] was complete to bark edge. This timber was felled in AD 128. Timber [612] was derived from the same tree.

Conclusions

Valuable dating evidence of three 1st- and 2nd-century structures has provided a framework for the earlier history of the southern part of the site. In two cases bark-edge dates of non-reused timbers provided the highest quality of dating and it can be suggested that these are likely to provide the actual construction dates of the structures from which the samples derived. The dating for the construction of Waterfront 3 is less certain, although a date in the early 2nd century seems likely.

6.14 The medieval pottery

Lyn Blackmore

Introduction

In all a total of 715 sherds of medieval pottery was recovered from the site; this is mainly of Late Saxon and early medieval date, with only one good later medieval group and only 12 post-medieval sherds. The assemblage was quantified by sherd-count and estimated vessel equivalent (EVE), but not by weight, and where percentages are quoted below these are based on sherd-counts only. For various reasons the assemblage is discussed here as one group, but chronological trends are also noted in the land-use descriptions. The Late Saxon pottery is in generally good condition, with some quite sizeable sherds and a number of rims. The 12th- to 15th-century sherds are mostly of average size and condition but those from [196] comprise substantial parts of six vessels. Table 21 expands the abbreviations used below, and Table 22 gives the frequency of the medieval ware types.

Table 21 Medieval and post-medieval fabric codes

Fabric	Expansion	Range
Medieval		
ANDE	Andenne-type ware	1050–1200
BADO	Badorf-type ware	900–1200
BLGR	Blue-grey ware	1050–1200
CBW	Coarse Border ware	1270–1500
EGS	Early German Stoneware	1250–1300
EMCH	Early Medieval Chalky ware	1050–1150
EMCW	Early Medieval Coarse Whiteware	1000–1150
EMFL	Early Medieval Flinty ware	970–1100
EMFL COAR	Abundant Flint-tempered ware	900–1050
EMGR	Early Medieval Grog-tempered ware	1050–1150
EMIS	Early Medieval Iron-rich Sandy ware	1050–1150
EMS	Early Medieval Sandy ware	970–1100
EMSH	Early Medieval Shelly ware	1050–1150
EMSS	Early Medieval Sand- and Shell-tempered ware	1000–1150
ESUR	Early Surrey ware	1050–1150
ESUR FL	Early Surrey ware + flint	1050–1150
HUY	Huy-type ware	875–925
KING	Kingston-type ware	1230–1400
KINGSL	Surrey Medieval Slipped Whitewares	1250–1400
LCALC	Calcareous London-type ware	1080–1200
LCOAR	Coarse London-type ware	1080–1200
LCOAR CALC	Calcareous LCOAR	1080–1200
LCOAR SHEL	Shelly Coarse London-type ware	1080–1200
LLON	Late London ware	1400–1500
LMHG	Late Medieval Hertfordshire Glazed ware	1340–1450
LOGR	Local Greyware	1050–1150
LOND	London-type ware	1080–1350
LSS	Late Saxon Shelly ware	900–1050
MG	Mill Green ware	1270–1350
NFRE	Misc North French Unglazed wares	900–1200
REDP	Red-painted ware	900–1250
REDP OLV	Red-painted ware olive fabric	900–1250
REDP WHT	Red-painted ware white fabric	900–1250
RHGR	Rhenish Greyware (Tiel type)	900–1100
SATH	Sandy Thetford-type ware	1000–1150
SHER	S Herts/Limpsfield Greywares	1140–1300
SHER FL	S Herts Greyware + flint	1150–1300
SIEG	Siegburg Unglazed Stoneware	1300–1500
SSW	Shelly Sandy ware	1140–1220
STAM	Stamford ware	1050–1150 (crucibles poss 1000+)
THET	Ipswich Thetford-type ware	1000–1150
TUDG	Tudor Green ware	1350–1500
Post-medieval		
DUTR	Dutch Red Earthenware	1300–1650
EBORD	Early Border ware	1480–1550
PMBL	Post-medieval Black-glazed ware	1580–1700
PMBR	Post-medieval Bichrome Redware	1480–1600
PMRE	Early Post-medieval Redware	1480–1600
PMSRG	Post-medieval Slip-coated Redware with green glaze	1480–1650
RAER	Raeren Stoneware	1480–1610
TGW	English Tin-glazed ware	1570–1800

Fabrics and forms

A total of 42 different medieval fabrics was recorded; wares which can be definitely dated to the 14th and 15th centuries are rare.

Late Saxon wares

Four fabrics can be dated to the period 900–1050. The earliest is the wheelthrown Late Saxon Shelly ware (LSS), which accounts for 20% of the medieval assemblage (144 sherds). This regional import was the dominant ware used in London from the late 9th or early 10th century onwards; the precise source is unknown, but was probably in Oxfordshire (Vince & Jenner 1991, 38–41, 49–54; Goffin 1995, 85; Mellor 1994, 37–44). Most sherds are from quite standard cooking pots with everted rims, but five rims are from bowls/dishes found in Building 9 (16.5: [168]), 16.2: [179]) and Open Area 4 (12.1: [212], [245], 12.7: [301]). One rim from Open Area 4 (12.1: [204]) has a perforation 5mm in diameter just below the rim wall, possibly to permit suspension, although rather small. As no other sherds were found the function of this piece must remain unclear; the fabric is also slightly atypical, having very fine shell.

A later and more locally made fabric is Early Medieval Sandy ware (EMS), which appeared sometime during the third quarter of the 10th century (63 sherds, 9% of the medieval assemblage). Again, most sherds are from cooking pots, but the rim of a bowl with thumbed decoration was found in Building 6 (13.2: [290]), while a spouted pitcher is represented by a long spout from below Building 14 (22.3: [25]; cf Vince & Jenner 1991, 58, fig 2.35, no. 61). Two sherds from a possible lamp were found in Open Area 4 (12.1: [212]).

Up to eight sherds are from East Anglia: two are of Thetford ware (THET), while six are of the sandy variant (SATH), 1% of the total assemblage. These wheelthrown greywares began to reach London during the 10th century, but are mainly found between 970–1050; they are generally rare in the City (Vince & Jenner 1991, 92). The identification of a few sherds from Open Area 4 (12.10: [469]) is uncertain: two are in a soft, loose sandy ware, while some laminated flakes of a harder micaceous ware are possibly Roman.

Late Saxon/early medieval wares

This period is represented by 10 fabrics (predominantly shell-tempered and sandy wares) which came into use between 1000 and 1050, and went out of use between 1100 and 1150 (Blackmore 1999, 42–4). The dominant shell-tempered ware is EMSS (73 sherds, 10%); fabric EMSH amounts to only 15 sherds (2%), but this is on the whole a normal pattern (Vince & Jenner 1991, 63, 65). The most common sandy fabric is Early Surrey ware (44 sherds), which appeared in London between c 1040–50 (Vince & Jenner 1991, 73–5; Goffin 1995, 85–6). Together with the finer variant EMIS (12 sherds) and the coarser variant with flint inclusions (ESUR FL, one sherd), these Surrey wares account for 8% of the total assemblage. In both groups cooking pots are the most common form; two vessels in EMSS have thumbed rims, one found in the disuse of the Roman Building 1 (6.25: [250]; cf Vince & Jenner 1991, fig 2.38, no. 70), the other in the fill of Building 7 (14.4: [280]). This decoration is also found on two bowls, one in EMSS from Building 8 (15.4: [153]), the other in EMSH from Building 11 (8.3: [463]).

Two related fabrics are Early Medieval Grog-tempered ware (EMGR) and the chalk-tempered ware EMCH. The former is represented by two sooted sherds from a spouted pitcher found in Building 6 (13.2: [296]); the rounded collared profile and slight lid-seating of the rim (diameter 110mm) are unparalleled in the published material from the City (cf Vince & Jenner 1991, 80–1). Fabric EMCH (four sherds) is represented by sherds from cooking pots and the spout from a pitcher found in Building 15 (25.4: [173]).

Two fabrics are characterised by the presence of flint inclusions. Of these, EMFL (Vince & Jenner 1991, 69–70) comprises 1.5% of the medieval assemblage. Forms include a bowl with a thumbed rim, and a socketed handle or spout from a bowl which has scorch marks on either side, both from Open Area 4 (12.10: [469]), and a large spout from a pitcher from Building 7 (14.6: [247]), the mouth of which has an unusual recessed profile. A much coarser fabric with abundant flint inclusions, here classified as EMFL COAR, has not been noted in any of the published waterfront assemblages, and is of uncertain date, but similar atypical coarsewares were found in early medieval deposits at Westminster Hall (Whipp & Platts 1976; Goffin 1995, 86). This ware is predominantly oxidised with a grey core; it is represented by 12 sherds from a spouted pitcher with decoration of applied thumbed strips and gridded circles which were found in an early pit in Open Area 4 (12.1: fills [245], [220], [212] and [204]). Stamped decoration is found on pitchers in LSS, EMS and EMSS, but seems to have been superseded by rouletting by 1100. The use of applied thumbed strips seems to have been an 11th-century innovation (Vince & Jenner 1991, 52, 58, fig 2.25, no. 30, fig 2.35, nos 61–2) which continued to be used on 12th-century pitchers in fabrics such as EMSS and EMCH (Vince & Jenner 1991, 62, 70–2, fig 2.41, nos 90–1). Indeed, the closest published parallel from London for the Suffolk House pitcher is in EMCH (Vince & Jenner 1991, fig 2.55, no. 138). Taken together with the stratigraphy, it would appear that this vessel is of mid 11th-century date. It could have been quite locally made, although the fact the ware is so rare in London might argue against this. Since Coarse London-type ware has now been found at Dover (J Cotter, pers comm), a possible source might be in southern Kent or Sussex, where coarser flint-tempered wares are more common in the early medieval period.

Medieval wares

Local wheelthrown wares first appeared in the last decades of the 11th century, but are rare until the mid 12th century (Vince 1991, 267–8). The earliest in this assemblage are LOGR (five sherds only) and a well-formed everted rim in LCOAR (from (14.4) [280]) which are probably of late 11th-century date (Vince & Jenner 1991, 76–9, 83). However, most finds of

LCOAR and the variants LCOAR SHEL and LCOAR CALC (total 45 sherds, 6%) are probably of mid to late 12th-century date and contemporary with the cooking pots in SSW (24 sherds, 3%). Vessels of note include a frying pan with socketed handle and stabbed decoration, and part of a curfew, both from Building 8 (15.4: [69]), and dated to 1100–1200.

Other 12th-century London-type wares include 10 sherds from a number of early-style jugs in London-type ware (LOND) and a large jug with broad strap handle in the calcareous variant LCALC ([204]). The latter has deep finger impressions on the inner wall below the handle junction. Later 12th-century forms in LOND include 11 sherds from up to six Rouen-style jugs and 13 sherds from up to seven jugs in the North French style which are now dated from c 1180 (Pearce et al 1985, 19, 29; Vince 1991, 268). Styles typical of the 13th century comprise two sherds from highly decorated jugs and 16 from baluster jugs which broadly date to between 1200–1350. Altogether, London-type wares comprise 78 sherds (10.8% of the medieval assemblage).

Kingston-type ware came into use c 1230 and should be contemporary with at least half of the London wares, but is much less common (4% of the medieval assemblage; see Table 22). Most of the 31 sherds are from two locations; 4 were associated with the construction of the first masonry building (23.1), while 19 are derived from two small rounded jugs found in a late 14th- or 15th-century pit in Open Area 5 (28.1: [196]). One of these, in a very fine fabric, has a slightly biconical profile and three girth grooves, similar to an example from Holy Trinity Priory (DUK77; Blackmore in prep; cf also Pearce & Vince 1988, no. 123). The other jug is in a much coarser ware. Other finds include a small biconical drinking jug with yellow-green glaze from Building 15 (25.5: [165]) (cf Pearce & Vince 1988, fig 83, no. 205).

The slightly later whiteware fabric CBW amounts to 32 sherds (4.5%), which derive from up to 12 vessels. Most are from Building 15 and further east (groups 25 and 26), and 15 are from the same pit as the Kingston wares (28.1: [196]). Three sherds are from jugs, but the rest are from cooking pots, three of which had flat-topped rims. Six sherds are from a cistern with internal and external white deposits, the fabric of which has been heat-altered.

Imports

These amount to 32 sherds (4.5% of the total medieval assemblage). Most of the early imports derive from the Rhineland. The Badorf-type wares include a sherd from a standard thick-walled amphora found in a post-Conquest pit fill in Building 6 (13.2: [290]) and an intrusive sherd from an early level in the Roman Building 1 (6.7: [51]). The latter is in a thin-walled coarse fabric closer to that of the earlier Walberberg-type ware (mainly 7th- to 8th-century) which is found in Middle Saxon *Lundenwic*. Given the absence of any other early material it seems unlikely that this is the first occurrence of Middle Saxon Walberberg ware in the City; it is either an atypical Roman sherd or indicates that early medieval London was receiving a wider range of later fabrics than previously thought.

Two types of red-painted-type ware are present (not all are decorated): a white-bodied ware, and an olive ware which is probably related to the later Pingsdorf ware (Vince & Jenner 1991, 100–2). Seven sherds are of Rhenish Greyware, including rim and body sherds from a globular cooking pot found in different fills of the early pit in Open Area 4 (12.1: [212], [204]). This fabric, previously classified as Thetford Whiteware (Vince & Jenner 1991, 94–5), was reidentified after it was matched with finds from the Netherlands, notably Tiel (M Bartels, pers comm). Red-painted wares and greywares were present in 10th-century levels at Bull Wharf, but are more common in 11th-century groups; globular cooking pots (*Kugeltopfe*) in Blue-grey ware (here represented by two sherds) are most common in waterfront groups of *c* 1050–1150 (Vince 1988, 241-2; Vince & Jenner 1991, 103–4). The frequency of all three types declines after 1150.

A single whiteware sherd found in a dumped layer in Open Area 4 (12.10: [470]) contains abundant fine clear white and yellowish quartz sand, and has a narrow applied strip under a yellowish-green glaze. Although rather thick-walled, it is similar in style to the Lime Street pitcher (Vince & Jenner 1991, fig 2.212, no. 270), which is now believed to be of 9th- or 10th-century date and from Huy (Giertz 1996, 47). Andenne wares include an intrusive pitcher rim from a Roman context in Open Area 3 (6.3: [100]) which has splashes of a poorly mixed iron-rich glaze. The profile is incomplete, but sufficient survives to show that it is of the deep collared type, which is the latest in the Andenne sequence (Vince & Jenner 1991, 104–6, fig 2.112, no. 274; Giertz 1996, 55, fig 6, nos 19–20). Further body sherds from Open Area 4 (12.1: [204]) are from a different pitcher with a yellow-green glaze; another, from Building 15 (25.5: [169]), has rouletted decoration.

North French wares mainly derive from cooking pots and spouted pitchers; two handle fragments are present, one with an applied thumbed strip (cf Vince & Jenner 1991, fig 2.121, no. 292).

Finally, there is a developed funnel-necked beaker in Siegburg Stoneware found in a late pit in Open Area 5 (28.1: [196]). This form, which dates from the early 15th century (Gaimster 1987, 341, fig 1, no. 3; 1997, 84), is one of the most common Rhenish stoneware exports, accounting for *c* 30% of the Rhenish wares found in early 15th-century contexts in the City (Vince 1988, 242). Most of the body is missing, and it is not known if this was decorated, but it may well have had an applied medallion or smaller roundels and possibly a handle (cf Hurst *et al* 1986, 176–9).

Discussion

The site of Suffolk House lies a short distance to the east of Queenhithe, and close by the site of the Steelyard, which from the 1170s, if not earlier, was the headquarters of German merchants visiting London. It is also a short distance upstream from London Bridge, and a little to the west of the waterfront sites of Seal House and Swan Lane. All these sites have produced important, but slightly different, ceramic sequences. That at Queenhithe starts in the very late 9th century, and continues

uninterrupted throughout the 10th century and into the medieval period. The Vintry sequence has not been published but starts a little later. The pottery from the Public Cleansing Depot site at Dowgate has been considered by Vince (1985), but that from the larger excavation at Thames Exchange remains to be studied in detail. An early riverside bank at Swan Lane was first thought to contain pottery dating to between the late 9th and early 11th centuries (Vince 1985, 86–7), but further analysis has shown that the earliest medieval pottery groups (Waterfront I) date to the late 11th or early 12th century (Vince 1992, 141).

The medieval pottery from Suffolk House is thus of interest as it has chronological and, in broad terms, spatial links with a number of different sites in the area. The sequence does not go back as early as at Queenhithe, but it would seem to be a little earlier than at Seal House or Swan Lane as there is a horizon which may date to between 1000–50. This is suggested by finds from Open Area 4 (12.1, 12.2 and 12.9), and Building 8 (15.4), and by the fact that 20% of the ceramic assemblage comprises a ware which went out of use before 1050 (albeit largely in residual contexts). Although no foreshore or revetment groups are present here, this early phase would appear to be broadly contemporary with the first waterfront groups at New Fresh Wharf and Billingsgate (Vince 1992, 140), and may well be of a similar date as the initial German base established at Dowgate.

The bulk of the Suffolk House assemblage comprises homogeneous groups of pottery dating to the later 11th and 12th centuries which are derived from a series of contemporary horizons across the excavated area. This activity is evidenced by the upper fill of pit (12.1), dated *c* 1050–80 to the early 12th century, the robbing of the Roman walls (12.7) and dumping (12.10), all in Open Area 4; by Building 11 (18.1), the cellared Building 9 (15.4) and occupation layers below Building 14. A similar group of pottery was recovered from layers dated to *c* 1040–70 at Westminster Abbey (Goffin 1995, 85–7). One vessel in particular is found in several contexts, the flint-gritted pitcher, in Open Area 4 for example (12.1: [212], [245]) and Building 7 (14.4: [265]), and offers a potential link between them; other links probably exist, but were less easy to detect in groups of small unglazed body sherds. Taken together with the contemporary groups associated with Waterfront I at Seal House and Swan Lane (Vince 1992, 141), this would suggest a general burst of activity in the area *c* 1050–80. Groups which can be dated to the mid 12th century include the backfill of the cellar of Building 9 and modifications (group 16), Building 12 (group 19) and pit fills in Open Area 5 (group 21).

The function of the site at this time appears from the pottery to have been primarily domestic; most sherds are from cooking pots, but the relatively larger number of spouted pitchers might suggest that the area was used for provisioning or catering as much as by more permanent residents. Ceramic evidence for commerce was limited, but the range of wares from the Rhineland, Low Countries and northern France fits well with the general pattern for the waterfront area in the late 11th century. The volume is much less here than in the area of the Hanse base at the Steelyard, but the latter is an exceptional case. The

Table 22 *The frequency of the medieval ware types*

Fabric	Sherds	% sherds	EVEs	% weight
ANDE	6	0.8	5	1.1
BADO	3	0.4	3	0.6
BLGR	2	0.3	2	0.4
CBW	32	4.5	12	2.5
EGS	1	0.1	1	0.2
EMCH	4	0.6	4	0.8
EMCW	4	0.6	1	0.2
EMFL	10	1.4	10	2.1
EMFL COAR	12	1.7	5	1.1
EMGR	2	0.3	2	0.4
EMIS	12	1.7	5	1.1
EMS	63	8.8	45	9.6
EMSH	15	2.1	13	2.8
EMSS	73	10.2	44	9.3
ESUR	44	6.2	37	7.9
ESUR FL	1	0.1	1	0.2
HUY	1	0.1	1	0.2
KING	30	4.2	11	2.3
KINGSL	1	0.1	1	0.2
LCALC	2	0.3	2	0.4
LCOAR	31	4.3	28	5.9
LCOAR CALC	5	0.7	4	0.8
LCOAR SHEL	9	1.3	6	1.3
LLON	10	1.4	2	0.4
LMHG	1	0.1	1	0.2
LOGR	5	0.7	5	1.1
LOND	78	10.8	44	9.4
LSS	144	20.1	99	21.0
MG	6	0.8	3	0.6
NFRE	9	1.3	5	1.1
REDP	1	0.1	1	0.2
REDP OLV	4	0.6	3	0.6
REDP WHT	1	0.1	1	0.2
RHGR	7	1.0	5	1.1
SATH	6	0.8	3	0.6
SHER	46	6.4	33	7.0
SHER FL	1	0.1	1	0.2
SIEG	4	0.6	1	0.2
SSW	24	3.4	16	3.4
STAM	1	0.1	1	0.2
THET	2	0.3	2	0.4
TUDG	2	0.3	2	0.4
Totals	**715**	**100**	**471**	**100**

large group of Red-painted and Blue-grey wares found on the foreshore at Dowgate (Dunning 1959, 73–8), for example, must have been used in an adjacent building belonging to German merchants or discarded from ships moored alongside (Vince 1985, 86; Blackmore 1999, 44).

There is little material dating to the late 12th century, and the amount of 13th- to 15th-century material is also limited. Groups (19) and (23), however, are possibly contemporary with those associated with Seal House Waterfront II (1163–92), and/or Waterfront III at Seal House and Swan Lane (dated to

1203–15). The mid 13th to 15th centuries are poorly represented, but some finds may relate to activity in the general area of the church (evidenced on other sites in the area: GM12, LPL73, LAU85, REC89), or be connected with the establishment of the Manor of the Rose/Pountney's Inn. The latter is the most likely source of the late medieval group from the rubbish pit in Open Area 5 (28.1: [196]).

Groups which could be dated to the late 12th century include a later deposit in Building 12 (19) and a layer predating the earliest masonry structure, Building 14 (23), the building itself being datable to the early 13th century.

6.15 The medieval and post-medieval finds

The site produced a small quantity of post-Roman finds, some of which appear to be intrusive in apparently secure Roman contexts. The excavator comments that there was a strong possibility of contamination from the side of the trench when shoring was removed. A medieval lead-alloy spangle from Open Area 2 <168> came from a context which otherwise produced material of 1st- or early 2nd-century date (1.5: [569]), and a possible lead-alloy mount <112> came from a dump associated with Waterfront 4 containing finds of 1st- to 2nd-century date (4.4: [689]).

The 1994 testpits yielded several objects. Two iron arrowheads <40> <28> came from the early medieval Building 9 (16.2: [179]) and the later Building 14 (23.1: [191]), and also a fragment of horseshoe <375> from later phases of Building 15, the first phase of the Manor of the Rose (25.5: [165]). Two wooden bowls <63> <64> were found in an early medieval pit (12.1: [298]). More wood was preserved in a late medieval or post-medieval well, probably located in the southern part of Building 15 (26.2: [532]), which produced part of a wooden box <389> (see Fig 72), a scale tang knife <362> and a fragment of cloth <361>. There was post-medieval glass in a 15th-century pit assemblage from Open Area 5 (28.1: [196]).

6.16 The medieval and post-medieval building material

Terence Paul Smith

Introduction

Medieval and post-medieval ceramic building materials from the site include bricks and roofing tiles, some of the latter of early forms. In the early medieval period too there was reuse of Roman materials, especially as make-up and in floors: large quantities of residual Roman material were therefore present in most medieval deposits. The 12th-century Building 12 in particular (group 19) contained quite large quantities of such material. Bricks were present in larger quantities (by weight) than were other materials (tegulae, imbrices and flue tiles, for example), suggesting that there may have been deliberate selection of the material which was regarded as more useful. From this building the percentages of Roman materials (by weight and ignoring a single tessera) were: bricks 68·7%, tegulae 12·5%, imbrices 10·5% and flue tiles 8·2% (total = 99·9%); by contrast with the percentages from the Roman townhouse, Building 3 (bricks 34·8%, tegulae 52·4%, imbrices 12·0% and flue tiles 0·7%: total = 99·9%). Flue tiles were probably under-represented in the Roman house, but the other percentage figures will bear comparison; particularly telling are the contrasts in the figures for bricks and tegulae. In later buildings – the 13th- to 14th-century Building 14 (group 21), for example – all Roman materials were present in far more meagre quantities, suggesting that the supplies available for reuse were far less ample after the end of the 12th century.

Ceramic building materials

Bricks

Bricks of medieval and post-medieval date were found in and sampled from a small number of contexts. As commonly in the London area, they fall into two main groups: (1) those in fabric 3033 and its variants, at this site fabrics 3039 and 3046; and (2) those in fabric 3032.

The first group is in an orange/red fairly sandy fabric, 3046 showing rather more sand than the more common 3033, and 3039 showing in addition yellow/white silty streaks. Almost certainly they were made within the London area itself. Examples from c 1380–1400 have been found at Billingsgate Fish Market in Lower Thames Street (BIG82; Keily 1998, 37), although their main period of use within central London seems to be from the later 15th century down to the Great Fire of 1666 or a little later, perhaps down to c 1700 (Crowley 1997, 200). In general, thicker examples (60mm and more, as here) are later, although caution is needed in using brick dimensions for dating: large bricks of late 15th-century date *are* known, for example in the surviving parts of London Wall in St Alphege Garden and in Old Hall at Lincoln's Inn.

Bricks of the second group (in fabric 3032) are darker red to purplish in colour, often with a yellowish tinge to the surfaces.

Table 23 Dimensions of sampled post-medieval bricks

Subgroup	Fabric	Dimensions (mm)
30.1	3039	230 × 105 × 60
30.1	3033	242 × 102 × 62
30.1	3033	235 × 100 × 65
31.1	3032	225 × 100 × 64
31.1	3046	? × 115? × ?
31.1	3032	? × 115 × 66

Among various inclusions are black burnt organic materials or voids where these have burned out altogether; these represent the 'Spanish' – domestic ash and other rubbish – deliberately added to the raw material in order to save on costs of fuel for firing. They were manufactured at a number of different yards within the London area and date from after the Great Fire of 1666 (Crowley 1997, 200); they were in use down to the 19th century. The dimensions of bricks sampled from this site are presented in Table 23, and fabric types are described in Table 24.

Roofing tiles

EARLY TYPES

Several fragments of early medieval roofing tiles were recovered from Buildings 8 (15.4), 9 (16.5), 12 (19.3–4), 15 (22.3, 23.1) and 16 (25.6). They are in a distinctive very sandy fabric, red but usually with a grey core (fabric 2273), probably made within the London area itself (Betts 1990, 221; 1997, 66–7). They are of three types: (1) flanged tiles; (2) curved tiles; and (3) shouldered peg tiles. Types (1) and (2) resemble Roman tegulae and imbrices and were used in the same way; type (3) were hung in the same way as the slightly later peg or plain tiles but are much larger, thicker and heavier; their shape is distinctive, having a narrowing at the top, where the peg hole was formed. All were glazed – in brown or darkish green – over the parts of their surfaces which would have been exposed to the weather.

These thick and relatively heavy tiles seem to have come into use in the 1130s in London (dates from Cheapside) and are seen most often in association with churches and other religious buildings (as also at some locations outside London such as Lewes Priory, East Sussex), although they also appear to have been used on high-status secular buildings. They probably represent the 'thick tiles' (*spissae tegulae*) with which several citizens of London covered their houses following a serious fire in 1135/6 (Riley 1859, 329); they continued in use down to the late 12th or early 13th century. The largest number from the site was associated with the 12th-century Building 12, and would seem to indicate that this building was of fairly high status. Several were associated with the slightly earlier Buildings 8 and 9, and single examples with Buildings 15 and 16; these last may well be residual. The shouldered tiles are individually heavy, had to be double-lapped and could not be laid at a pitch of less than 40°. The resulting roof would itself have been extremely heavy: these were probably the least satisfactory roofing tiles ever used in London, and yet they seem to have had a high-status value. The flanged and curved tiles could be single-lapped and laid at a pitch of only 30°, and the resulting roof would have been quite light; but they were difficult to manufacture and lay. It is not surprising that both these early types of tiled roofing were later superseded entirely by peg tiles.

PEG TILES

Peg-tile fragments were recovered from several areas (an asterisk indicating the presence of glazed tiles): Buildings 12 (19.3*–4*), 15 (23.1*–2*) and 16 (25.3, 25.4*–6, 26.1, 26.3–4), Open Areas 5 (21.5, 28.1*) and 7 (26.7). Most are in the common

Table 24 Museum of London building material fabric types (all periods). The numbers refer to the ceramic building materials fabric collection held by the Museum of London Specialist Services

Fabric	Description
2271	Red or orange/red, sometimes with grey cores; fine texture with little quartz, scatter of muscovite mica in certain tiles, with red iron oxide and calcium carbonate
2273	Orange/red or light brown, commonly with grey core; sandy with common quartz and calcium carbonate
2276	As 2271 but distinguished by fine moulding sand
2452	Red, orange or brown; fairly fine with varying amounts of quartz and usually with scatter of calcium carbonate, siltstone and iron oxide (part of 2815 group)
2453	Pink or yellow/brown; numerous off-white clay inclusions in often mottled clay matrix with scatter of iron oxide; some with frequent quartz; often with red moulding sand
2454	Yellow, yellow-grey, pink or off-white; hard, well-fired fabric with varying amounts of red quartz and scatter of iron oxide; occasionally with red moulding sand
2455	Light brown, pink or orange; soft, fine, smooth clay with scatter of quartz and calcium carbonate inclusions
2456	Grey core with light brown margins; frequent shelly inclusions
2459A	Red, orange or brown; fine sandy fabric with small quartz and occasional scatter of calcium carbonate and iron oxide (part of 2815 group)
2459B	As 2459A but distinguished by fine moulding sand (part of 2815 group)
2459C	As 2459A but distinguished by organic moulding medium (part of 2815 group)
2586	As 2271 but more sandy
2587	Orange or light brown; fine sandy matrix with common quartz and iron oxide, usually with scatter of fine black iron oxide, red iron oxide and silty inclusions
2815	A fabric group comprising the individual fabrics 2452, 2459A/B/C, 3004 and 3006, not all of which are represented at this site
3004	Orange, red or brown; sandy with common quartz and occasional iron oxide and calcium carbonate (part of 2815 group)
3006	Red, orange or brown; covers the range between 2459A and 3004 with varying quartz; most have occasional iron oxide and calcium carbonate (part of 2815 group)
3009	Light brown/orange with grey upper margin; sandy with abundant quartz and large clay, siltstone, sandstone and iron oxide inclusions
3019	Light brown/orange, sometimes with light grey core; abundant siltstone inclusions and iron oxide with scatter of quartz and occasional calcium carbonate
3022	Light brown, orange, pink or off-white; frequent red or colourless quartz with occasional iron oxide and calcium carbonate in fine clay matrix; sandy version of 2454
3023	Red, orange or brown; sandy with abundant quartz and frequently with common black iron oxide specks; silty and red iron oxide inclusions scattered through sandy clay matrix
3028	Orange with common, well-sorted, medium quartz (<0.4mm); few to common rounded silty inclusions (<6mm) and red iron oxide (<1mm); some examples have bands of light-coloured silty clay
3032	Red or purplish red, often with yellow speckling to surfaces; hard texture with yellow or white carbonate specks and often with dark organic inclusions or voids where these have burned out during firing
3033	Orange or red; soft, sandy with moderate quartz and black iron oxide
3039	As 3033 but with white or yellowish streaky inclusions
3046	As 3033 but much more sandy
3050	Orange or reddish-pink; frequent dark red quartz with varying amounts of colourless quartz and occasional iron oxide and calcium carbonate; clay matrix, with occasional cream-coloured mottling, may have silty bands and streaks
3054	Light brown; abundant quartz with frequent red iron oxide; common grog inclusions of red and cream tile inclusions
3059	Fine orange to red fabric with common coarse quartz (<1mm) and a scatter of red iron oxide inclusions (<1mm); characterised by varying amounts of chaff temper and distinctively curved voids
3060	Red, orange or brown fabric with frequent fine quartz (<3mm), with common very fine black iron oxides (<0.1mm) and a scatter of very coarse red iron oxides (2mm)
3061	Orange or dark red; frequent quartz and red iron oxide with common white/cream clay lenses or pellets
3069	Orange or light brown; frequent quartz and red iron oxide with common white/cream clay lenses or pellets
3236	Orange to red; background matrix similar to 2452, with frequent rounded mottled pink/white calcareous inclusions and occasional dark red quartz crystals

fabrics 2271 and 2586. Some had mortar on broken edges, showing that they had been either reused at a later date or used for some purpose other than roofing (eg as 'fillers' or rubble) from the start: this was a common practice in most periods and was a way of utilising material broken in transit or at the building site. But complete tiles too were sometimes used for non-roofing purposes. A wall in Building 15 (25.4) used broken tiles in this way.

Peg tiles are difficult to date and those in the two main fabrics were in use from the later 12th century down to quite recent times. When pantiles were introduced during the 17th century, they were largely restricted to utilitarian or low-status buildings, or else hidden from view at street level on the upper pitches of mansard roofs: they never, despite claims sometimes made to the contrary, superseded peg tiles in south-east England. Peg tiles remained the normal method of roofing in London down to the advent of Welsh slate in the late 18th century and, even more particularly, following the development of the bulk freight railway system in the 19th century.

The two main fabrics are 2271, in various shades of red or orange-red and with a well-fired fine texture, and 2586, a more sandy version of 2271; tiles in both are almost certainly local products. Some peg tiles from Building 8 (15.4: [69]), however, are in fabric 2273 (see above), certainly indicating a medieval, and probably an early medieval, date, reflected by that of the building itself. The glazed tiles in other fabrics, present in many of the contexts (see above, group numbers marked with an asterisk), are also medieval, since in London glazed tiles were not used after the late 15th century. The glaze was applied either as splash-glaze – in small spots splashed on to the surface, perhaps using a brush in a 'spatter' technique – or as a more continuous cover-glaze. Some of the tiles are in fabric 2587, orange to light brown in colour and distinguished by silty inclusions and by tiny black iron-oxide inclusions, and these date from before the middle of the 15th century: they were recovered from Buildings 8 (15.4), 12 (19.3) and 16 (24.3, 25.4–5) and Open Area 5 (21.4, 28.1); nearly all are glazed.

Most of the roofing tiles from the site, where their peg/nail holes were preserved at all, have round holes; these were used throughout the period in which such tiles were made. An example from the fabric of a well in Building 15 (26.1: [521]), however, has diamond-shaped holes, an indication of a 15th-century or later date. Some tiles in Building 15 (25.5: [164]) are in fabric 2276, distinguished by its fine moulding sand though otherwise similar to 2271; such tiles were not manufactured until the end of the 15th century; in fact, the well-made examples from this context appear to be even later, perhaps of the 18th century.

From (26.6: [843]) came part of a curved ridge tile in fabric 2587; this is usually of medieval date. There are a few spots of brown glaze – possibly accidental. At the apex is a round hole, cut before firing, 8mm in diameter: it may have been intended to hold a rod or peg for fitting a ceramic finial. A possible ridge tile, in fabric 2271, was recovered from Building 8 (15.4: [69]).

Non-ceramic building materials

Roofing slate

Roofing slate was recovered from Building 14 (23.1: [200]), dated to the 13th to 14th centuries. This is Welsh slate, not normally found in London before the 18th century; it is, however, a tiny fragment and may therefore be intrusive.

Stone rubble

Much of the building material recovered for inspection was probably of Roman origin. Kentish rag rubble was present in many post-Roman contexts, including make-ups associated with Buildings 8 (15.1, 15.4) and 9 (16.5). Small abraded fragments of ferruginous sandstone were recovered (16.2: [179]) associated with dumps for a new floor within Building 9. Oolitic limestone rubble in the post-Roman dumping over Building 3 (12.13:

[367]) was possibly from the quarries at Barnack in Northamptonshire, and was found together with other Roman rubble including the Tuscan column.

Paving and inlay

Pieces of possible paving slabs or inlay included a piece of thin fine-grained laminated limestone from an occupation surface in Building 9 (16.2: [179]). Small fragments of sandstone and a worn piece of rag were found in pit fills in Open Area 4 near the Roman Tuscan order column (12.1, 12.13): these and a further sandstone fragment from Building 11 (18.1) may have been used for paving. So too may have been a smooth, worn piece of Kentish rag from Building 8 (15.4).

Miscellaneous

A fragment of oolitic limestone and a piece of fine glauconitic sandstone, both burnt, were noted in the same deposit (12.13: [358]) that produced the oolitic limestone column.

Daub

As well as residual Roman material, the early medieval Buildings 6, 7 and 8 yielded daub, which may be from external or internal walls. Other pieces – all very fragmentary – were not associated with specific structures.

6.17 The medieval and post-medieval plant remains

Lisa Gray

Introduction

Of the 13 samples from the site selected for further analysis, five were of post-Roman date (Table 25), and it is these which are discussed here. The methodology for the analysis was the same as that outlined in 6.10 above. Full details about the species present will be found in Table 26.

Results

Early medieval pit 1

{36} [267]; {37} [285]; {40} [298] (12.1) OA4
This feature contained plant remains preserved by waterlogging and mineralisation.

HABITAT
Weeds of cultivated land and waste and disturbed ground dominated these samples, for example sun spurge (*Euphorbia helioscopia* L), black nightshade (*Solanum nigrum* L) and fat hen.

Table 25 Provenance of medieval and post-medieval environmental samples

Period	Land use	Subgroup	Context no.	Sample no.	Feature type
Early medieval	OA4	12.1	267	36	fill of pit
Early medieval	OA4	12.1	285	37	fill of pit
Early medieval	OA4	12.1	298	40	fill of pit
Early medieval	OA4	12.8	630	55	fill of robber trench
Medieval/post-medieval	Building 16	26.2	532	50	fill of chalk-lined well

Four charred seeds were recovered, including an oat (*Avena* sp) grain, campion/catchfly, curled dock and an indeterminate grass (Poaceae) seed, all found in disturbed and cultivated ground. Also present were the arable weed corncockle (*Agrostemma githago* L) and a possible Roman nettle (*Urtica pilulifera* L), which are also found on waste ground (Polunin 1969, 58).

One seed of bogbean (*Meyanthes trifoliata* L) was present. This plant is found in shallow water, bogs and fens (Stace 1991, 638) and was the only purely aquatic taxon found in this feature, although seeds of the semi-aquatic spike-rush were also recovered.

ECONOMIC USES

The mineralised remains of economic plants consisted of edible fruit stones of sloe/blackthorn (cf *Prunus spinosa* L), cherry (*Prunus cerasus avium*), stem fragments and concretions, and plum (*Prunus domestica* L).

The waterlogged remains were dominated by cereal bran fragments. Remains of edible fruits were also present, including plum/bullace, apple/pear, cherry stones, blackberry/raspberry and abundant elder seeds. Other edible remains consisted of one waterlogged rye (*Secale cereale* L) grain and a coriander capsule fragment. One charred oat (*Avena* sp) grain was present, and charred grains of bread wheat, barley and spelt wheat.

Early medieval pit 2

{55} [630] (12.8) OA4
Waterlogging and mineralisation were the main forms of preservation of taxa in this sample.

HABITAT

Remains of plants from woodland/scrub/hedgerow and grassland habitats dominated this sample. Blackberry/raspberry and elder seeds were present in abundance. Seeds of flax, sedge, goosefoot and mallow were represented in lesser amounts.

ECONOMIC USES

Edible plant remains dominated. Elder and blackberry/raspberry seeds were abundant, and mineralised apple (*Malus* sp) seeds moderately so. Mallow seeds were also present in large quantities. Very small amounts of sedge and flax seeds were recovered, so these are unlikely to have been economically significant here.

Medieval/post-medieval well

{50} [532] (26.2) B16
Waterlogging and mineralisation were the main forms of preservation for the remains in this sample. The only charred remain was one ribwort plantain (*Plantago lanceolata* L) seed.

HABITAT

The range of habitat preferences for plants represented by the remains in this sample was quite evenly spread. Six taxa were from aquatic/semi-aquatic environments and included water plantain (*Alisma* sp) and fine-leaved water dropwort (cf *Oenanthe aquatica* L).

Most taxa were from waste/disturbed ground and included many of the plants to be found in earlier phases, but here included black mustard (*Brassica nigra* L), marigold (cf *Calendula* sp) and stinking mayweed (*Anthemis cotula* L).

ECONOMIC USES

Waterlogged cereal bran fragments dominated this sample. Next in abundance were hazelnut shell fragments. Other remains of edible plants included plum/bullace, fig and hop seeds.

Discussion

Early medieval pit 1: Open Area 4

The taxa in this sample contained the remains of plants growing in waste/disturbed ground and semi-aquatic habitats, but it is not possible to interpret them in terms of the immediate local environment because of their presence in dumped refuse. The presence of mineralised remains along with waterlogged bran fragments, however, means that cess may have been deposited in this pit and, although mineralised remains are difficult to identify, this process does suggest that the taxa arrived as probable food waste.

Edible fruit remains dominated this assemblage: the stones of cherry and sloe/blackthorn were mineralised but waterlogged examples were also present. The large number of elder seeds present could just reflect the fact that elder produces a large number of seeds anyway, but equally they could have been gathered specifically for jam or winemaking, or for medicinal reasons. Culpeper notes several uses for elderberries when boiled in wine. These include bringing down 'women's courses', dyeing hair black and boiling the berries in honey to cure earache (Culpeper 1853, 128). The waterlogged rye grain and coriander capsule may have been from plants growing wild locally or from cultivated plants.

Early medieval pit 2: Open Area 4

The plant remains from this second pit give a similar picture of the local environment: generally waste ground, some scrub/woodland edge habitats, and patches of semi-aquatic land or still water, but for the same reasons as for the first pit it would not be correct to interpret these samples in this way because of their uncertain origin.

Table 26 Details of medieval and post-medieval botanical remains

Land use			Early medieval pit OA4 (12.1) [267] {36}	Early medieval pit OA4 (12.1) [285] {37}	Early medieval pit OA4 (12.1) [298] {40}	Medieval well B3 (8.34) [523] {50}	Medieval pit OA4 (12.9) [630] {55}
Bulk sample volume (litres)			18	10	10	10	17
Flot volume (millilitres)			25ml	250g subsample	250g subsample	200ml 259g subsample	55ml
Scientific name	English name	Habitat and use codes					
Charred remains							
Indeterminate wood fragments	–	–	++++	+	–	++++	++++
Poaceae	Grass family seeds	ABCDEFH	I	–	–	–	–
Silene sp	Campion/catchfly	ABCDF	–	I	–	–	–
Avena sp	Oat	AFI	I	–	–	–	–
Rumex crispus L	Curled dock	BC	I	–	–	–	–
Plantago lanceolata L	Ribwort	D	–	–	–	I	–
Mineralised remains							
Indeterminate seeds			–	+	–	–	–
Indeterminate stem fragments			–	+++	–	–	–
Malus sp	Apple	CFHI	–	–	–	–	++
cf Prunus spinosa L	Sloe/blackthorn	CFG	–	+	–	–	–
Prunus avium/cerasus	Sloe/cherry	CGFI	–	+	–	–	–
Waterlogged remains							
Sonchus asper (L) Hill	Spiny milk-/sow-thistle	AB	–	–	–	+	–
Stellaria media L	Chickweed	AB	+	–	++	–	–
Urtica urens L	Small nettle	AB	+	–	–	–	–
Agrostemma githago L	Corncockle	AB	+	+	++	+	–
Chenopodium murale L	Nettle-leaved goosefoot	AB	+	–	+	–	–
Lamium sp	Dead-nettle	ABC	+	–	+	–	–
Polygonum sp	Knotgrass	ABCDEFG	–	–	–	+	–
Rumex sp	Dock	ABCDEFG	–	+	–	+	–
Ranunculus acris/repens/bulbosus	Buttercups	ABCDEG	–	–	++	–	–
Silene sp	Campion/catchfly	ABCDF	+	–	–	+	–
Chenopodium sp	Goosefoot	ABCDFH	–	–	+	–	+
cf Mentha sp	Mint	ABCEFGI	–	+	–	–	–
cf Carduus/Cirsium	Thistles	ABDEG	–	–	+	–	–
Carduus/Cirsium sp	Thistles	ABDEG	–	–	–	+	–
Sonchus arvensis L	Milk-/sow-thistle	ABE	–	+	–	–	–
Polygonum persicaria L	Persicaria	ABEH	–	–	–	+	–
Atriplex sp	Orache	ABFGH	–	–	–	+	–
Brassica/ Sinapis sp	Cabbage/mustard	ABFGHI	+	–	–	–	–
cf Brassica/ Sinapis sp	Cabbage/mustard	ABFGHI	–	–	+	–	–
Chenopodium album L	Fat hen	ABFH	+	+	+++	+	–
Polygonum aviculare L	Knotgrass	ABG	–	+	+	–	–
Anthemis cotula L	Stinking mayweed	ABGH	–	–	–	+	–
Papaver sp	Poppy	ABGHI	–	+	–	–	–
cf Rumex acetosella	Sheep's sorrel	AD	–	+	–	–	–
Rumex acetosella L	Sheep's sorrel	AD	–	–	+	+	–
Daucus carota L	Wild carrot	ADFGI	–	–	–	+	–
cf Daucus carota L	Wild carrot	ADFGI	–	–	+	–	–
Linum sp	Flax	ADHI	–	–	–	–	+

(*Table 26 cont*)

Land use			Early medieval pit OA4 (12.1) [267] {36}	Early medieval pit OA4 (12.1) [285] {37}	Early medieval pit OA4 (12.1) [298] {40}	Medieval well B3 (8.34) [523] {50}	Medieval pit OA4 (12.9) [630] {55}
Bulk sample volume (litres)			18	10	10	10	17
Flot volume (millilitres)			25ml	250g subsample	250g subsample	200ml 259g subsample	55ml
Scientific name	**English name**	**Habitat and use codes**					
Euphorbia helioscopia L	Sun spurge	AGI	+	−	+	−	−
Rumex crispus L	Curled dock	BC	−	−	+	+	−
Fragaria/Potentilla	Strawberry/cinquefoil	BCDEFGH	+	−	−	−	−
Potentilla sp	Cinquefoil/tormentil	BCDEFGH	−	−	+	−	−
Urtica dioica L	Stinging nettle	BCDEFGH	+	+	−	+	−
Malus cf sylvestris	Mallow	BCDF	−	−	−	−	++
Prunella vulgaris L	Self-heal	BCDG	−	−	−	+	−
Sambucus nigra L	Elder	BCFGH	+	+	+++	−	++++
Solanum nigrum L	Black nightshade	BF	+	−	+	−	−
Brassica nigra L	Black mustard	BFHI	−	−	−	+	−
cf Calendula sp	Marigold	BI	−	−	−	+	−
Hypochoeris radicata L	Cat's ear	CD	−	−	−	+	−
Stellaria graminea L	Lesser stitchwort	CD	−	−	−	+	−
cf Potentilla erecta	Tormentil	CDEGH	−	−	+	−	−
Cyperaceae	Sedges	CDEH	−	−	−	+	−
Corylus avellana L	Hazelnut shell fragment	CF	+	−	−	++	−
Rubus fruticosus/idaeus	Blackberry/raspberry	CFGH	+	++	+	−	+++
Prunus avium/cerasus	Sloe/cherry	CFGI	−	−	+	−	−
Prunus domestica L	Plum/bullace	CFI	+	−	+	+	−
Humulus lupus L	Hop	CGHI	−	−	−	++	−
Alisma sp	Water plantain	E	−	−	−	+	−
cf Oenanthe aquatica L	Fine-leaved water dropwort	E	−	−	−	+	−
Eleocharis sp	Spike-rush	E	+	+	+	+	−
cf Eleocharis palustris L	Common spike-rush	E	+	−	−	−	−
Potamogeton sp	Pondweed	E	−	−	−	+	−
Ranunculus scleratus L	Celery-leaved crowfoot	E	−	−	−	+	−
Meyanthes trifoliata L	Bogbean	EFG	−	+	−	−	−
Ranunculus flammula L	Lesser spearwort	EG	−	−	−	++	−
Coriandrum sativum L	Coriander	FGI	−	−	+	−	−
Ficus carica L	Fig	FGI	−	−	−	+	−
Secale cereale L	Rye	FI	−	−	+	−	−
Urtica pilulifera L	Roman nettle	−	−	−	+	−	−
Indeterminate Bryophyta sp	−	−	−	++	+	+	−
Indeterminate leaf fragments	−	−	−	−	−	++++	−
Indeterminate bud fragment	−	−	−	−	−	+	−
Indeterminate cereal bran	−	−	−	++++	++++	+++	−
Indeterminate stem fragments	−	−	−	++	−	−	−
Indeterminate wood fragments	−	−	++++	++	−	++++	−

Key

Habitat/use codes: A – weeds of cultivated land; B – ruderals, weeds of waste places and disturbed ground; C – plants of woods, scrub and hedgerow; D – open grass-land/heath; E – plants of damp/wet environment and aquatics; F – edible plants; G – medicinal and poisonous plants; H – commercial/industrial use; I – cultivated plants

Estimated levels of abundance: + = 1–10; ++ = 11–50; +++ = 51–150; ++++ = many 100s

Potential economic taxa were more numerous. The pit sample contained abundant waterlogged elder and blackberry/raspberry seeds which could have been used for jam, winemaking or for medicinal uses. Mineralised apple (*Malus* sp) seeds were present. This mode of preservation also suggests that faecal remains may have been deposited in the pit. Mallow seeds were abundant: no mention is made of the use of the seeds in Culpeper, but the whole plant is considered as being beneficial for bowel and bladder problems (Culpeper 1853, 223).

Medieval/post-medieval well: Building 15

Like the earlier pit groups, a variety of habitats were represented, but merely represent dumping; this is particularly the case here, as the well was almost certainly within a building, and therefore beyond the influence of the local environment.

The well contained cereal bran fragments, small numbers of plum/bullace stones and fig seeds, suggesting that cess or food waste was deposited in this feature, presumably after it was used for supplying drinkable water. Hop seeds were present, which may mean that they were being processed for their medicinal use or for brewing.

6.18 The medieval and post-medieval animal bone

Introduction

The animal bone for the post-Roman period was assessed, but not considered sufficiently significant for further analysis; the following summary has been compiled from the assessment report by Charlotte Ainsley.

Animal bone was recovered from a number of features representing the early medieval to post-medieval occupation of the site. The assemblages include three from occupation levels in Buildings 9 and 15 (the Manor of the Rose) which almost certainly largely represent waste within food-preparation areas, and two from later features: a chalk-lined well and a cesspit. These principal assemblages are described below.

Results

Early medieval sunken-floored building

[182] (16.2); [131] (16.6) B9
An assemblage from an early floor in the sunken-floored Building 9 (16.2) was mainly comprised of unspecified rat head, mouse/vole upper limb and unidentified fish vertebrae. It was unusual in its lack of the three main domesticates. In addition 0.009kg of oyster shell fragments were recovered. In a later fill (16.6), chicken, represented by a single head, and unidentified fish remains were present, along with a wider range of species including remains of butchered pig bones, and cattle-size and juvenile sheep-size fragments. Rodent presence was indicated by unspecified mouse/vole head fragments.

Late medieval hearth

[164] (25.5) B15
A varied selection of animal remains was recovered from the fill of a post-medieval hearth in Building 15. The majority of the bones were fragmentary, being less than 25mm in size. Large mammals were represented by a single cattle-size butchered pelvis, a number of vertebrae and ribs of sheep-size mammals, and a juvenile pig tibia. A range of upper and lower limb bones of chicken, unspecified mouse and rat were also recovered. Of the latter, a single mandible was also present. A notable find from this context is a rabbit humerus. Unidentifiable fish remains and 0.099kg of shell, the majority of which was oyster, were also recovered

Medieval/post-medieval well

[532] (26.2) B16
The majority of the bones from this feature were fragmentary and had clear indications of being burned. Butchery was present on cattle- and sheep-size limb bones. A single chicken limb bone, dog pelvis and metatarsal, and a range of rodent skeletal parts (unspecified rat and mouse) all showing signs of burning, were recovered. Unidentifiable fish remains and 0.759kg of marine shell comprising mostly cockles, winkles and oysters were also present.

Post-medieval cesspit

[627] (27.1) OA8
The largest single assemblage found at the site came from the later fill of a cesspit, possibly of post-medieval date. High occurrences of cattle, pig and sheep/goat dominated the assemblage. In addition, a dog humerus, a horse femur, the metacarpal of a roe deer and an unidentified bird humerus were present.

Discussion

Little was recovered from the earlier medieval period, and although preservation was good with low-level fragmentation, the size of the assemblage is too small to be used to assess the age and size of the animals at death, which would have allowed primary and possibly secondary usage of the animals to be interpreted. It is also not possible to say much about diet, although the three main domesticates and other species such as rabbit, chicken and fish were clearly exploited.

Despite the frequency of burning within the later medieval or post-medieval contexts, identification to species was often possible, although more profitable data could not be extracted due to the comparatively high degree of fragmentation.

The main domesticates were present together with rabbit and chicken, but also non-food animals such as horse and dog. The wild species that were present are indicative of both their exploitation for food (deer, a range of shellfish and fish) and the presence of vermin (rats and mice), but again, the sample is too small either for further analysis or for valid comparisons to be made with other sites.

The presence of vermin in floor or occupation levels in close proximity to food debris does, however, seem to indicate poor domestic hygiene, which is perhaps to be expected in the earlier medieval Building 9, but not within the high-status Manor of the Rose (B15–16), although the area is interpreted as an undercroft beneath the ground-floor or first-floor chapel.

FRENCH AND GERMAN
SUMMARIES

Résumé

En 1969 durant une opération de surveillance pendant la
construction de Suffolk House, Upper Thames Street, Peter
Marsden a relevé des éléments de maçonnerie importants qu'il
a interprété comme étant les restes d'un hôtel particulier romain
de taille assez importante rattaché au 'Palais du Gouverneur'
sous la station Cannon Street. Un projet de réaménagement du
site par Argent Real Estate a permis de faire de plus amples
recherches sur ce site et a donné lieu à une évaluation en
1994–5 et des fouilles et opération de surveillance en 1996–7.
Le nouveau bâtiment a été renommé la Maison du Gouverneur
(Governor's House). Le 'Palais' est classé et sa préservation
est par conséquent extrêmement importante; les travaux
archéologiques ont été conçus pour faire partie d'un ensemble
de mesures visant à réduire le plus possible les dégâts qui
pourraient être apportés au reste de l'archéologie.

Malgré la nature limitée des fouilles, on a retrouvé et relevé
un marais préhistorique jusque là inconnu. Deux structures au
sud-ouest du site construites avec du bois provenant d'arbres
qui, il semble, avaient été abattus en 84 apr. J.C. retenaient
un quai orienté nord-sud à une hauteur de 2.1m OD. Ceci
représente sans doute l'extrèmité est d'un quai situé le long
de la rivière sous Upper Thames Street qui s'étendait sur 120m
jusqu'à l'embouchure de la Walbrook; à cet endroit l'extrèmité
ouest en a été retrouvée à la station Cannon Street en1988. Dans
la partie est du site, un revêtement de poteaux et planches a été
construit en 100–20 apr. J.C. et montait jusqu'à 1.3m OD; il
était en partie construit avec des bois de construction récupurés.
Une zone supplémentaire fut asséchée au sud de Suffolk House
probablement vers 125–6 apr. J.C. quand une canalisation
encaissée fut placée au-dessus du revêtement de poteaux et
planches, s'étendant au-delà des limites des fouilles. Il est
presque certain que ces structures prédatent les phases
principales du site. Plus avant pendant le 2ème siècle, un
système de canalisation fait de tuyaux creux en chêne apportait
l'eau vers l'ouest.

Les murs et les sols de plusieurs bâtiments ont été retrouvés
sur les terrasses qui surplombent la rivière; ils comprennent
deux structures anciennes qui prédatent la phase de l'hôtel
particulier. L'un de ces bâtiments, au nord-est, était peut-être
les locaux d'un orfèvre, un second à l'ouest fut probablement
reconstruit pour former l'aile nord de l'hôtel particulier. Des
détails supplémentaires sur l'hôtel particulier ont été ajoutés
aux observations faites en 1969, en particulier à l'emplacement
de l'aile ouest où un système de chauffage sous le sol a été
retrouvé. Des fragments du tambour et du châpiteau d'une
colonne romaine d'ordre Tuscan qui avaient déjà été vus en 1994
ont été retrouvés en 1996 dans une fosse médiévale placée
au-dessus de l'angle sud-est du bâtiment. On a aussi retrouvé
les restes d'un ou deux bâtiments contemporains situés â l'est
de l'hôtel particulier.

Il semblerait que l'occupation romaine du site ait continué
au moins jusque vers la fin du 4ème siècle quand l'hôtel
particulier fut démoli; ses murs ont cependant survécu sur une
hauteur considérable.

Les fosses du début du 11ème siècle furent remplacées à la fin du 11ème et au début du 12ème siècle par une série de bâtiments comprenant des sols enfoncés ou des caves construits dans le sol noir (dark earth) accumulé au-dessus des restes romains. A ces bâtiments succédèrent des murs médiévaux en calcaire le long des façades de Laurence Pountney Lane et au sud de Rectory House; des fondations en calcaire et en gravier placés sur des pieux fendus en hêtre ont été retrouvées dans la partie sud du site, elles sont d'un type caractéristique de la première partie du 12ème siècle. Le long de Suffolk Lane, on a retrouvé des murs appartenant à au moins deux phases de la Pountney's Inn du 14ème siècle, plus tard nommé le Manoir de la Rose. Un puits revêtu de calcaire et une fosse d'aisance associés au manoir ont été probablement utilisé jusqu'au 17ème siècle.

Trois des chapitres de ce volume portent sur le développement du site en commençant par le marais préhistorique, continuant durant la longue période d'occupation romaine et jusqu'aux époques médiévales anciennes et récentes (chapîtres 2–4). Les données stratigraphiques se trouvent dans les contributions fournies par des spécialistes et sont d'une part intégrées au texte et d'autre part présentées d'une manière plus détaillée dans les appendices. Nous avons également essayé de voir si les résultats obtenus durant les deux phases du projet ont contribué à répondre avec succès aux questions de recherche posées avant le commencement de chaque phase et révisées par la suite. Nous avons aussi examiné le succès de la stratégie de mitigation et ses conséquences pour la gestion future des sites archéologiques (chapître 5).

Zusammenfassung

1969 fand Peter Marsden bei einer Probegrabung während der Bauarbeiten am Suffolk House, Upper Thames Street, reichlich Mauerwerk, das er als Überreste eines bedeutenden, zum Gouverneurspalast unter der Station Cannon Street gehörenden Stadthauses interpretierte. Vor dem Beginn neuerlicher Bauarbeiten durch Argent Real Estate ergab sich noch einmal die Gelegenheit zu weiteren archäologischen Untersuchungen, d.h. nach einer Prüfung der Erfolgsaussichten 1994/5 fanden 1996/7 Kontroll- und schließlich endgültige Ausgrabungen statt. Da die Palastgegend unter Denkmalschutz steht, kam der Erhaltung höchste Bedeutung zu. Die archäologischen Arbeiten standen daher unter dem Vorrang der Schadensbeschränkung an den verbleibenden archäologischen Resten.

Trotz dieser Beschränkungen wurde bisher dort nicht vermutetes Sumpfgebiet gefunden. Zwei aus AD 84 gefällten Bäumen errichtete Konstruktionen dienten der Befestigungen einer Nord-Süd verlaufenden Anlegestelle, ca. 2,1m ü.d.M.. Diese war vermutlich das östliche, unter der Thames Street gelegene Ende einer Werft, die sich etwa 120m bis zur Walbrook-Mündung erstreckte, wo das westliche Ende 1988

unter der Station Cannon Street belegt ist. Im östlichen Teil der Ausgrabung befand sich ca. 1,3m ü.d.M. eine zwischen AD 100–20 errichtete Pfosten/Bohlen-Uferbefestigung, die z.T. aus gebrauchtem Bauholz gebaut war. Weitere Landgewinnung fand vermutlich zwischen AD 125/6 südlich von Suffolk House statt, als eine gedeckte Drainage über die Uferbefestigung und über die Grenze der Ausgrabung hinaus verlegt wurde. Diese Anlagen datieren fast mit Sicherheit vor den größeren Bauphasen. Später im 2.Jh. leiteten Röhren aus ausgehöhlten, geviertelten Eichen Wasser nach Westen.

Auf der Terrasse über dem Fluß wurden Mauern und Fußböden mehrerer Gebäude freigelegt. Dazu gehören auch zwei vor der Stadthäuserphase liegende Bauwerke. In dem im Nordwesten gelegenen Gebäude mag Gold geschmiedet worden sein, das westliche wurde umgebaut und mag den Nordflügel des von Marsden gefundenen Stadthauses gebildet haben. Weitere Einzelerkenntnisse zum Stadthaus wurden den 1969iger Beobachtungen hinzugefügt, insbesondere zum Westflügel, in dem eine Fußbodenheizung freigelegt wurde. Teile einer Säulentrommel und eines Kapitells einer römisch-toskanischen Säulenordnung, zuerst 1994 geortet, wurden aus einer mittelalterlichen Grube geborgen, die über dem Südwestteil des Gebäudes lag. Östlich des Stadthauses wurden die Überreste zweier Häuser aus derselben Zeit gefunden.

Die römische Besiedlung dieser Gegend reicht mindestens bis ins späte 4. Jh., als das Stadthaus zerstört wurde, dessen Wände jedoch in beträchtlicher Höhe überlebten.

Den Gruben des 11. Jhs. folgten im späten 11. bis frühen 12.Jh. eine Reihe von Senkböden oder unterkellerten Gebäuden, die in den Darkearth-Lagen oberhalb der römischen Reste errichtet wurden. Diesen folgten später mittelalterliche Kalksteinfundamente und -wände entlang der Straßenfront der Laurence Pountney Lane und südlich des Rectory House. Ein Kalkstein- und Kiesfundament über gespaltenen Buchenpfählen im südlichen Teil der Ausgrabung gehört zu der Art, wie sie vom 12.Jh. an gefunden wird. Entlang Suffolk Lane wurden wenigstens zwei Phasen des Pountney Inns, später 'Manor of the Rose', aus dem 14.Jh. gefunden. Ein mit Kalkstein ummauerter Brunnen und eine Abtrittsgrube, die dem Gut zugeordnet werden, mögen bis ins 17. Jh. in Benutzung gewesen sein.

In den Kapiteln 2–4 wird die geschichtliche Entwicklung von dem vorgeschichtlichen Sumpfgebiet, über die langzeitliche römische Besiedlung, bis in das frühe und späte Mittelalter besprochen. Beiträge von Spezialisten unterstützen das stratigrafische Material. Die Ergebnisse sind in den Anhang eingearbeitet. Es wird auch versucht festzustellen, ob die Resultate der beiden Ausgrabungsphasen des Projektes die vorher aufgestellten und später aktualisierten Forschungsfragen beantwortet haben. Kapitel 5 behandelt den Erfolg der schadensbeschränkenden Maßnahmen und deren Auswirkungen auf zukünftiges Vorgehen unter derartigen Umständen.

BIBLIOGRAPHY

Abbreviations
BAR   British Archaeological Reports
CBA   Council for British Archaeology
MoL   Museum of London
MoLAS   Museum of London Archaeology Service

This bibliography lists archive reports relating to the site, including assessments, project designs, excavation and evaluation reports, as well as main sources consulted. Those volumes cited as being in preparation at the time of going to press are intended to form a part of the MoLAS monograph series; titles and authors are in some instances provisional, and may be subject to change.

The Research Archive

Ainsley, C, Conheeney, J, Corcoran, J, Giorgi, J, Scaife, R & Sidell, J, 1996 *Assessment of the environmental material from Suffolk House, City of London (SUF94)*

Brigham, T, Sloane, B & Malt, R, 1998 *An archaeological investigation at Suffolk House, EC4 City of London: an updated project design*

Brigham, T & Watson, B, 1995 *Suffolk House, 5 Laurence Pountney Hill & 154–156 Upper Thames Street, London, EC4: an archaeological interim report*

Goodburn, D, 1996 *The woodwork*

Hughes, R, 1994a *Suffolk House, an archaeological desk study*, Ove Arup & Partners

Hughes, R, 1994b *Suffolk House, conditions of engagement*, Ove Arup & Partners

Mackie, P & McCann, W, 1997 *Suffolk House: ground penetrating radar survey*, Clark Laboratory

Tyers, I & Boswijk, G, 1996 *Dendrochronological spot dates for 82 timbers from Suffolk House (SUF94), City of London, Three Ways Wharf (LTS95), City of London Guys Hospital (GHL89 & GHD90), Southwark, Lafone St (LAF96), Southwark, Jacob's Island (JAC96), Southwark, & Atlantic Wharf (FTW96), Tower Hamlets*, ARCUS Dendrochronology

Woodger, A, 1996a *An archaeological investigation at Suffolk House, 5 Laurence Pountney Hill & 154–156 Upper Thames Street, London EC4*

Woodger, A, 1996b *Suffolk House, 5 Laurence Pountney Hill & 154–156 Upper Thames Street, London EC4: an archaeological assessment*

Woodger, A, 1997 *Suffolk House, 5 Laurence Pountney Hill & 154–156 Upper Thames Street, London EC4: an updated project design*

Bibliography

Place of publication given for books published outside the United Kingdom.

Adkins, L & Adkins, R A, 1982 *The handbook of British archaeology*

Allason-Jones, L & Miket, R, 1984 *The catalogue of small finds from South Shields Roman fort*

Andersen, S Th, 1970 'The relative pollen productivity and pollen representation of north European trees, and correction factors for tree pollen spectra', *Danm Geol Unders* ser II, 96–9

Andersen, S Th, 1973 'The differential pollen productivity of trees and its significance for the interpretation of a pollen diagram from a forested region', in *Quaternary plant ecology* (ed H J B Birks & R G West), 109–15

Ayre, J & Wroe-Brown, R, with Malt, R, in prep *Queenhithe: excavations at Thames Court, City of London, 1989–1997*, MoLAS Monograph

Bailey, K C, 1929 *The Elder Pliny's chapters on chemical subjects*, part I

Baker, C A, Moxey, P A & Oxford, M, 1978 'Woodland continuity and change in Epping Forest', *Fld Stud* 4, 645–69

Barham, A J, 1990 *Report on the sedimentological characteristics of monolith samples from the basal stratigraphy of Vintry House, London (VRY89)*, Geoarchaeological Service Facility Rep 90/03

Bateman, N, 1986 'Bridgehead revisited', *London Archaeol* 5, 233–41

Bateman, N, 1998 'Public buildings in Roman London: some contrasts', in B Watson 1998b, 47–57

Bateman, N & Milne, G, 1983 'A Roman harbour in London: excavations and observations near Pudding Lane, City of London 1979–82', *Britannia* 14, 207–26

Bayley, J, 1991 'Archaeological evidence for parting', *Archaeometry '90*

Bayley, J, 1992a 'Goldworking in Britain from Iron Age to medieval times', *Interdisciplinary Science Reviews* 17, 4, 314–21

Bayley, J, 1992b 'Non-ferrous metalworking in England Late Iron Age to early medieval', PhD thesis, University of London, 104–13, unpub

de la Bédoyère, G, 1991 *The buildings of Roman Britain*

Bennett, K D, Whittington, G & Edwards, K J, 1994 'Recent plant nomenclatural changes and pollen morphology in the British Isles', *Quat Newsl* 73, 1–6

Bentley, D, 1984 'A recently identified valley in the City', *London Archaeol* 5, 13–16

Betts, I M, 1990 'Appendix 3: building materials', in 'Medieval buildings and property development in the area of Cheapside' (ed J Schofield, P Allen & C Taylor), *Trans London Middlesex Archaeol Soc* 41, 220–9

Betts, I M, 1997 'Ceramic building materials', in *St Bride's Church, London: archaeological research 1952–60 and 1992–5* (ed G Milne), English Heritage Archaeol Rep 11, 60–8

Betts, I M, Black, E W & Gower, J, 1994 *A corpus of relief-patterned tiles in Roman Britain*, J Pottery Stud 7

Birks, H J B, 1989 'Holocene isochrone maps and patterns of tree spreading in the British Isles', *J Biogeogr* 16, 503–40

Birks, H J B, Deacon, J & Peglar, S, 1975 'Pollen maps for the British Isles 5000 years ago', *Proc Royal Soc B* 189, 87–105

Bishop, M C & Coulston, J C N, 1993 *Roman military equipment*

Blackmore, L, 1999 'Aspects of trade and exchange evidenced by recent work on Saxon and medieval pottery from London', *Trans London Middlesex Archaeol Soc* 50, 38–54

Blackmore, L, in prep 'The pottery', in *Excavations at Holy Trinity Priory Aldgate, London* (ed J Schofield & R Lea), MoLAS Monograph

Blagg, T F C, 1977 'Schools of stonemasons in Roman Britain', in *Roman life and art in Britain*, part 1 (ed J Munby & M Henig), BAR 41(i), 51–73

Blagg, T F C, 1984 'An examination of the connexions between military and civilian architecture', in *Military and civilian in Roman Britain* (ed T F C Blagg & A C King), BAR 136, 249–64

Brigham, T, 1990a 'The late Roman waterfront in London', *Britannia* 21, 99–183

Brigham, T, 1990b 'A reassessment of the second basilica in London, AD 100–400: excavations at Leadenhall Court, 1984–86', *Britannia* 21, 53–97

Brigham, T, Goodburn, D, Tyers, I, with Dillon, J, 1995 'A Roman timber building on the Southwark waterfront, London', *Archaeol J* 152, 1–72

Brigham, T & Watson, B, in prep *Excavations at Regis House*, MoLAS Monograph

Brigham, T, Watson, B, Tyers, I & Bartkowiak, R, 1996 'Current archaeological work at Regis House in the City of London', *London Archaeol* 8, 31–7 (pt 1), 63–8 (pt 2)

Brodribb, G, 1987 *Roman brick and tile*

Brunning, R, 1996 *Waterlogged wood*, English Heritage Guidelines

Burch, M & Hill, J, 1988 *Excavations at Cannon Street Station*, MoL Archive Rep

Burnham, B C, 1987 'The morphology of Romano-British "small towns"', *Archaeol J* 144, 156–90

Callender, M H, 1965 *Roman amphorae*

Carlin, M & Belcher, V, 1989 'Gazetteer', in M D Lobel, 63–99

Clapham, A R, Tutin, T G & Moore, D M, 1987 *Flora of the British Isles*, 3rd ed

Clifford, E M, 1954 'The Roman villa, Witcombe, Gloucestershire', *Trans Bristol Gloucestershire Archaeol Soc* 73, 5–69

CoL 1992 *A directory of conservation areas and listed buildings and scheduled monuments in the City of London*, Corporation of London, Department of Planning Report

Collingwood, R G, 1930 *The archaeology of Roman Britain*

Cool, H E M, 1991 'Roman metal hairpins from southern Britain', *Archaeol J* 147, 148–82

Cool, H E M, 1995 'Glass vessels of the fourth and early fifth century in Roman Britain', in *Le Verre de l'antiquité tardive et du haut moyen age: typologie-chronologie-diffusion, Association française pour l'archéologie du verre* (ed D Foy), Musée Archéologique Départementale du Val d'Oise, 11–23

Cowan, C, 1992 'A possible *mansio* in Roman Southwark: excavations at 15–23 Southwark Street, 1980–86', *Trans London Middlesex Archaeol Soc* 43, 3–191

Cowan, C, in prep *The development of north-west Roman Southwark: excavations at Courage's Brewery, 1974–90*, MoLAS Monograph

Crowley, N, 1997 'Ceramic building material', in C Thomas et al, 195–201

Crummy, N, 1983 *The Roman small finds from excavations in Colchester 1971–9*, Colchester Archaeol Rep 2

Culpeper, N, 1853 ed *Culpeper's complete herbal*

Devoy, R J N, 1979 'Flandrian sea-level changes and vegetational history of the lower Thames estuary', *Phil Trans Royal Soc London B* 285, 355–407

Devoy, R J N, 1980 'Post-glacial environmental change and man in the Thames estuary: a synopsis', in *Archaeology and coastal change* (ed F H Thompson), 134–48

van Driel-Murray, C, 1998 'The leatherwork from the fort', in *Roman Castleford*, vol 1: *The small finds* (ed H E M Cool & C Philo), Yorkshire Archaeol 4

Dunning, G C, 1959 'Pottery of the late Anglo-Saxon period in England', in *Anglo-Saxon pottery: a symposium* (G C Dunning, J G Hurst, J N L Myres & F Tischler), *Medieval Archaeol* 3, 31–78

Dunwoodie, L & Brigham, T, in prep *Excavations at 168 Fenchurch Street*, MoLAS

Dyson, T, 1978 'Two Saxon land grants for Queenhithe', in *Collectanea Londoniensia: studies in London archaeology and history presented to Ralph Merrifield* (ed J Bird, H Chapman & J Clark), London Middlesex Archaeol Soc Spec Pap 2, 200–15

Dyson, T, 1990 'King Alfred and the restoration of London', *London J* 15, 99–100

Dyson, T, 1992 'The early London waterfront and the local street system', in K Steedman *et al*, 122–31

Ekwall, E, 1954 *Street names of the City of London*

Ellison, R A & Zalasiewicz, J A, 1996 'Palaeogene, Neogene', in *British regional geology: London and the Thames Valley* (ed M A Sumbler), 4th ed

English Heritage, 1991 *Management of archaeological projects*

Flude, K, 1980 *Excavations in the G.P.O. Tunnel, Upper Thames Street, 1977*, MoL Archive Rep

Gaimster, D, 1987 'The supply of Rhenish stoneware to London 1350–1600', *London Archaeol* 5, 339–47

Gaimster, D, 1997 *German stoneware 1200–1900*

Gale, S & Hoare, J, 1991 *Quaternary sediments*

Gibbard, P L, 1994 *Pleistocene history of the lower Thames Valley*

Giertz, W, 1996 'Middle Meuse Valley ceramics of Huy-type: a preliminary analysis', *Medieval Ceram* 20, 33–64

Girling, M A, 1987 'The bark beetle *Scolytus scolytus* (Fabricius) and the possible role of elm disease in the early Neolithic', in *Archaeology and the flora of the British Isles* (ed M Jones), 34–8

Girling, M A & Greig, J, 1985 'A first fossil record for *Scolytus scolytus* (F) (Elm Bark Beetle): its occurrence in elm decline deposits from London and the implication for the Neolithic elm decline', *J Archaeol Sci* 12, 347–51

Glasbergen, W & Groenman-Van Waateringe, W, 1974 *The pre-Flavian garrisons of Valkenburg ZH*

Godwin, H, 1940 'Pollen analysis and forest history of England and Wales', *New Phytol* 39, 370–400

Goffin, R, 1995 'The pottery', in 'Excavations at the dorter undercroft, Westminster Abbey' (P S Mills), *Trans London Middlesex Archaeol Soc* 46, 79–87

Goodburn, D, 1991a 'A Roman timber-framed building tradition', *Archaeol J* 148, 182–204

Goodburn, D, 1991b 'Wet sites as archives of ancient landscapes', in *Wet site excavation and survey* (ed J Coles & D Goodburn)

Goodburn, D, 1992 'Wood and woodland: carpenters and carpentry', in *Timber building techniques in London c 900–1400* (ed G Milne), London Middlesex Archaeol Soc Spec Pap 15, 106–30

Goodburn, D, 1995 'From tree to town', in T Brigham *et al*, 33–59

Goodburn, D, 1998 'The death of the wildwood and birth of woodmanship in SE England', in *Hidden dimensions* (ed K Bernick), 130–8

Goodburn, D, in prep 'New light on aspects of Roman woodwork from Regis House', in T Brigham & B Watson

Goodfellow, A V & Thornton, J H, 1966 *Romano-British shoes in the Guildhall Museum* (typescript held in MoL, unpub)

Greensmith, J & Tucker, E, 1973 'Holocene transgressions and regressions on the Essex coast and outer Thames estuary', *Geol en Mijnb* 52, 193–202

Greig, J R A, 1982 'Garderobes, sewers, cesspits and latrines', *Current Archaeol* 85, 49–52

Greig, J R A, 1989 'From lime forest to heathland – five thousand years of change at West Heath Spa, Hampstead, as shown by the plant remains', in *Excavations at the Mesolithic site on West Heath, Hampstead 1976–1981* (ed D Collins & D Lorimer), BAR 217, 89–99

Greig, J R A, 1991 'The botanical remains', in *Excavation and salvage at Runnymede Bridge 1978: the Late Bronze Age waterfront site* (ed S P Needham), 234–61

Grime, J P, Hodgson, J G & Hunt, R, 1990 *The abridged comparative plant ecology*

Groenman-van Waateringe, W, 1967 *Romeins lederwerk uit Valkenburg Z.H.*

Guido, M, 1978 *The glass beads of the prehistoric and Roman periods in Britain and Ireland*, Soc Antiq London Research Commitee Rep 35

Hanf, M, 1983 *The arable weeds of Europe – with their seedlings and seeds*

Harben, H A, 1918 *A dictionary of London*

Harden, D B, 1960 'The Wint Hill hunting bowl and related glasses', *J Glass Stud* 2, 44–81

Harden, D B, 1973 'The glass', in *Excavations at Shakenoak Farm near Wilcote, Oxfordshire* 4 (ed A C C Brodribb, A R Hands & D R Walker), privately printed, 98–107

Hassall, M W C & Tomblin, R S O, 1996 'Roman inscriptions in Britain in 1995', *Britannia* 27, 439–57

Hawthorne, J G & Smith, C S, 1979 *Theophilus: On divers arts*

Hill, C, Millett, M & Blagg, T, 1980 *The Roman riverside wall and monumental arch in London*, London Middlesex Archaeol Soc Spec Pap 3

Hill, J & Rowsome, P, in prep *Excavations at 1 Poultry: the Roman sequence*, MoLAS Monograph

Hill, J & Woodger, A, 1999 *Excavations at 72–75 Cheapside/83–93 Queen Street, City of London*, MoLAS Archaeol Studies 2

Hillam, J & Tyers, I, 1987 'Sapwood estimates and the dating of short ring sequences', in *Applications of tree-ring studies: current research in dendrochronology and related areas* (ed R G W Ward), BAR Int ser 333, 165

Hillman, G C, 1972 *Distinguishing chaff remains of emmer and einkorn: summary of the criteria applied to the charred remains from Mycenae*

Hoevenberg, J, 1993 'Leather artefacts', in *The Valkenburg excavations 1985–1988* (ed R M van Dierendonck, D P Hallewas & K E Waugh), Nederlandse Oudheden 15 Valkenburg Project 12

Horsman, V, Milne, C & Milne, G, 1988 *Aspects of Saxo-Norman London, I: Building and street development*, London Middlesex Archaeol Soc Spec Pap 11

Howe, M D, Perrin, J R & MacKreth, D F, 1980 *Roman pottery from the Nene Valley: a guide*, Peterborough City Museum Occ Pap 2

Hurst, J G, Neal, D S & van Beuningen, H J E, 1986 *Pottery produced and traded in north-west Europe 1350–1650*, Rotterdam Papers VI

Isings, C, 1957 *Roman glass from dated finds*, Groningen

Jones, D M & Rhodes, M, 1980 *Excavations at Billingsgate Buildings 'Triangle', Lower Thames Street, 1974*, London Middlesex Archaeol Soc Spec Pap 4

Keene, D, 1988 *Social and economic study of medieval London: interim report on the Bank of England area*, Institute of Historical Research report, unpub

Keily, J, 1998 'The fabric of the medieval London house', in *The medieval household: daily living c 1150–1450* (ed G Egan), Medieval finds from excavations in London 6, 24–41

Kingsford, C L, 1917 'Historical notes on medieval London houses', *London Topographical Record* 11, 28–81

Kingsford, C L, 1971 ed *Stow's Survey of London* [1603]

Lloyd-Morgan, G, 1977 'Mirrors in Roman Britain', in *Roman life and art in Britain* (ed J Munby & M Henig), BAR 41(ii), 231–52

Lobel, M D (ed), 1989 *The British atlas of historic towns, III: The City of London from prehistoric times to c 1520*

Loeschcke, S, 1919 *Lampen aus Vindonissa*, Zurich

Manning, W, 1985 *Catalogue of the Romano-British iron tools, fittings and weapons*, British Museum

Marsden, P, 1965 'A boat of the Roman period discovered on the site of New Guy's House, Bermondsey, 1958', *Trans London Middlesex Archaeol Soc* 21.2, 118–31

Marsden, P, 1975 'The excavation of a Roman palace site in London, 1961–1972', *Trans London Middlesex Archaeol Soc* 26, 1–102

Marsden, P, 1976 'Two Roman public baths in London', *Trans London Middlesex Archaeol Soc* 27, 1–70

Marsden, P, 1987 *The Roman forum site in London: discoveries before 1985*

Marsden, P, 1994 *Ships of the port of London: first to eleventh centuries AD*, English Heritage Archaeol Rep 3

Meddens, F M, 1996 'Sites from the Thames estuary wetlands, England, and their Bronze Age use', *Antiquity* 70, 325–34

Mellor, M, 1994 'A synthesis of Middle and Late Saxon, medieval and early post-medieval pottery in the Oxford region', *Oxoniensia* 59, 17–217

Merrifield, R, 1965 *The Roman city of London*

Merrifield, R, 1983 *London: city of the Romans*

Miller, L M B, 1982 'Miles Lane: the early Roman waterfront', *London Archaeol* 4, 143–7

Miller, L M B & Rhodes, M, 1980 'Leather footwear', in D M Jones & M Rhodes

Millett, M, 1990 *The Romanization of Britain: an essay in archaeological interpretation*

Millett, M, 1998 'Introduction: London as capital?', in B Watson 1998b, 7–12

Milne, G, 1985 *The port of Roman London*

Milne, G (ed), 1992 *From Roman basilica to medieval market: archaeology in action in the City of London*

Milne, G, 1995 *Roman London*

Milne, G, 1996 'A palace disproved: reassessing the provincial governor's presence in 1st-century London', in *Interpreting Roman London: papers in memory of Hugh Chapman* (ed J Bird, M Hassall & H Sheldon), Oxbow Monograph 58, 49–56

Milne, G & Wardle, A, 1993 'Early Roman development at Leadenhall Court, London, and related research', *Trans London Middlesex Archaeol Soc* 44, 23–170

Moore, D T & Oddy, W A, 1985 'Touchstones: some aspects of their nomenclature, petrography and provenance', *J Archaeol Sci* 12:1, 59–80

Morris, J, 1982 *Londinium: London in the Roman Empire*

de Moulins, D, 1990 'The environmental analysis', in *The archaeology of London, vol 1: The upper Walbrook Valley in the Roman period* (C Maloney with D de Moulins), The archaeology of

Roman London 1, CBA Res Rep 69, 85–115

Norman, P, 1901 'Sir John de Poulteney and his two residences in London, Cold Harbour and the Manor of the Rose, together with a few remarks on the parish of St Laurence Poultney', *Archaeologia* 57 (pt 2), 257–84

O'Sullivan, A, 1998 'Woodmanship and the supply of underwood and timber to Anglo-Norman Dublin', in *Dublin and beyond the Pale* (ed P Healy), 59–69

Padley, T G, 1991 'The Roman shoes', in T G Padley & S Winterbottom

Padley, T G & Winterbottom, S (eds), 1991 *The wooden, leather and bone objects from Castle Street, Carlisle: excavations 1981–2*, Cumberland & Westmorland Antiquarian & Archaeol Soc Research ser no. 5

Peacock, D P S & Williams, D F, 1986 *Amphorae and the Roman economy: an introductory guide*

Pearce, J E & Vince, A G, 1988 *A dated type-series of London medieval pottery, part 4: Surrey Whitewares*, London Middlesex Archaeol Soc Spec Pap 10

Pearce, J E, Vince, A G & Jenner, M A, 1985 *A dated type-series of London medieval pottery, part 2: London-type ware*, London Middlesex Archaeol Soc Spec Pap 6

Perring, D, 1991 *Roman London*

Perring, D & Roskams, S, with Allen, P, 1991 *The early development of Roman London west of the Walbrook*, The archaeology of Roman London 2, CBA Res Rep 70

Pevsner, N & Cherry, B, 1973 *London, 1: The cities of London and Westminster*, The Buildings of England ser

Pipe, A, 1997 *The marine crustacea from Regis House*, MoLAS Archive Rep

Polunin, O, 1969 *Flowers of Europe: a field guide*

Rackham, O, 1976 *Trees and woodland in the British landscape*

Rauxloh, P & Symonds, R P, in prep 'The Roman pottery: a comparison between the data contained in the spot-date files and quantified data from selected contexts', in C Cowan

RCHM (Royal Commission on Historical Monuments) 1928 *London, III: Roman London*

RCHM (Royal Commission on Historical Monuments) 1929 *London, IV: The City of London*

Rhodes, M, 1982 'The finds', in *Medieval waterfront development at Trig Lane, London* (ed G Milne & C Milne), London Middlesex Archaeol Soc Spec Pap 5, 84–92

Riley, H T (ed), 1859 *Munimenta Gildhallae Londiniensis*, vol 1: *Liber Albus*

Rodwell, W & Rowley, T (eds), 1975 *The 'small towns' of Roman Britain*, BAR 15

Rowsome, P, 1999 'The Huggin Hill baths and bathing in London: barometer of the town's changing circumstances?', in *Roman baths and bathing* (ed J DeLaine and D Johnston), J Roman Archaeol Suppl Ser 37, 262–77

Scaife, R, 1980 'Late Devensian and Flandrian palaeoecological studies in the Isle of Wight', PhD thesis, University of London, unpub

Scaife, R, 1987 'The Late Devensian and Flandrian vegetation of the Isle of Wight', in *Wessex and the Isle of Wight: field guide* (ed K E Barber), 156–80

Schmid, E, 1972 *Atlas of animal bones: for prehistorians, archaeologists and Quaternary geologists*

Schofield, J, 1991 'The construction of medieval and Tudor houses in London', *Construction History* 7, 3–28

Schofield, J, 1995 *Medieval London houses*

Schofield, J, Allen, P & Taylor, C, 1990 'Medieval buildings and property development in the area of Cheapside', *Trans London Middlesex Archaeol Soc* 41, 39–238

Schofield, J, with Maloney, C (eds), 1998 *Archaeology in the City of London, 1907–1991: a guide to records of excavations by the Museum of London and its predecessors*, Archaeol Gazetteer ser 1, MoL

Selkirk, A, 1988 'Roman London: a Christmas address to the Society of Antiquaries of London, 15th December 1988', unpub lecture

Sidell, J, Cotton, J, Rayner, L & Wheeler, L, in prep *The topography and prehistory of Southwark and Lambeth*, MoLAS Monograph

Sidell, J, Wilkinson, K, Scaife, R & Cameron, N, 2000 *The Holocene evolution of the London Thames: archaeological excavations (1991–1998) for the London Underground Limited Jubilee Line Extension Project*, MoLAS Monograph 5

Simmons, I G & Tooley, M, 1981 *The environment in British prehistory*

Smith, A G, 1970 'The influence of Mesolithic and Neolithic man on British vegetation: a discussion', in *Studies of the vegetational history of the British Isles* (ed D Walker & R G West)

Smith, A G & Pilcher, J R, 1973 'Radiocarbon dates and the vegetational history of the British Isles', *New Phytol* 72, 903–14

Spoerry, P, 1993 *Archaeology and legislation in Britain*

Stace, C, 1991 *New flora of the British Isles*

Steedman, K, Dyson, T & Schofield, J (eds), 1992 *Aspects of Saxo-Norman London, III: The bridgehead and Billingsgate to 1200*, London Middlesex Archaeol Soc Spec Pap 14

Stephenson, A, 1996 *Cannon Place, London EC4*, MoLAS Assessment Rep

Stuiver, M, Reimer, P J, Bard, E, Beck, J W, Burr, G S, Hughen, K A, Kromer, B, McCormac, F G, van der Plicht, J & Spurk, M, 1988 'Calibration curve', *Radiocarbon* 40, 1041–83

Sutherland, C H V, 1959 *Gold: its beauty, power and allure*

Symonds, R P, 1998 'Quelques aperçues sur le port romain de Londres, provoqués par les travaux du Projet César', *SFECAG, Actes du Congrès d'Istres*, 339–48

Symonds, R, in prep 'The Roman pottery', in T Brigham & B Watson

Thomas, C, Sloane, B & Phillpotts, C, 1997 *Excavations at the Priory and Hospital of St Mary Spital, London*, MoLAS Monograph 1

Thompson, R & Oldfield, F, 1986 *Environmental magnetism*

Todd, M, 1970 'The small towns of Roman Britain', *Britannia* 1, 114–30

Troels-Smith, J, 1955 'Characterization of unconsolidated sediments', *Danm Geol Unders* ser IV, 3, 38–73

Turner, J, 1962 'The Tilia decline: an anthropogenic interpretation', *New Phytol* 61, 328–41

Vince, A G, 1985 'Saxon and medieval pottery in London: a review', *Medieval Archaeol* 29, 25–93

Vince, A G, 1988 'The date and frequency of German imports in the City of London from the 10th to 15th centuries', in *Zur Keramik des Mittelalters und der beginnenden Neuzeit im Rheinland* (ed D R M Gaimster, M Redknap & H-H Wegner), BAR Int ser 440, 241–2

Vince, A, 1990 *Saxon London: an archaeological investigation*

Vince, A G, 1991 'Early medieval London: refining the chronology', *London Archaeol* 6, 263–71

Vince, A G, 1992 'Finds catalogue', in K Steedman et al, 139–42

Vince, A & Jenner, A, 1991 'The Saxon and early medieval pottery of London', in *Aspects of Saxo-Norman London, II: Finds and environmental evidence* (ed A Vince), London Middlesex Archaeol Soc Spec Pap 12

Wacher, J, 1998 *Roman Britain*

Walthew, C V, 1975 'The town house and the villa house in Roman Britain', *Britannia* 6, 189–205

Watson, B, 1998a '"Dark earth" and urban decline', in B Watson 1998b, 100–6

Watson, B (ed), 1998b *Roman London: recent archaeological work*, J Roman Archaeol, supp ser 24

Watson, B, Brigham, T & Dyson, T, 2001 *London Bridge: 2000 years of a river crossing*, MoLAS Monograph 8

Weinreb, B & Hibbert, C (eds), 1983 *The London encyclopaedia*

Westman, A (ed), 1994 *Archaeological site manual*, MoLAS, 3rd ed

Whipp, D & Platts, E, 1976 'Westminster Hall excavation', *London Archaeol* 2:14, 351–5

Wild, J P, 1970 'Button-and-loop fasteners in the Roman provinces', *Britannia* 1, 137–55

Williams, T, 1993 *Public buildings in the south-west quarter of Roman London*, The archaeology of Roman London 3, CBA Res Rep 88

Wilcox, G H, 1977 'Exotic plants from Roman waterlogged sites in London', *J Archaeol Sci*, 269–82

Wilmott, T, 1991 *Excavations in the middle Walbrook Valley, City of London, 1927–1960*, London Middlesex Archaeol Soc Spec Pap 13

Winterbottom, S, 1991 'The sheet leather objects', in T G Padley & S Winterbottom

Woodger, A, in prep *Further evidence of Saxo-Norman and medieval occupation in the Cheapside area*, MoLAS

Zohary, D & Hopf, M, 1993 *Domestication of plants in the Old World*, 2nd ed

INDEX

Compiled by Susanne Atkin

Page numbers in **bold** refer to illustrations